Profitable
Personnel Services

Profitable Personnel Services

Start and Run a Money-Making Business

Kristi Mishel
John J. Thomas

TAB Books
Division of McGraw-Hill, Inc.
New York   San Francisco   Washington, D.C.   Auckland   Bogotá
Caracas   Lisbon   London   Madrid   Mexico City   Milan
Montreal   New Delhi   San Juan   Singapore
Sydney   Tokyo   Toronto

©1995 by **McGraw-Hill, Inc.**
Published by TAB Books, a division of McGraw-Hill, Inc.

pbk   1 2 3 4 5 6 7 8 9 <<DOH/DOH>> 9 9 8 7 6 5

Library of Congress Cataloging-in-Publication Data

Mishel, Kristi
    Profitable personnel services : start and run a money-making
business / by Kristi Mishel and John J. Thomas.
        p.   cm.
    Includes index.
    ISBN 0-07-042369-5
    1. Employment agencies—United States—Handbooks, manuals, etc.
2. New business enterprises—United States—Handbooks, manuals, etc.
I.Thomas, John J., 1950- .II. Title.
HD5875.M57   1995
331.12'8'0973—dc20   94-36919
                                                          CIP

Acquisitions editor: Jeff Worsinger
Editorial team: Robert E. Ostrander, Executive Editor
               Sally Glover, Book Editor
Production team: Katherine G. Brown, Director
               Lisa M. Mellott, Coding
               Rose McFarland, Desktop Operator
               Nancy K. Mickley, Proofreading
               Jodi L. Tyler, Indexer   TAB1
Designer: Jaclyn J. Boone   0423695

Kristi Mishel wishes to thank her loving parents, Paul and Helen Nall, and her remarkable daughter, Sandy Roberts, for all their unwavering love and support. John Thomas wishes to thank his loving sister, JoAnne Rosensteel, for her constant devotion.
In tender, loving memory of Patricia Nall, John Edward, and Sara Jane Thomas.

Contents

Introduction

Personnel professionals, executives, sales managers, and entrepreneurs are generally overwhelmed by the prospect of starting a personnel agency. Although they have the transferable skills, they often fail because they do not know enough about how to run a prosperous business.

The purpose of this book is to provide a comprehensive and practical business guide that shows you how to establish and operate a successful and profitable personnel placement agency. The book provides a simple system for achieving maximum profitability in a business start-up operation.

There are three significant levels of professionals who will benefit from reading this book:

- Enterprising personnel management professionals who have completed training in the personnel department of a large company and have decided to put that intricate knowledge to work.
- Established personnel placement service owners or managers or someone considering buying an existing agency. This book will aid in managing the business more efficiently and professionally.
- Industrious professionals with a management, sales/customer service, or strong entrepreneurial background who are looking for ways to transfer their existing skills or abilities into a new and exciting business opportunity.

These are the areas covered: the joys, benefits, frustrations, and excitement of becoming self-employed, and how to determine whether you have what it takes to be successful; time-tested tools for staying competitive in this fast-paced business environment; simplified instructions for the fundamental start-up of your business, i.e., market research, business plans, selecting company name and logo, location, licenses, forms, furniture, stationery, business equipment, suppliers, phone systems, signage, and expansion. We also provide the tools for establishing your outside professional support network, i.e., accountant, attorney, computer consultant, management consultant, financial adviser, insurance agent, and printer and graphics professionals.

A full chapter is devoted to covering the financial aspects of the business: starting capital, credit lines, cash flow crises, investment resources, and investments. Legal information required to protect the agency from pending suits is included, covering such areas as required state and federal postings, hiring, laws on retaining and firing, reference-checking laws, application revisions, and small-claims court procedures.

You'll also find information on: protecting your agency through business insurance, general liability, automobile liability, worker's compensation, and fire insurance; comprehensive medical plan options; retirement coverage; structuring the agency to ensure maximum profitability by selecting the type of placement service best suited to your area; types of placement categories; fee schedules; operating schedules; employer and applicant participation in payment of fees; territory definition; additional support services; creating the administrative structure for all accounting functions; interoffice communications; filing systems; applicant testing; inventory control; closing orders; screening and selecting interviewees for new positions; tracking your competition; updating the business plan; policy letters for every circumstance.

There's also an uncomplicated look at the internal operations of the business, covering interviewing techniques, scheduling, negotiating hires, taking job orders, screening applicants, running credit checks, recruiting, and managing time and crises. All requisite forms are included in each section when required, i.e., applications, job orders, contracts, etc.

One of the most crucial components of any business involves staffing. This book includes job descriptions and requirements, pay structures, salary and performance evaluations, bonus and incentive plans, benefit packages, a complete employee handbook, training manuals, and hiring and firing policies.

Understanding the marketing and public relations aspect of the business will ensure quicker success. Some of the key points covered are marketing plans, exclusive accounts, networking, business associations, public speaking engagements, company image, networking, customer service, media advertising strategies, mailing lists, free advertising ideas, bartering, and generating repeat business.

Competition in the placement business is fierce, and this book gives you all the tools you'll ever need to not only stay competitive in the marketplace, but also beat the competition almost every single time!

Taxes are perhaps the most crucial issue of all, and often the most overlooked. We thoroughly explain all of the state and federal requirements, payroll taxes, personal income tax, expense deductions, depreciation, and tax audits.

We hope you'll enthusiastically pursue the creation, upgrade, or expansion of a reputable and successful personnel agency. Our approach is friendly, instructional, and specifically designed for you to become the owner of your own prosperous business, finally realizing your self-employment dream.

I

So you want to create a personnel agency?

Within a few short months after opening my own agency, I began to experience a whole new set of emotions. These sensations had never been present through all my years as an employee. I didn't have to answer to anyone!

Every single decision made, goal accomplished (no matter how small), and dollar earned came completely from my own resources. Because there was no one looking over my shoulder suggesting possible solutions to my everyday problems, or offering creative ideas, the triumphs, each time, no matter how large or small, became mine and mine alone.

I felt as if a huge gate had finally opened, giving me the freedom to explore my untapped potential and finally accomplish my own set of professional goals. Whenever a mistake was made in judgment, I was more than willing to own the error. Each time, I considered the mistake a hard lesson and I learned from it. Each error became a series of stumbling, standing up, shaking off, and continuing forward. But I was always learning. The freedom to maximize my thoughts, ideas, decisions, and accomplishments was far more internally satisfying than anything I had ever experienced during my many years of training.

Timing is the key to everything! This is your time to put to good use all those years of careful preparation and hard-learned lessons. Immense personal pleasure, self-satisfaction, and feelings of self-confidence are your rewards when you finally make the decision to give back what you've learned.

WHY I STARTED A PERSONNEL AGENCY

In 1972 I was a young, married, 22-year-old mother with only a high-school diploma, a light clerical background, and plenty of common sense. Luckily, I discovered the satisfaction and joy of the personnel placement industry.

I started working for a full-range permanent and temporary placement service as their receptionist. My natural personality demands that I do the best possible job I can do, and my work reflected it. So during my first week of employment, my manager offered me a wonderful long-term goal. She said, "It'll take me ten years to teach you everything I've learned in this field, and by that time I'll be 62 years old and ready to retire, and you'll be 32 and ready to manage."

This situation is an excellent example of encouraging, and at the same time, motivating, employees. With the proper incentives, employees will work their hardest and stay with the company to achieve their long-term goals. This promotes a win-win atmosphere beneficial to all parties. The stimulus might not lead to ownership, but perhaps it will lead to a management position within the firm.

During this period she slowly and patiently taught me how to manage, operate, and eventually own my own business. Not only was she my teacher/mentor, but we also became good friends. I have always felt extremely fortunate and thankful to have had this opportunity before I opened my own agency.

So you might say I was destined to become an agency owner. The plan evolved to buy out the absentee owner at the end of my training, but a sagging economy in the early 1980s forced the company to lay me off instead. What a shock! I was primed and ready, with no options other than developing my own, and that left me with no other choice but to do exactly that.

I started North Coast Personnel Agency in the spring of 1982 with nothing more than the knowledge I'd gained during training, an established reputation in the field, a desk, a chair, a telephone, and a yellow notepad. My starting capital was only $2,000!

If I can open and operate a successful personnel agency with only a high-school education during one of the worst recessions in this century, with only a $2,000 investment, so can you!

COMPETITION

In order to stay competitive in your business, always follow these three basic rules in life. Do not lie, do not steal, and do not cheat. These simple maxims apply to your personal life as well as your professional environment. Remember these basic tools every time you make a decision, no matter how insignificant it is. It's essential to be consistently honest and ethically reliable in every situation you encounter. By using these standards, you'll be very surprised at how quickly your reputation for integrity spreads into the business community.

When you work hard every day to meet the needs of each client with sensitivity and sound business practices, the return will be astounding. Repeat business and referrals is the name of the game and the primary goal for any business owner. It's what they strive so diligently for and work towards. Large employment agencies sometimes lose the "personal" touch and can't retain that valuable client year after year.

QUALITY SERVICE

Do what you say you're going to do, every single time, and always follow up on the details. Try not to favor one client over another, as this practice will eventually come back and bite you when you least expect it. The general public quickly recognizes a consistently reliable, honest, quality service. This naturally encourages those valuable, long-term relationships that are so essential to the growth and profitability of your company.

You do not need an extensive personnel background or tremendous training to be successful in this field. I deliberately chose to hire people without personnel background. The traits that I looked for in a successful personnel employee were honesty, sensitivity, and commitment. Common sense should be a fundamental element used in almost every situation you encounter. So rely on your basic intuition and understanding of people and their nuances.

BUYING AN EXISTING AGENCY

This can sometimes be a simple shortcut to ownership. You can find the advertisements for businesses on the marketplace in the local newspapers, trade publications, and rental agents.

Most businesses are sold lock, stock, and barrel. This includes fixtures, equipment, inventory, and all of the office supplies. You might prefer to only buy the fixtures, equipment, and leasehold improvements and stay free to create your own image.

Before you buy an existing business, follow these essential instructions first:
- Find out why the business is for sale. Do an investigation.
- Is the location suitable for you? Is there competition close by?
- Sit in on the business for a few days, and take a close look at the daily volume and clientele.
- Is there going to be additional cost for redecorating the existing facility to upgrade the image? If so, does this negate the advantage of buying?
- Look carefully at the business's financial records for the last three years and also for the year to date. Compare sales tax records with the owner's claims.

TIME, PATIENCE, AND PERSEVERANCE

We all know that life is a constant series of ups and downs, and being self-employed certainly lets you experience this reality early on. Just be prepared, going in, to stay in it for the long haul through thick and thin. One way to accomplish this is to learn how to take pleasures in the little things. Make an effort to enjoy your daily accomplishments instead of just focusing on the long-term disappointments. This can mean the simple difference between sticking it out during the rough periods, or backing out when things get too frustrating.

It's a great idea to set up long-range plans, with a fall-back position (plan B) in case of emergencies. We'll go into the planning of your business, in more detail, in the business plan in chapter 2. You will never be able to guarantee the outcome of all your business transactions, even though you work with the best intentions. Since that's the case, just do not get caught without a net or alternate plan. Far too many new business owners have not been prepared for the unexpected, and they're the ones that fold very quickly when things get shaky. Learn to be flexible with your business decisions. Be adaptable and aware of constant change.

When you learn how to work "on" your business, and not "in" your business, the daily operations will always go more smoothly. This means keeping the big picture in mind, all the time. It's very easy to get lost in the daily whirl of various business demands and victories and lose sight of your long-range goals.

A very good friend of mine taught me years ago how to take minivacations when things get stressful. This didn't mean a trip somewhere physically, since that was obviously out of the question. I learned how to take a few minutes of escape, in my mind, from immediate business pressures. For example, I'd recall a serene snowfall in my apple orchard (very rare) or a loving and peaceful day with my daughter Sandy. I quickly found that as long as it was a memory that made me smile and feel calm, but wasn't related in any way to my business, it worked like a charm. These breaks were an essential part of my steady workday and always helped me make clearer decisions and sound business deals when the pressures were mounting. I was able to relax more often and be more productive.

USING THIS BOOK

Whether you are a novice in the personnel agency business or a tried-and-true professional with years behind you, read every chapter slowly and carefully. Tailor the style to meet your own special business, but trust the tools. They are time-tested and proven through 20 years of trial and error.

2
Initial start-up functions

To some people, the very idea of creating a business, let alone operating an existing firm, seems daunting. It might feel like trying to climb a mountain with no preparation, gear, or knowledge. Unfortunately, some never, ever get to the top, let alone stay there for long and prosper.

This chapter is devoted to carefully outlining the steps necessary to start the self-employment process. We'd like you to consider each of these tasks as steps toward the goal. In a very short time, and after each project is successfully completed, you'll see that the mountaintop is quite reachable after all.

ASSESSING YOUR TRANSFERABLE SKILLS

Many individuals from a variety of training environments can move directly into the field of personnel placement with confidence. The backgrounds can also be gained from many different kinds of professions: management (in any industry, and at any level), customer service, marketing, directing, teaching, counseling, sales (wholesale or retail, inside or outside). A strong service industry background is very helpful, but product-related industries have customer service requirements, too. The final category included in this list is my favorite because it's a combination of the previously listed skills: mother or father! It takes a little bit of all of those skills to successfully raise a child. Don't you agree?

As you can see from the skills inventory listed in the following, in order to be successful in any of the above professions, you have to have a good mixture of learned skills, basic characteristic traits, and style. This combination is also the formula for success for the new agency owner. We have listed the combination requirements for your review:

Skills inventory

Organized, detail oriented, good planner, information specialist, good memory, innovative, competitive, image conscious, priority oriented, growth and goal oriented, list maker, disciplined, excellent communicator (both verbal and written), troubleshooter, and problem solver.

Characteristic traits and style

Ethical, patient, flexible, adaptable, optimistic, curious, thorough, strong-willed, sensitive, self-confident, intuitive, gentle, great sense of humor, and good common sense. The only strengths added to this are a strong personal family, friend, and/or business support system and, of course, innate intelligence.

If your background, training, or education is in the personnel industry already, you will easily recognize yourself in this picture. Isn't it interesting how many other professionals share your skills and personality? Fortunately for you, whether you're upgrading an existing agency or considering opening one of your own, the training time will be shortened because of your familiarity with personnel terminology and industry systems.

MARKET RESEARCH

After you've conducted a complete market analysis of your potential territory, it'll be much easier to project your sales and make sound business decisions. Listed in the following are a few basic steps to follow in order to assess your potential target market and thereby project income:

1. Establish your territory parameters (city/county/state).
2. Take a look at any existing agencies in the area and find out their current gross receipts.
3. Research the area's buying power.
4. Look at how the immediate population spends its money and on what types of resources.
5. Figure out what part of the existing agency market you can logically expect to gain.

When you're doing this valuable research, you can begin to build your competitors' profiles. The information you gather from these rival agencies will include everything from current fee structures to a copy of their application and contract. These files should be kept current at all times and will be invaluable data whenever it's time to make any decisions regarding the expenditure of your marketing budget dollars.

A lot of the information that you gather will come from diligent phone calls and fancy footwork. Quite a bit of the research is already available to the general public in the form of studies and reports put together by government agencies, other businesses within the territory, and trade publications.

Start first with the Yellow Pages to learn how many businesses are already operating in your chosen area. You can see by the size of the display ads how financially stable much of the competition is. Also, check the daily "help-wanted" listings in the local newspapers. These are the two primary advertising resources for employment agencies and should give you a pretty good idea of the competitive marketplace. Be sure to look in the Sunday paper, as it consistently has more employment ads than any other day of the week.

It's crucial that you select an office location that's easily accessible to the general public. The chamber of commerce can give you maps of the major trading areas, as well as the local city newspaper office. For the best traffic patterns, look for freeways and main thoroughfares that are close to your chosen site.

The business development division of the chamber of commerce welcomes inquiries from potential business owners. In their current membership newsletter, they include monthly statistics regarding the number of business inquiries, tourist information, and potential relocation residents.

Another valuable resource is to check with the advertising manager at the local newspaper for any articles that have been published as business profiles. This will give you valuable information about the income stream of the community and its purchasing power. Remember the radio and television stations, too. They are constantly conducting surveys of all types that might be of tremendous help.

Finally, take a careful look at the types of businesses that are predominant in your selected area. How many large employers are there? Is there growth potential? Is there consistent expansion? Are they currently hiring? You have to be sure of a stable local economy if you expect to realistically participate in the payroll picture. Be careful to avoid an area that has large peaks and valleys in employment, such as resort areas and agriculturally based industries. These seasonal businesses will adversely affect your steady cash flow.

More often than not, a new agency owner will already be familiar with the area that's being targeted. Just use your plain common sense and logical business evaluations, and there should be little problem with your choice.

After gathering the market research data, you can carefully select a market research firm to gather specific data regarding present market, market share of competition, and future market. If you do your homework ahead of time, you will save considerable expense when using this type of professional service. We'll discuss more on site selection later in this chapter.

PREPARE A BUSINESS PLAN

The business plan is considered the snapshot of your business and is primarily designed to use as a tool for implementing the creation and development of your company. Too much emotional connection with the ups and downs of the company make it difficult to make the spontaneous, yet sound business decisions so vital in a growing firm. A carefully prepared, well-thought-out business plan forces you to take an objective and realistic look at the areas of your business that might need special attention. Consider the business plan an operating tool that you, as well as your managers, will use in making valuable decisions that affect the bottom line.

If you ever choose to seek financing, your loan proposal will be developed using the information prepared on the business plan. Financial institutions can readily see your professionalism and thorough research when you present a sound and viable business plan in the loan process.

The following information is geared toward developing and using your company business plan not only as an operating tool but also for preparing a loan proposal for financing. Almost all business plans follow a standard formula, and we have included the order in which the material should be prepared:

- Title page.
- Statement of purpose.
- Table of contents.
- Business summary and description.
- Financial data.
- Supporting documents.

Purchase a professional-looking cover for the package. Try to find something in more of a subdued banking style instead of a flashy color. We suggest blue, black, or brown for the presentation folder. Put the name of your business, the name(s) of the principals of the business, the address, and the phone number on the title page. You can also include your logo if it's professional and businesslike. This dresses up the package a bit.

The statement of purpose follows the title page. You could also use the word "summary." In the case of financing, this section lets the reader know exactly what you are looking for in the very beginning of the proposal. Be specific and clear and support the request with as much information as possible.

Included in this section are: a description of the nature of your business, whether it's a sole proprietorship, partnership, corporation, etc.; the amount of financing requested; your proposed repayment schedule; how much equity share of the borrower is involved; the equity-debt ratio after the loan is granted; your security; and/or collateral available. Next is the table of contents. Although this is prepared last, it's an essential part of the package.

The description of your business is considered to be the heart of this proposal. Put "Description of Business" at the top of the page and then prepare the information carefully and thoroughly. You are far more involved, and therefore more aware of your company's marketplace, operating costs, systems and procedures, and industry requirements than any of the people who are assessing your proposal. It's advisable to work with your professional support people to target the funding level required.

The financial summary is the projected income and expenses of your business for the next three years. Included are a monthly breakdown for the entire first year, and then, only on a quarterly basis, a breakdown for the following two years. Since your profit and loss projections only show the projected profit or loss at the end of each period, you will also have to prepare a pro forma cash flow statement as well. Your business management consultant, accountant, or financial adviser can help you understand what's required in this section of your business plan.

The supporting documents in the plan could include the personal information of the principals of the company. In the case of financing, the lenders like to see the background of their clients because it's one of the primary factors in issuing a loan. Your dedication, professionalism, qualifications, and tenacity are definitely considered when making a funding decision.

We felt that the following information was most appropriate to include at the end of the business plan section. It's the standard list of reasons for a business failure:

- Poor client relationships.
- Competition ignored.
- Poor budgeting.
- Inefficient credit and collection systems.
- Illness of key personnel.
- Lack of adequate staff training.
- Inefficient control over quality of service.
- Underpricing your services.
- Inadequate financial records.
- Inability of management to see and act on problems.
- Extending too much credit to clients.
- Bad accounts receivable system.

- Failure to promote strong company image.
- Loss of enthusiastic sales drive.
- Inability to compete in the marketplace.
- Undercapitalized.
- Not enough insurance.
- Inability to recognize current financial problems.
- Overborrowing.
- Loss of key personnel.
- Unwillingness to use professional support system.
- Ignoring market trends that affect the business.
- Failure to maximize tax savings.

The following section is included to both acquaint you with making your own (worksheet) spreadsheets and help you visualize the viability of your personnel placement business.

Cash flow and income statement spreadsheet

This plan was created in EXCEL 5.0™ and can be used as an attachment to your business plan. These are generic spreadsheets and should be modified to reflect the specifics of your company. Before making any modifications, type in the information in the columns and rows exactly as listed. Review the formulas and then, after understanding what they do and what they influence, make the changes that will reflect the structure of your company and the applicable state and federal laws.

"Columns" run vertically across the worksheet (spreadsheet) and "rows" are horizontal. Formulas and data are entered in "cells." In referring to "cells," the "column" is listed first and then the "row" number. For example, in cell "B4," "Jan" is listed. In cell "B35" the formula "=SUM(B6:B33)" is entered.

Open EXCEL, and if there is not a new worksheet displayed, open a new one. Type in the formulas as listed in the lettered columns and numbered rows. Format the sheet as follows:
- Columns A–AK, rows 1–4, centered and bold.
- Columns B–AM, rows 6–127, currency ($).

Criteria for formulas and cell notations are as follows:
- Anytime a calculation is desired, the entry in the cell is preceded by an "=".
- Cell ranges are designated by the cell addresses separated by ":". For example, "B6:AK33" encompasses the sales data for your company, spanning a three-year period.
- "SUM" in a formula means you want to add the contents of the listed cells. For example, "=SUM(B6:B33)" lets the worksheet know that cells B6 through B33 are to be added and the result placed in the cell where the formula resides.
- "*" in a formula means to multiply. For example, "=B35*0.6" causes the contents of cell B35 to be multiplied by 0.6. Say the number 200 is the contents of cell B35. The following would be produced, 200 * 0.6 = 120, and 120 would appear in the cell where the formula resides.
- "/" in a formula, means you want to divide. For example, "=B35/0.6" causes the contents of cell B35 to be divided by 0.6. Say the contents of cell B35 are the number 200. The following would be produced: 200/0.6 = 333.33, and 333.33 would appear in the cell where the formula resides.

A full explanation concerning worksheets and formulas can be obtained in the product manuals or books from your library or bookstore.

Cash flow projections

In Fig. 2-1, cells A1 through AM72 (A1:AM72) contain the "CASH FLOW PROJECTIONS." Cells A2, N2, and Z2 should be modified to list your company name. Column "A" lists the descriptions for the data that will be entered in B6:AK33, B45:AK54, and B56:AK68. In these data cells, type the projected income and expenses for your company. Rows 35, 38–40, 42, 55, 70, and 72 are calculated fields, and no data, other than the formulas, are to be entered.

The starting month in cell B4 should be modified to reflect the projected start-up month for your company and the subsequent months listed in cells C4:AK4. "Total Sales" (row 35) are derived by adding the projected figures for each month, rows 6–33.

In the "Cash Receipts" section, monthly sales are broken into three periods. Most clients will pay their bills in full. However, some will elect to pay in installments. To reflect this, row 38 takes 60 percent of the projected total monthly sales (row 35) and places that figure in the current month. Row 39 takes 25 percent of the projected monthly sales and places that figure in the next monthly period. Row 40 takes 15 percent of the projected monthly sales and places that figure in the next monthly period. "Total Receipts" adds up these adjusted monthly figures to reflect a staggered or installment cash flow. Because of this, there's a two-month lag period after the three-year projections. This two-month lag period is reflected in cells AL39:AM42, AL72, and AM72. This two-month lag period is not reflected in the "INCOME STATEMENT" as it would be reported.

"Withholding" in row 55 was calculated using 22 percent of "Salaries" (row 54), but "Withholding" should be adjusted to reflect current withholding tax standards. Row 67 indicates an outstanding business loan and should be modified to indicate any capital your company borrows. "Total Disbursements" (row 70) are derived by adding the projected figures for each month, rows 45–68. "Net Cash From Operations" are calculated by subtracting "Total Disbursements" (row 70) from "Total Receipts" (row 42).

Income statement

In Fig 2-2, cells A1 through AM72 (A1:AM72) contain the "INCOME STATEMENT" for your company. Cell A77 should be modified to list your company name. Column "A" lists the descriptions for the data that will be calculated from the figures in the "CASH FLOW PROJECTIONS." Cells B80:B127 reflect your first year of operation. Cells C80:C127 show the second year, and cells E80:E127 display the third year. Cells D80:D127 reflect the percentage of change from the first year to the second, and cells F80:F127 disclose the percentage of change from the second year to the third.

"Gross Sales," row 80, add up the month to year totals from "Total Sales," row 35. "Installment Income Variance," row 81, subtracts the adjusted "Total Receipts," row 42, from the "Total Sales," row 35, to reflect the influence of installment payments. "Net Sales," row 82, adds up the month to year totals from "Total Receipts," row 42.

	A	B	C	D	E	F
1	CASH FLOW PROJECTIONS					
2	(YOUR COMPANY NAME)					
3						
4		Jan	Feb	Mar	Apr	May
5	Sales:					
6	Permanent Placement					
7	Temporary Placement					
8	Secretarial Service					
9	Resume Preparation					
10	Cover Letters					
11	Typing & Word Processing					
12	Faxing					
13	Mail Receiving Services					
14	Copy Service					
15	Message Service					
16	Audio Tape Editing					
17	Transcribing Service					
18	Laser Printing					
19	Graphic Design					
20	Typesetting					
21	Newsletter Preparation					
22	Brochures					
23	Mailing Lists					
24	Label Making					
25	Collating					
26	Editing					
27	Notary Public					
28	Computor Tutorial					
29	Workshops					
30	Resourcing					
31	Interviewing Skills					
32	Dress Codes					
33	Payrolling					
34						
35	Total Sales	=SUM(B6:B33)	=SUM(C6:C33)	=SUM(D6:D33)	=SUM(E6:E33)	=SUM(F6:F33)
36						
37	Cash Receipts					
38	First Month	=B35*0.6	=C35*0.6	=D35*0.6	=E35*0.6	=F35*0.6
39	Second Month		=B35*0.25	=C35*0.25	=D35*0.25	=E35*0.25
40	Third Month			=B35*0.15	=C35*0.15	=D35*0.15
41						
42	Total Receipts	=SUM(B38:B40)	=SUM(C38:C40)	=SUM(D38:D40)	=SUM(E38:E40)	=SUM(F38:F40)
43						
44	Cash Disbursements					
45	Rent/Lease/Mortgage					
46	Telephone					
47	Utilities					
48	Structure Insurance					
49	Vehicle Insurance					
50	Bond					
51	Office Equipment rental					
52	Advertising					
53	Postage					
54	Salaries					
55	Withholding	=B54*0.22	=C54*0.22	=D54*0.22	=E54*0.22	=F54*0.22
56	Telemarketing Commissions					
57	Employee Profit Sharing					
58	(Given Every Quarter)					
59	Professional Services					
60	Office Supplies					
61	Office Expense					
62	Vehicle Expense					
63	Education					
64	Research					
65	Dues, Memberships, Subscriptions					
66	Travel & Entertainment					
67	Initial Investment ($25,000) Loan Payment					
68	Miscellaneous					
69						
70	Total Disbursements	=SUM(B45:B68)	=SUM(C45:C68)	=SUM(D45:D68)	=SUM(E45:E68)	=SUM(F45:F68)
71						
72	Net Cash From Operations	=B42-B70	=C42-C70	=D42-D70	=E42-E70	=F42-F70
73						

2-1 Cash flow projections.

	G	H	I	J	K	L	M
1							
2							
3	1st Year						
4	Jun	Jul	Aug	Sep	Oct	Nov	Dec
5							
6							
7							
8							
9							
10							
11							
12							
13							
14							
15							
16							
17							
18							
19							
20							
21							
22							
23							
24							
25							
26							
27							
28							
29							
30							
31							
32							
33							
34							
35	=SUM(G6:G33)	=SUM(H6:H33)	=SUM(I6:I33)	=SUM(J6:J33)	=SUM(K6:K33)	=SUM(L6:L33)	=SUM(M6:M33)
36							
37							
38	=G35*0.6	=H35*0.6	=I35*0.6	=J35*0.6	=K35*0.6	=L35*0.6	=M35*0.6
39	=F35*0.25	=G35*0.25	=H35*0.25	=I35*0.25	=J35*0.25	=K35*0.25	=L35*0.25
40	=E35*0.15	=F35*0.15	=G35*0.15	=H35*0.15	=I35*0.15	=J35*0.15	=K35*0.15
41							
42	=SUM(G38:G40)	=SUM(H38:H40)	=SUM(I38:I40)	=SUM(J38:J40)	=SUM(K38:K40)	=SUM(L38:L40)	=SUM(M38:M40)
43							
44							
45							
46							
47							
48							
49							
50							
51							
52							
53							
54							
55	=G54*0.22	=H54*0.22	=I54*0.22	=J54*0.22	=K54*0.22	=L54*0.22	=M54*0.22
56							
57							
58							
59							
60							
61							
62							
63							
64							
65							
66							
67							
68							
69							
70	=SUM(G45:G68)	=SUM(H45:H68)	=SUM(I45:I68)	=SUM(J45:J68)	=SUM(K45:K68)	=SUM(L45:L68)	=SUM(M45:M68)
71							
72	=G42-G70	=H42-H70	=I42-I70	=J42-J70	=K42-K70	=L42-L70	=M42-M70
73							

2-1 Continued.

	N	O	P	Q	R	S
1	CASH FLOW PROJECTIONS					
2	(YOUR COMPANY NAME)					
3						2nd Year
4	Jan	Feb	Mar	Apr	May	Jun
5						
6						
7						
8						
9						
10						
11						
12						
13						
14						
15						
16						
17						
18						
19						
20						
21						
22						
23						
24						
25						
26						
27						
28						
29						
30						
31						
32						
33						
34						
35	=SUM(N6:N33)	=SUM(O6:O33)	=SUM(P6:P33)	=SUM(Q6:Q33)	=SUM(R6:R33)	=SUM(S6:S33)
36						
37						
38	=N35*0.6	=O35*0.6	=P35*0.6	=Q35*0.6	=R35*0.6	=S35*0.6
39	=M35*0.25	=N35*0.25	=O35*0.25	=P35*0.25	=Q35*0.25	=R35*0.25
40	=L35*0.15	=M35*0.15	=N35*0.15	=O35*0.15	=P35*0.15	=Q35*0.15
41						
42	=SUM(N38:N40)	=SUM(O38:O40)	=SUM(P38:P40)	=SUM(Q38:Q40)	=SUM(R38:R40)	=SUM(S38:S40)
43						
44						
45						
46						
47						
48						
49						
50						
51						
52						
53						
54						
55	=N54*0.22	=O54*0.22	=P54*0.22	=Q54*0.22	=R54*0.22	=S54*0.22
56						
57						
58						
59						
60						
61						
62						
63						
64						
65						
66						
67						
68						
69						
70	=SUM(N45:N68)	=SUM(O45:O68)	=SUM(P45:P68)	=SUM(Q45:Q68)	=SUM(R45:R68)	=SUM(S45:S68)
71						
72	=N42-N70	=O42-O70	=P42-P70	=Q42-Q70	=R42-R70	=S42-S70
73						

	T	U	V	W	X	Y	Z
1							CASH FLOW PROJECTIONS
2							(YOUR COMPANY NAME)
3							
4	Jul	Aug	Sep	Oct	Nov	Dec	Jan
5							
6							
7							
8							
9							
10							
11							
12							
13							
14							
15							
16							
17							
18							
19							
20							
21							
22							
23							
24							
25							
26							
27							
28							
29							
30							
31							
32							
33							
34							
35	=SUM(T6:T33)	=SUM(U6:U33)	=SUM(V6:V33)	=SUM(W6:W33)	=SUM(X6:X33)	=SUM(Y6:Y33)	=SUM(Z6:Z33)
36							
37							
38	=T35*0.6	=U35*0.6	=V35*0.6	=W35*0.6	=X35*0.6	=Y35*0.6	=Z35*0.6
39	=S35*0.25	=T35*0.25	=U35*0.25	=V35*0.25	=W35*0.25	=X35*0.25	=Y35*0.25
40	=R35*0.15	=S35*0.15	=T35*0.15	=U35*0.15	=V35*0.15	=W35*0.15	=X35*0.15
41							
42	=SUM(T38:T40)	=SUM(U38:U40)	=SUM(V38:V40)	=SUM(W38:W40)	=SUM(X38:X40)	=SUM(Y38:Y40)	=SUM(Z38:Z40)
43							
44							
45							
46							
47							
48							
49							
50							
51							
52							
53							
54							
55	=T54*0.22	=U54*0.22	=V54*0.22	=W54*0.22	=X54*0.22	=Y54*0.22	=Z54*0.22
56							
57							
58							
59							
60							
61							
62							
63							
64							
65							
66							
67							
68							
69							
70	=SUM(T45:T68)	=SUM(U45:U68)	=SUM(V45:V68)	=SUM(W45:W68)	=SUM(X45:X68)	=SUM(Y45:Y68)	=SUM(Z45:Z68)
71							
72	=T42-T70	=U42-U70	=V42-V70	=W42-W70	=X42-X70	=Y42-Y70	=Z42-Z70
73							

2-1 Continued.

	AA	AB	AC	AD	AE	AF
1						
2						
3					3rd Year	
4	Feb	Mar	Apr	May	Jun	Jul
5						
6						
7						
8						
9						
10						
11						
12						
13						
14						
15						
16						
17						
18						
19						
20						
21						
22						
23						
24						
25						
26						
27						
28						
29						
30						
31						
32						
33						
34						
35	=SUM(AA6:AA33)	=SUM(AB6:AB33)	=SUM(AC6:AC33)	=SUM(AD6:AD33)	=SUM(AE6:AE33)	=SUM(AF6:AF33)
36						
37						
38	=AA35*0.6	=AB35*0.6	=AC35*0.6	=AD35*0.6	=AE35*0.6	=AF35*0.6
39	=Z35*0.25	=AA35*0.25	=AB35*0.25	=AC35*0.25	=AD35*0.25	=AE35*0.25
40	=Y35*0.15	=Z35*0.15	=AA35*0.15	=AB35*0.15	=AC35*0.15	=AD35*0.15
41						
42	=SUM(AA38:AA40)	=SUM(AB38:AB40)	=SUM(AC38:AC40)	=SUM(AD38:AD40)	=SUM(AE38:AE40)	=SUM(AF38:AF40)
43						
44						
45						
46						
47						
48						
49						
50						
51						
52						
53						
54						
55	=AA54*0.22	=AB54*0.22	=AC54*0.22	=AD54*0.22	=AE54*0.22	=AF54*0.22
56						
57						
58						
59						
60						
61						
62						
63						
64						
65						
66						
67						
68						
69						
70	=SUM(AA45:AA68)	=SUM(AB45:AB68)	=SUM(AC45:AC68)	=SUM(AD45:AD68)	=SUM(AE45:AE68)	=SUM(AF45:AF68)
71						
72	=AA42-AA70	=AB42-AB70	=AC42-AC70	=AD42-AD70	=AE42-AE70	=AF42-AF70
73						

	AG	AH	AI	AJ	AK	AL	AM
1							
2							
3							
4	Aug	Sep	Oct	Nov	Dec		
5							
6							
7							
8							
9							
10							
11							
12							
13							
14							
15							
16							
17							
18							
19							
20							
21							
22							
23							
24							
25							
26							
27							
28							
29							
30							
31							
32							
33							
34							
35	=SUM(AG6:AG33)	=SUM(AH6:AH33)	=SUM(AI6:AI33)	=SUM(AJ6:AJ33)	=SUM(AK6:AK33)		
36							
37							
38	=AG35*0.6	=AH35*0.6	=AI35*0.6	=AJ35*0.6	=AK35*0.6		
39	=AF35*0.25	=AG35*0.25	=AH35*0.25	=AI35*0.25	=AJ35*0.25	=AK35*0.25	
40	=AE35*0.15	=AF35*0.15	=AG35*0.15	=AH35*0.15	=AI35*0.15	=AJ35*0.15	=AK35*0.15
41							
42	=SUM(AG38:AG40)	=SUM(AH38:AH40)	=SUM(AI38:AI40)	=SUM(AJ38:AJ40)	=SUM(AK38:AK40)	=SUM(AL38:AL40)	=SUM(AM38:AM40)
43							
44							
45							
46							
47							
48							
49							
50							
51							
52							
53							
54							
55	=AG54*0.22	=AH54*0.22	=AI54*0.22	=AJ54*0.22	=AK54*0.22		
56							
57							
58							
59							
60							
61							
62							
63							
64							
65							
66							
67							
68							
69							
70	=SUM(AG45:AG68)	=SUM(AH45:AH68)	=SUM(AI45:AI68)	=SUM(AJ45:AJ68)	=SUM(AK45:AK68)		
71							
72	=AG42-AG70	=AH42-AH70	=AI42-AI70	=AJ42-AJ70	=AK42-AK70	=AL42-AL70	=AM42-AM70
73							

2-1 Continued.

	A	B	C	D
76	**INCOME STATEMENT**			
77	**(YOUR COMPANY NAME)**			
78		1st Year	2nd Year	
79	Revenue			%
80	Gross Sales	=SUM(B35:M35)	=SUM(N35:Y35)	=(C80-B80)/B80
81	Installment Income Variance	=(SUM(B42:M42))-(SUM(B35:M35))	=(SUM(N42:Y42))-(SUM(N35:Y35))	=(C81-B81)/B81
82	Net Sales	=SUM(B42:M42)	=SUM(N42:Y42)	=(C82-B82)/B82
83				
84	Sales Expense			
85	Advertising	=SUM(B52:M52)	=SUM(N52:Y52)	=(C85-B85)/B85
86	Telemarketing	=SUM(B56:M56)	=SUM(N56:Y56)	=(C86-B86)/B86
87	Employee Profit Sharing	=SUM(B57:M57)	=SUM(N57:Y57)	=(C87-B87)/B87
88	Travel & Entertainment	=SUM(B66:M66)	=SUM(N66:Y66)	=(C88-B88)/B88
89				
90	Total Sales Expense	=SUM(B85:B88)	=SUM(C85:C88)	=(C90-B90)/B90
91				
92	Administrative Expense			
93	Insurance	=SUM(B48:M49)	=SUM(N48:Y49)	=(C93-B93)/B93
94	Bond	=SUM(B50:M50)	=SUM(N50:Y50)	=(C94-B94)/B94
95	Salaries	=SUM(B54:M54)	=SUM(N54:Y54)	=(C95-B95)/B95
96	Withholding	=SUM(B55:M55)	=SUM(N55:Y55)	=(C96-B96)/B96
97	Professional	=SUM(B59:M59)	=SUM(N59:Y59)	=(C97-B97)/B97
98				
99	Total Administrative Expense	=SUM(B93:B98)	=SUM(C93:C98)	=(C99-B99)/B99
100				
101	General Expense			
102	Rent/Lease/Mortgage	=SUM(B45:M45)	=SUM(N45:Y45)	=(C102-B102)/B102
103	Telephone	=SUM(B46:M46)	=SUM(N46:Y46)	=(C103-B103)/B103
104	Utilities	=SUM(B47:M47)	=SUM(N47:Y47)	=(C104-B104)/B104
105	Office Equipment Rental	=SUM(B51:M51)	=SUM(N51:Y51)	=(C105-B105)/B105
106	Postage	=SUM(B53:M53)	=SUM(N53:Y53)	=(C106-B106)/B106
107	Office Supplies	=SUM(B60:M60)	=SUM(N60:Y60)	=(C107-B107)/B107
108	Office Expense	=SUM(B61:M61)	=SUM(N61:Y61)	=(C108-B108)/B108
109	Vehicle Expense	=SUM(B62:M62)	=SUM(N62:Y62)	=(C109-B109)/B109
110	Education	=SUM(B63:M63)	=SUM(N63:Y63)	=(C110-B110)/B110
111	Research	=SUM(B64:M64)	=SUM(N64:Y64)	=(C111-B111)/B111
112	Dues, Membership, Subscriptions	=SUM(B65:M65)	=SUM(N65:Y65)	=(C112-B112)/B112
113	Loan Payment ($25,000 @10% 3 Years)	=800.06*12	=800.06*12	=(C113-B113)/B113
114	Miscellaneous	=SUM(B68:M68)	=SUM(N68:Y68)	=(C114-B114)/B114
115				
116	Total General Expense	=SUM(B102:B114)	=SUM(C102:C114)	=(C116-B116)/B116
117				
118	Total Operating Expenses	=B116+B99+B90	=C116+C99+C90	=(C118-B118)/B118
119				
120	Total Operating Income	=B82-B118	=C82-C118	=(C120-B120)/B120
121	State Tax	=B120*0.05	=C120*0.05	=(C121-B121)/B121
122				
123	Pretax Income	=B120-B121	=C120-C121	=(C123-B123)/B123
124	Federal Tax	=B123*0.25	=C123*0.25	=(C124-B124)/B124
125				
126	Net Income	=B123-B124	=C123-C124	=(C126-B126)/B126

2-2 Income statement.

	E	F
76		
77		
78	3rd Year	
79		%
80	=SUM(Z35:AK35)	=(E80-C80)/C80
81	=(SUM(Z42:AK42))-(SUM(Z35:AK35))	=(E81-C81)/C81
82	=SUM(Z42:AK42)	=(E82-C82)/C82
83		
84		
85	=SUM(Z52:AK52)	=(E85-C85)/C85
86	=SUM(Z56:AK56)	=(E86-C86)/C86
87	=SUM(Z57:AK57)	=(E87-C87)/C87
88	=SUM(Z66:AK66)	=(E88-C88)/C88
89		
90	=SUM(E85:E88)	=(E90-C90)/C90
91		
92		
93	=SUM(Z48:AK49)	=(E93-C93)/C93
94	=SUM(Z50:AK50)	=(E94-C94)/C94
95	=SUM(Z54:AK54)	=(E95-C95)/C95
96	=SUM(Z55:AK55)	=(E96-C96)/C96
97	=SUM(Z59:AK59)	=(E97-C97)/C97
98		
99	=SUM(E93:E98)	=(E99-C99)/C99
100		
101		
102	=SUM(Z45:AK45)	=(E102-C102)/C102
103	=SUM(Z46:AK46)	=(E103-C103)/C103
104	=SUM(Z47:AK47)	=(E104-C104)/C104
105	=SUM(Z51:AK51)	=(E105-C105)/C105
106	=SUM(Z53:AK53)	=(E106-C106)/C106
107	=SUM(Z60:AK60)	=(E107-C107)/C107
108	=SUM(Z61:AK61)	=(E108-C108)/C108
109	=SUM(Z62:AK62)	=(E109-C109)/C109
110	=SUM(Z63:AK63)	=(E110-C110)/C110
111	=SUM(Z64:AK64)	=(E111-C111)/C111
112	=SUM(Z65:AK65)	=(E112-C112)/C112
113	=800.06*12	=(E113-C113)/C113
114	=SUM(Z68:AK68)	=(E114-C114)/C114
115		
116	=SUM(E102:E114)	=(E116-C116)/C116
117		
118	=E116+E99+E90	=(E118-C118)/C118
119		
120	=E82-E118	=(E120-C120)/C120
121	=E120*0.05	=(E121-C121)/C121
122		
123	=E120-E121	=(E123-C123)/C123
124	=E123*0.25	=(E124-C124)/C124
125		
126	=E123-E124	=(E126-C126)/C126

2-2 Continued.

"Advertising," row 85, adds up the month to year totals from "Advertising," row 52. "Telemarketing," row 86, adds up the month to year totals from "Telemarketing," row 56. "Employee Profit Sharing," row 87, adds up the month to year totals from "Employee Profit Sharing," row 57.

"Travel and Entertainment," row 88, adds up the month to year totals from "Travel and Entertainment," row 66. "Total Sales Expense," row 90, adds the four categories within "Sales Expense" of the "INCOME STATEMENT." "Insurance," row 93, adds up the month to year totals from both "Insurance" categories, rows 48 and 49.

"Bond," row 94, adds up the month to year totals from "Bond," row 50. Check with your state and local officials if this is required. "Salaries," row 95, adds up the month to year totals from "Salaries," row 54.

"Withholding," row 96, adds up the month to year totals from "Withholding," row 55. "Professional," row 97, adds up the month to year totals from "Professional Services," row 59. "Total Administrative Expense," row 99, adds the five categories within "Administrative Expense" of the "INCOME STATEMENT."

"Rent/Lease/Mortgage," row 102, adds up the month to year totals from "Rent/Lease/Mortgage," row 45. "Telephone," row 103, adds up the month to year totals from "Telephone," row 46. "Utilities," row 104, adds up the month to year totals from "Utilities," row 47.

"Office Equipment Rental," row 105, adds up the month to year totals from "Office Equipment Rental," row 51. "Postage," row 106, adds up the month to year totals from "Postage," row 53. "Office Supplies," row 107, adds up the month to year totals from "Office Supplies," row 60.

"Office Expense," row 108, adds up the month to year totals from "Office Expense," row 61. "Vehicle Expense," row 109, adds up the month to year totals from "Vehicle Expense," row 62. "Education," row 110, adds up the month to year totals from "Education," row 63. "Research," row 111, adds up the month to year totals from "Research," row 64.

"Dues, Membership, Subscriptions," row 112, adds up the month to year totals from "Dues, Membership, Subscriptions," row 65. "Loan Payment," row 113, multiplies the monthly payment times 12. This should change according to your situation. "Miscellaneous," row 114, adds up the month to year totals from "Miscellaneous," row 68.

"Total General Expense," row 116, adds the 13 categories within "General Expense" of the "INCOME STATEMENT." "Total Operating Expenses," row 118, adds "Total Sales Expense," row 90, "Total Administrative Expense," row 99, and "Total General Expense," row 116.

"Total Operating Income," row 120, subtracts "Total Operating Expenses," row 118 from "Net Sales," row 82. "State Tax," row 121, multiplies "Total Operating Income," row 120 by 5 percent. This 5 percent will vary according to the state.

"Pretax Income," row 123, subtracts "State Tax," row 121 from "Total Operating Income," row 120. "Federal Tax," row 124, multiplies "Pretax Income," row 123 by 25 percent. This will vary from year to year. "Net Income," row 126, subtracts "Federal Tax," row 124 from "Pretax Income," row 123.

BUSINESS OWNERSHIP

Once you've decided to start the business, you have to consider under which legal form it will take.

- Sole proprietorship.
- Partnership.
- Limited partnership.
- Corporation.

Sole proprietorship

This means that the business will have only one owner. There will not even be silent partners allowed in a sole proprietorship. It's the easiest method of starting a business. You don't have to have any legal papers other than the business license and a fictitious-name filing. There are no separate income tax returns like you would need for other types of businesses. Each year, the income and expenses that you report will be filed on a Schedule C of IRS Form 1040. Also, the FICA taxes are less for the owner than in other forms.

The only true disadvantage of the sole proprietorship is that the creditors of your firm can attach your personal property and bank accounts. Your personal credit can be ruined, and you can be harassed for years after the business closes.

Partnership

General

This legal form of operation is extremely dangerous. If the partnership has two or more people involved, each becomes liable for the others' actions. If there is any legal action, each partner can be sued personally, with bank accounts and property attached. One partner can be left with a major mess if the other partner skips town.

Very few partnerships survive without severe conflicts, and this usually causes the business to eventually fail. Do not try to form a partnership on a verbal agreement and a handshake. Your attorney fees for forming this style of ownership are about the same as for the other choices, so be sure your attorney draws up the appropriate formal contracts.

The IRS requires that a Form 1065 be filed as the tax return. You must also secure a Federal Employee Identification number using Form SS-4. The partnership itself does not pay any of the year-end taxes with its tax return. Each partner reports his or her share of the profit and losses on his or her own individual tax return, and each pays the taxes on those profits.

Limited partnerships

Limited partnerships are very similar to corporations. Investors in the partnership are only liable for their individual investment. But that's all they can lose. The silent partner situation is one where one or more partners put up capital, and the other partner(s) run the business. A limited partnership protects the assets of prosperous silent partners. This form of ownership is usually used for real-estate syndications. The 1986 Tax Reform Act now limits the amount of losses limited partners can deduct on their personal tax return.

Corporation

A corporation is considered the most realistic way to start a business because the corporation is a separate entity from you. The corporation is solely responsible for the business actions and debts. You become protected in most situations because you are considered to be an employee of the corporation. This happens even though you might own all or most of the stock. If you don't operate the corporation in the required financial or legal manner, you might lose this protection.

In a corporation, you can enjoy many executive privileges that are hard to justify in a partnership or sole proprietorship. Shareholders that are forming a corporation can divide the ownership into shares. Corporate minutes can define the responsibilities. One of the shareholders can leave without much legal pressure and without forcing the business to dissolve.

Set up a shareholders' agreement that provides for the purchase of one shareholder's portion in the event of his or her death. This agreement can grant the other shareholders the right of first refusal.

One disadvantage is double taxation. The corporation must pay taxes on the net income, and you must also pay taxes on the dividends received from the corporation. Some business owners increase their own salaries in order to reduce the corporate profits. This lowers the possibilities of having the profits taxed twice.

Subchapter S corporation

Subchapter S allows profits or losses to travel directly through the corporation to you and other shareholders. If your firm produces a substantial profit, forming a Subchapter S corporation would be smart. This is because the profits will be added to your personal income and taxed at an individual rate.

The qualifications for filing Subchapter S corporations are:
- Corporation must be a domestic.
- Corporation must not be a member of an affiliated group.
- Corporation must not have more than 35 shareholders.

For more information on Subchapter S corporations, contact your local IRS office.

SELECT COMPANY NAME AND LOGO

What's the identity of this new enterprise of yours? Picture how it will sound when your receptionist answers the phone, "Good morning . . ." Do you like how it sounds? What will the symbol be that represents your firm and appears on all your documentation and advertising? Does it grow on you?

Company name

One of the most enjoyable projects in the creation of your agency is the professional identification. Your personal dream of becoming self-employed becomes very real when there's a name attached to the concept. Be sure to choose one that is distinctive and professional sounding, and one that will be effective for employers and applicants alike. It's always a good idea to try to select a company title that indicates what type of business you are operating. When choosing the name for my own company, I picked North Coast Personnel Agency because it was indicative of the area in which I wanted to serve (North Coast) and clearly described the type of service I was offering to the general public (personnel). The agency that I worked in during my training period was named Redwood Empire Employment Agency. Again, the area in which we targeted clientele was in the Redwood Empire, and Employment Agency stated the type of service. It should be easy and fun to find a good name. Ask your friends, family, and business associates for their ideas, too. It's always a good idea to get as many choices as possible and try them out on a few people until you find the one that sounds the best to you.

Try to picture what the name would look like in the Yellow Pages display advertising of the telephone book and in the newspaper want ads. The name will be on all your business cards, letterhead, and envelopes, so pick a name that is easy to say, easy to understand, and easy to announce when you answer your phone. "Good morning, North Coast Personnel . . . ."

One of the things you want to avoid is opting for a personal name such as Roberts Personnel Agency. The reason for this is simple. If at some point in the future you want to sell your firm, it's very difficult to find someone else who thinks like you, works like you, and does business exactly like you. Through all your diligent effort, your reputation in the industry has been firmly established, and the last thing in the world you want is someone negatively affecting all your hard work in the creation of the business. It doesn't happen often, but sometimes the new owner doesn't represent your service in the way you did, so why take the chance on having them destroy your name, as well as your business?

Logo

Creating a strong company image is not only done in the selection of a name, but also in the visual trademark. You want a business image that represents you and your firm and is easily reprintable with all your future advertising, stationery, etc. You might eventually want to have some advertising specialties designed for your marketing (coffee cups, pens, calendars, etc.) programs. It would be difficult to expect even the most professional firm to try to effectively reproduce tiny images or intricate pictures.

Look in the Yellow Pages display advertising of your phone book for some examples of logos. There are certainly many types. See which ones catch your eye at a quick glance and which ones get lost or skimmed over in the process.

Fortunately, there are several avenues to choose from for the selection of the design for your company image. Graphics firms offer the service, and now there are computer programs available that help you select your own. If the start-up cost is a major factor for your business (which is most likely), then you might opt for the individualized approach. Either way, take your time, be careful, and pick something you will be comfortable with for years and years. The odds are it will never change.

FICTITIOUS BUSINESS NAME STATEMENT: D.B.A. (DOING BUSINESS AS)

If the name of your agency is different from your personal name, you might be required to register it with a county, city, or state agency. Contact your local county clerk's office to find out if that's required in your selected area. They will mail you the necessary forms and give you any information requested on the subject.

There is a registration fee, and the cost will vary per state. It ranges between $10 and $100. In some states, as part of the legal procedure, you are required to run a fictitious business name statement in a local newspaper. North Coast Personnel Agency was in California. The requirement was to post a four-week consecutive run in a paper within the county. The cost for this was minimal, but I suggest you call all the papers in your area and get price quotes from each one for the four-week run. Since this is not to be considered part of your advertising budget, select the least expensive quote.

One other way to find out if you will be required to have a fictitious name notice is to contact the bank that will be acting as your business financial entity. Ask if the bank requires the certification in order to open your business bank account. If they do, ask them where you need to go to get the proper form.

Sole proprietors and partnerships are required to follow this procedure when they choose distinctive names for business. Corporations don't need to apply for the fictitious business name statement in most states unless they are doing business under a different name. If you choose incorporation, these legal documents act as the fictitious filing requirement.

BUSINESS LICENSE

In order to show compliance with most city and county regulations, a business license will be required for your new company. There is a minimal fee to operate your business, which again, varies per area. Some cities receive a percentage of your gross revenue receipts.

The license will be processed through the zoning or planning department, and they will check to see if a personnel agency falls within the proper legal zoning requirements. They will determine if there are enough parking facilities to accommodate your type of business. If you are planning to open your business in an area where there are several other service oriented companies, you should have very few problems with zoning.

LOCATION

The location of your business is every bit as important as the name you pick or the style and reputation you develop.

Community

Several questions need to be answered at this crucial stage:
- Are you planning to service a densely populated area or a relatively small community?
- Would the current population support a business like yours?
- Are there other agencies already providing this service, and if so, how many and what types?
- Is there a stable economic base in the community?
- Do high-school and college graduates tend to seek employment outside the area?

- Is there a broad-minded chamber of commerce?
- Are there good public services and school systems?

These are just a few of the questions you'll want to examine before you begin to get too serious about setting up an agency. When you research the community, try to find the answers to all of these questions. Generally, new agency owners are totally familiar with their chosen communities, but if not, be sure to do your homework!

Site

One of the idioms in business that I find most appropriate in site selection is: location, location, location. You must be easily locatable for all your clients. Be sure there is a freeway access close by your office, and that the city streets are well maintained and clearly marked. Since you'll need plenty of parking for the applicants registering with your service, try to find a facility where the parking is free, or at least minimal. The last thing you or your applicant want to do is worry about the parking meter ticking while a counseling session is in process.

The professional demeanor of your office complex is another extremely important consideration. This is the snapshot by which clients evaluate the character, personality, and style of your service. Take as much time as you need to select a business environment that is pleasant and appealing to anyone stopping by. Above all, make sure it's clean and comfortable.

When I first opened North Coast, I chose an office building that housed other types of service businesses within the building structure. There was a bookkeeping service, attorney services, notary public, and small publishing firm. This automatically gave me a group of employer/clients who quickly became completely aware of, and loyal to, my services. Since I saw these individuals on a daily basis, we were able to create a friend/business relationship that evolved into a more trusting friendship than with most clients. We were able to satisfy the staffing requirements for each of these firms for several years, and we made a great deal of revenue from the automatic referrals they sent our way from their business contacts.

Eventually, you might decide to move your practice into a single residence, such as a one- or two-bedroom house, on a busy thoroughfare. This should only be done after you have outgrown your initial space, established a strong reputation, and developed an exclusive client list that will follow you, no matter where you move the business. Take special care when choosing your home away from home. Since you are the only one deciding, make sure it's where you want to spend the majority of your time.

STATIONERY, LETTERHEAD, ETC.

You should be able to buy all your stationery, letterhead, envelopes, business cards, and necessary record-keeping forms for around $200 at your local discount office-supply store. Larger retailers, such as Office Plus, Office Discounts, Costco, etc., will have a wide variety of forms for your personal selection. Look in the Yellow Pages for listings under "Office Supplies," "Paper Products-Wholesale," or "Stationers-Retail."

Since your business materials are a snapshot of your professionalism and style, be sure to get the best quality available for the best price. Don't skimp on this part of your business start-up, as it could cause you to lose valuable style and reputation points with those valuable clients in the future.

If you decide to have a logo created and letterhead with envelopes printed, contact several of the larger printing houses in your area and get several bids from each of them for your specific project. Since your stationery is a reflection of your image in the business community, be picky! Watch out for the volume discount quotes. When talking with the printer about cost, it always sounds great to get a larger volume at a reduced rate, but remember, you might decide to change things a few times in the beginning stages of your new enterprise. Until your systems are finally refined, the business forms might change several times. So don't get trapped in the initial ordering process with too much of a product that makes your upgrading choices limited.

There are several software programs on the market that are designed to help entrepreneurs create the images of their choice. The look you create for your business can be extremely professional and very personal. Try the Paint program that comes with Windows. Also try the graphics programs that comes with the packaged "office" programs.

Business cards are one of the most inexpensive source of advertising known. They are distributed to a variety of potential clients in numerous situations and at several locations. Every time someone asks for your card, give them two. Ask them to keep one for themselves and pass the second one on to someone else. This type of advertising brings in more business than you can imagine. Get your business cards in as many hands as possible. Include it every time you send out a piece of business correspondence or your brochure. Don't put too much information on the card. It's frustrating for the reader if it's too "busy." Keep it short and simple: logo, company name, your name, short byline, address, phone number, and fax number when appropriate. Use the same type style for all the information on the card.

Lay all the business cards you've accumulated on a table and see what attracts your attention. Look for the markings that catch your eye and focus your attention. Remember, don't try to "reinvent the wheel." If you see one that works for you, tailor the style for your own. Use what works, and you'll be far better off.

You might want to design a grand opening announcement card and envelope. This can be sent to all of your friends, the businesses you currently know, and all the future businesses you want to develop. Be sure to make it a personalized mailing and include two business cards in each one. Before sending the announcement, telephone the company first, ask for the name of the hiring source within the firm, and address it directly to this individual. When the receptionist asks why you want the name, be sure to tell them it's for an announcement notice for the opening of your new firm. Be sure to answer any questions they might have when you call. When selecting the size of the announcement, look through one of the mail order business catalogues that have business forms and office supplies, or visit your local printer's office or stationery shop. (See Fig. 2-3.)

When I opened my own firm, I also designed an "introduction to the interview" card. This was taken by the applicant to each job interview and handed to the interviewer prior to the meeting. This small card not only gave my company a classier presentation, but the employer had one more piece of paper with the North Coast name attached. (See Fig. 2-4.)

Color, texture, and style are very important! Again, look at the choices that are available to you, as there are many. Pick a color that's easy on the eyes, and select a

2-3 New company announcement card.

2-4 Interview announcement card.

print style that flows smoothly. The feel of the paper is as important as the color. There are several grains and weights to choose from. Take the time to do this part of the setup carefully, and you'll always be glad you did. It feels good when you're complimented on the choices you made. Since your business materials reflect the company image, and that image is you, they should always be of the highest quality.

BUSINESS FORMS

A personnel agency is an extremely detail-oriented business and requires numerous forms to make the operation run more smoothly. All of the forms listed in the following section have been carefully refined and tested over the years, and they have proven to work remarkably well in a very busy practice.

Job applications

Every time an applicant comes into your office for an interview, he or she will be given this standard business form to fill out before talking with an employment counselor. The receptionist needs to be sure they fill out this form completely, even if they have brought a résumé. Unfortunately, very few people enjoy this particular part of looking for work. Sometimes they act as though it's tedious, time-consuming, and a general pain in the neck! Actually, it's one of the most valuable tools the interviewer has to gather the necessary information for valuable future employer introductions.

The paper stock (weight) for the application should be a slightly larger bond than the business stationery, as it will be handled often and can easily get damaged if it's too flimsy. I used a weight similar to the business card stock since it was often paper-clipped to job orders.

When picking the color, make sure that it's easy on the eyes, not bright. Select a clear and concise print style with plenty of space for writing. Also, keep the color scheme consistent for all your stationery. (See Fig. 2-5.)

Fee schedule (applicant)

The second form handed to the new applicant, along with the application, is the explanation of fees (Fig. 2-6 at the end of chapter). Because of its importance, the fee schedule is one of the first pieces of information applicants should see. No one should ever be surprised that the services you offer cost money. Some will not choose to pay the fee or be involved with a charge for services at any level, so it's always best to find this out quickly and up front, so as not to waste anyone's time. Sometimes an order comes in that's fee paid. This means the employer is held responsible for the entire fee. Some applicants might only want to be contacted for those openings.

Fee schedule (employer)

Most of the time, employers will be contacting your office by telephone to make a request for a new employee. The discussion of fees usually happens during this conversation, and ordinarily only on the first job order given from this particular firm. After the phone call, when the letter confirming the job order is prepared, also include and send a copy of the employer fee schedule (Fig. 2-7 at the end of chapter) at the same time.

Credit applications

If you decide to offer your services as an applicant-paid-fee agency, or split-fee agency, then it's very important to have the client fill out a credit application (Fig. 2-8) at the same time they fill out the placement contract (Fig. 2-9). This will aid you in your decision to extend credit to this individual in the future. Detailed credit application information will be covered in chapter 9, under "RUNNING CREDIT CHECKS."

Placement contracts

The agency counselors should have a book of contracts numbered and bound in packages of 50 at their desks. Each contract should have two copies, one that is removed from the binder and given to the applicant, after signing, and one that remains bound in the packet and left at the counselor's desk. They are always prepared individually for each applicant and employer introduction made by your company.

Before an applicant goes to an interview, he or she needs to read and sign the placement contract for that specific job order. This agreement includes all of the pertinent data directly related to the job order and potential placement. The information includes: name and address of applicant, current date, date and time of interview, name and address of company placing the order, contract number, job order num-

2-5 Application for employment.

(COMPANY NAME)
APPLICATION
(Please Print)

Position Desired _____ Salary Required _____

PERSONAL

Name _____

Address _____ City _____ Zip _____

Telephone Number _____ Message Number _____

How did you hear about this agency? _____

Is there any information we would need about your name or use of another name for us to be able to check your work record?

_____

Have you ever been convicted of a felony? _____ No _____ Yes (If yes, please explain) _____

EDUCATION

	School Name/Location	Years Completed	Degree/Diploma
High School			
College			
Tech. Training			
Other			
Special Study			
Special Skills			

EMPLOYMENT RECORD
(Please include employment for at least 10 years)

1. _____

Company Name (Current/Most Recent)	Your Position/Title
	Dates Employed

Address		From	To

Manager/Supervisor	Telephone	Wage/Salary

Reason For Leaving _____

2. _____

Company Name	Your Position/Title
	Dates Employed

Address		From	To

Manager/Supervisor	Telephone	Wage/Salary

Reason For Leaving _____

3. _____

Company Name	Your Position/Title
	Dates Employed

Address		From	To

Manager/Supervisor	Telephone	Wage/Salary

Reason For Leaving _____

4. _____

Company Name	Your Position/Title
	Dates Employed

Address		From	To

Manager/Supervisor	Telephone	Wage/Salary

Reason For Leaving _____

1. _____   _____
   Name   Years Known

   _____   _____
   Address   Telephone

   _____
   Occupation

2. _____   _____
   Name   Years Known

   _____   _____
   Address   Telephone

   _____
   Occupation

3. _____   _____
   Name   Years Known

   _____   _____
   Address   Telephone

   _____
   Occupation

PLEASE READ CAREFULLY BEFORE INTERVIEWING:

Should I accept employment with an employer or employers through the information and services of (Company), I agree to pay the said agency a fee in the amount equal to, as follows:

PERMANENT EMPLOYMENT (Lasting longer than 90 days):

<table>
<tr><td>75% of First Month's Salary
(3 Equal Payments in 90 Days)</td><td>* No Registration Fee
* No Charge until placed
* 5% Discount if all payments are made on time
* 10% Discount if paid within 5 working days of placement
* Visa and MasterCard accepted</td></tr>
</table>

TEMPORARY PLACEMENT (Lasting less than 90 days):

1/90th of permanent fee for each calendar day employed. Payments for temporary positions are to be made as paychecks are received.

The applicant further understands and agrees that if within 180 days after an introduction to an employer arranged by (Company), the applicant should accept any position offered by said employer, even though it is not the position originally outlined, or as a result of information directly or indirectly by this agency, the applicant agrees to pay or the services as shown above.

I agree to pay all collection costs, including Attorney's fees, on all delinquent accounts when so ordered by the court.

I authorize investigation of all statements in this application. I hereby certify that the answers given by me to the questions and statements herein are true and correct to the best of my knowledge.

Today's Date _____   _____
                                          Signature of Applicant

                                          _____
                                          Social Security Number

2-8 Application for credit.

NAME _____

ADDRESS _____

CITY _____ STATE _____ ZIP CODE _____

TELEPHONE NUMBER _____

CAR DESCRIPTION _____

DRIVERS LICENSE # _____ CAR LICENSE # _____

PINK SLIP _____ (WHO OWNS THE CAR)

BANK NAME _____ ACCOUNT # _____

BANK BRANCH _____ # _____

FINANCIAL REFERENCES:

1. NAME _____ ADDRESS _____

    CITY _____ STATE _____ ZIP CODE _____

2. NAME _____ ADDRESS _____

    CITY _____ STATE _____ ZIP CODE _____

3. NAME _____ ADDRESS _____

    CITY _____ STATE _____ ZIP CODE _____

PAYMENT PLANS (PLEASE CIRCLE ONE)

1. PLAN A - Pay within 5 days of placement and receive a 10% discount.
             Mastercard and Visa accepted.

2. PLAN B - 10% down (payable within five (5) days of hire), THEN, a three
             equal payments (one per month) for ninety (90) days. A 5%
             discount will be granted if all payments are made on time.

DATE _____ SIGNATURE _____

2-9 Placement contract.

(COMPANY)
1111 First Street, Anytown, USA
(222) 333-4444

Contract # _____
Appt. Date _____
Appt. Time _____
Meet With _____

Job Order # _____

Total Amount of Estimated Fee

$ _____

_____ 19___

In consideration of the sum of $_____ to be paid by_____

_____ of which is hereby acknowledged as received, we agree to furnish correct information by which he or she shall

be able to SECURE EMPLOYMENT as _____

with _____

located at _____

CONDITIONS OF EMPLOYMENT

Rate of Wages _____ per _____

Hours per day_____ Work will last _____

Labor Contract ___ Yes___ No   Union Membership Required ___ Yes___ No   Labor Dispute ___ Yes ___ No

Amount of fee, if any, paid by employer _____

Amount of fee, if any, advanced by employer _____

Other terms or understandings : 10% of the Fee MUST be paid within five (5) days of employment. Balance of the Fee MUST
be paid within ninety (90) days of employment, in three (3) equal monthly payments.
* Late charges of 1.5% per month or 18% per year will be added to ALL past due accounts.

How order was given _____ Date _____

Report for position to _____ (name of person to interview)

(COMPANY)

By : _____

This contract is the property of the APPLICANT and must not be taken from him or her. NO FEES UNLESS HIRED.

Signature of Applicant _____

Address _____ Phone _____

Contract Expiration Date _____ 19 _____ .

The applicant shall be responsible for only one full fee for any single placement, whether or not employment is secured through
the assistance of more than one employment agency. (Section 9975, Business and Professions Code)

In no instance in which the employment secured is subsequently terminated shall the fee charged an applicant by an employment agency be greater
than the total gross earnings of the applicant in such employment. (Section 9974.3 Business and Professions Code)

A refund, when due shall be made with 10 working days after requested in writing by the applicant. (Section 9974.7, Business and Professions Code)

If the applicant making a deposit on a fee for placement fails to obtain employment, the employment agency shall upon demand therefor, repay the
amount of the deposit to the applicant. Unless the deposit is returned within 48 hours after demand, the employment agency shall pay the applicant an
additional sum equal to the amount of the deposit. (Section 9977, Business and Professions Code)

ber, contract expiration date, and the financial relationship and time schedule for payments of services rendered for the applicant's share of the placement fee.

The individual signing the placement contract is held legally responsible for the cost of your services only if he or she is hired by the client company. That individual must also earn income for at least 90 days for the full placement fee to be awarded.

The counselor can fill in all the required information on the blank spaces, and then have the applicant read it carefully and sign it before the introduction interview with the employer.

Signing the placement contract does not obligate a client to accept the position, nor does it guarantee the job will be offered. It only guarantees the timely payment for your services if the placement is agreed on by both parties.

One of the biggest problems in sending an applicant to an interview without his or her signature on the agency contract is that the applicant might decide to accept the offered position, and after much headache on your part, the applicant will not be required by a court of law to pay for your services. All the applicant has to say is that he or she heard about the job opening through the grapevine or a friend, and not through your direct referral. If this matter goes to court, the judge will rule in favor of the applicant because there is no contract to back up your case! Unfortunately, I've seen this problem happen with my associates in the placement field. So be very careful and have all the required documentation taken care of before you send the applicant out on an interview.

Job orders

Each time a company requests assistance in recruiting a new employee, a form is filled out detailing all the pertinent information (Fig. 2-10). This exhaustive questionnaire enables the job counselor to cover all the necessary questions regarding the specific requirements of the opening. It's ridiculous to assume that all the pertinent points can be covered, or even remembered, without it. There are simply too many points to cover.

The job orders should also be numbered and bound in packets of 50 for each counselor to have at his or her desk. Just like the placement contracts, the job order book should have duplicate copies so the original can be torn out of the book and used conveniently. The copy stays bound in the packet for record-keeping purposes. This system of tracking the orders will alleviate any future frustration with lost orders.

Eventually, the same job order will be called into the agency by the same employer again and again. So instead of asking all the same questions when they call and wasting valuable time, it's much easier, and more time effective, to take the basic information and pull the previous job order from the inactive files. Detailed job order information is covered in chapter 7, under "TAKING JOB ORDERS."

Long-distance telephone calls

Prepare the form shown in Fig. 2-11 and distribute a copy of it to each of your employees for every month. It will help you avoid the shock when you receive your telephone bill at the end of the month and can't figure out why the charges are so high. When the employees are given this form, they are more likely to curb their personal calls. It will make life much easier, believe me!

2-10 Job order.

(COMPANY)   Job Order #_____
1111 First Street
Anytown, USA   Date_____
(222) 333-4444

JOB TITLE _____

COMPANY NAME_____ PHONE NUMBER_____

ADDRESS_____ TYPE OF BUSINESS_____

MAILING_____ CROSS STREET_____

CO. SIZE_____CONFIDENTIAL?_____ PREFERRED START DATE_____

REQUIREMENTS: TYPE SPEED_____ S/H_____ W/P_____ COMPUTER_____

MVR_____ SMOKING_____ WILL TRAIN_____GROWTH POTENTIAL_____

DUTIES_____

_____

_____

_____

_____

QUALIFICATIONS_____

_____

_____

_____

_____

RATE OF WAGES_____ PER_____ HOURS PER DAY/WEEK_____ DAYS PER WEEK_____

COMMISSION ESTIMATE 1 YR $_____ 5 YR $_____ MILEAGE_____ PAYDAYS_____

BENEFTS: MEDICAL(when)____DENTAL (when)_____OPTICAL____NONE_____OTHER_____

NEW POSITION ___REPLACEMENT___REASON_____PREFERRED START DATE_____

ORDER PLACED PHONE_____LETTER_____IN PERSON_____EXCLUSIVE_____

PLACED BY_____INTERVIEWED BY_____

SALES CALL DATE_____ BY_____

PERSON HIRED_____

START DATE_____SALARY_____

DATE	TIME	NAME	RESULTS

2-11 Log of long-distance calls.

For the month of: _____

Date	Phone #	Name	Appl.	Empl.	Bkpg.	Pers.
_____	_____	_____	_____	_____	_____	_____
_____	_____	_____	_____	_____	_____	_____
_____	_____	_____	_____	_____	_____	_____
_____	_____	_____	_____	_____	_____	_____
_____	_____	_____	_____	_____	_____	_____
_____	_____	_____	_____	_____	_____	_____
_____	_____	_____	_____	_____	_____	_____
_____	_____	_____	_____	_____	_____	_____
_____	_____	_____	_____	_____	_____	_____
_____	_____	_____	_____	_____	_____	_____
_____	_____	_____	_____	_____	_____	_____
_____	_____	_____	_____	_____	_____	_____
_____	_____	_____	_____	_____	_____	_____
_____	_____	_____	_____	_____	_____	_____
_____	_____	_____	_____	_____	_____	_____
_____	_____	_____	_____	_____	_____	_____
_____	_____	_____	_____	_____	_____	_____
_____	_____	_____	_____	_____	_____	_____
_____	_____	_____	_____	_____	_____	_____
_____	_____	_____	_____	_____	_____	_____
_____	_____	_____	_____	_____	_____	_____
_____	_____	_____	_____	_____	_____	_____
_____	_____	_____	_____	_____	_____	_____

Help-wanted advertising tracking form

Every time you call your newspaper and place the help-wanted advertisements for recruitment purposes, fill out a tracking form (Fig. 2-12). Scatter ads are listed by individual titles and short descriptions and are run alphabetically throughout the ad section. A "laundry list" is the full index of all your current job openings, by title, and is generally placed at the beginning of the help-wanted section.

The help-wanted advertising tracking form lets each employee within your office know what to expect when the incoming calls start flooding in the first thing Monday morning. Then each person answering the phone can intelligently answer any questions regarding the advertisement. They can describe the job, screen and record the phone call, possibly schedule the appointment for the counselor, or refer the call to the appropriate individual in the office.

2-12 Log of newspaper advertisements.

Date of Ad _____

ORDER #	JOB TITLE	# OF CALLS
_____	_____ CO. _____	_____
_____	_____ CO. _____	_____
_____	_____ CO. _____	_____
_____	_____ CO. _____	_____
_____	_____ CO. _____	_____
_____	_____ CO. _____	_____
_____	_____ CO. _____	_____
_____	_____ CO. _____	_____
_____	_____ CO. _____	_____
_____	_____ CO. _____	_____
_____	_____ CO. _____	_____
_____	_____ CO. _____	_____

Use this form religiously, and it will save countless hours of frustration when the onslaught begins. I call it an onslaught because our phones rang every 15 seconds on Monday morning, with inquiries and appointment scheduling taking up a majority of the telephone time.

Placement tally

The form shown in Fig. 2-13 is a convenient control tool for the quick-and-easy reference of job placements made each month. It not only gave me great incentive each month at a quick glance, but it also kept me abreast of the monthly productivity of my staff.

This placement tally form is used to record the date a specific job order was filled, the position title requested on the job order, the company name making the request, the name of the applicant placement, and finally the placement fee for services rendered.

Memorandum

All busy and productive offices use memos. They guarantee recognition and memory of items mentioned and sometimes forgotten. Some staff members, as well as management, use this form of communication religiously. It always gets the attention of their coworkers.

The memo might be brief, calling a meeting for a certain date and time, or it might be an explanation of policy to better aid new employees. For whatever purpose, this long-standing form has its many uses and will definitely be around for a long, long time (see Fig. 2-14).

Sales report form

It's crucial that a record be kept of all past, present, and potential future business contacts (see Fig. 2-15). Nothing is more embarrassing than to contact a company, thinking it's a new call, only to learn that the firm has received a letter or call from your agency just recently. It suddenly appears to the potential client that the left hand of your company doesn't seem to know what the right hand is doing.

It's not only frustrating, but it's also bad business. The sales report form keeps you from ever having this problem. It gives the date of the sales contact, name of the company, address and phone number, the contact name within the business, who made your agency contact, and what was the response to the sales call. Keep this form updated continuously and require all of your sales staff to submit a weekly account of all contacts made.

Employee review forms

Each employee should have a 90-day probationary review, a three- to six-month review, and annual review. These reviews are designed to keep the business relationship between staff and management on track. This is the best time to air any frustrations, teach any new policy changes, and listen carefully to the input from the individual doing the job. Sometimes it's easy to overlook some of the difficulties of

2-13 Placement tally.

FROM: _____ TO: _____

DATE	COMPANY	APPLICANT

_____

_____   _____

FEE: _____ 75% _____ 65% _____

_____

_____   _____

FEE: _____ 75% _____ 65% _____

_____

_____   _____

FEE: _____ 75% _____ 65% _____

_____

_____   _____

FEE: _____ 75% _____ 65% _____

_____

_____   _____

FEE: _____ 75% _____ 65% _____

_____

_____   _____

FEE: _____ 75% _____ 65% _____

_____

_____   _____

FEE: _____ 75% _____ 65% _____

_____

_____   _____

FEE: _____ 75% _____ 65% _____

_____

_____   _____

FEE: _____ 75% _____ 65% _____

_____

_____   _____

FEE: _____ 75% _____ 65% _____

_____

_____   _____

FEE: _____ 75% _____ 65% _____

MEMORANDUM

To: _____ Date: _____

Subject: _____

Message: _____

_____

_____

_____

_____

_____

_____

_____

_____

_____

_____

_____

Signed: _____

2-14 Memorandum form.

the position, and since time has a tendency to change all things, the original position might have grown into something entirely different from what you originally designed. Always give the original of the employee review form (Fig. 2-16) to the employee for his or her employment file, and keep a copy for your employee file records.

Contract expiration

On each employment contract there is a blank space available to write in the 180-day or six-month expiration date. The contract expiration form (Fig. 2-17) gives you the closing date for each consecutive contract. It isn't practical to assume that the contact has an open-ended time frame. If the applicant is hired in the firm after the contract expiration date has passed, there is no fee.

The contract expiration form provides all the information necessary to call the company in six months and innocently ask if the applicant is available. If they act as though you've reached a wrong number, or appear to be baffled by the request, you're safe from any problems.

I designed this particular form in order to ensure that every placement fee earned by myself and my staff was received by the appropriate individual or company. Unfortunately, sometimes the employer and the applicant join together in agreement and decide that the match should be made without the agency's knowledge. I've seen many dishonest employers and applicants who kept the placement confidential and, in so doing, eliminated the agency involvement.

2-15 Sales report form.

DAILY CONTACTS

DATE	COMPANY NAME	INDIVIDUAL NAME	CALL	RESULTS

2-16 Employee review form.

Employee Name: _____ Date: _____
Position: _____ Hire Date: _____

Description of Responsibilities:
_____
_____
_____

On a Scale of 1 to 10 with 10 being Outstanding - Exceptional Performance and
1 being Poor - Below Expectations

	Self-Appraisal Rating	Manager's Rating
Professional Performance		
1. Understanding our Services	_____	_____
2. Grasp of Instruction	_____	_____
3. Understanding our Customers	_____	_____
4. Judgment & Ability to Solve Problems	_____	_____
5. Productivity / Results	_____	_____
6. Quality of Work	_____	_____
7. Working within "System"	_____	_____
8. Written Communication Skills	_____	_____
9. Ability to Plan, Schedule & Complete Work	_____	_____
10. Verbal Communication Skills	_____	_____
11. Ability to Meet Deadlines	_____	_____
Personal Development And Leadership Skills		
1. Professional Demeanor / Appearance	_____	_____
2. Acceptance of Suggestions / Input Ideas	_____	_____
3. Assumption of Responsibility	_____	_____
4. Training / Motivation of Assistants	_____	_____
5. Attitude Towards Associates / Customers	_____	_____
6. Dependability / Credibility	_____	_____
Overall Appraisal Rating	_____	_____

2-17 Contract expiration form.

COMPANY	NAME	JOB ORDER #	CONTRACT #	EXPIRATON DATE

Job order control sheet

The form shown in Fig. 2-18 is used to keep a running tally of all job orders received and the activity for each order. The information listed on the job order control sheet is: the job order number, the date the order was received, the company name and address, the business phone number, the name of the caller, the job title of the employee requested, the list of names of applicants sent to the interviews, the placement contract number, contract expiration number, and whether or not an applicant was hired. This form of record keeping was a tool that was used at North Coast many times for quick reference when employers called to renew job orders.

Competitive agency employer client list

I designed the competitive agency employer client list (Fig. 2-19) so I could keep track of all the bits and pieces of information that came my way in applicant interviews, association meetings, and lunch appointments. I generally passed the collected data on to my sales staff, and they made new potential client contacts. It's invaluable to know which agency is handling the placements for which companies. It also indicates that the firms are familiar with the placement agency procedure and might or might not be satisfied with their immediate agency. It's certainly worth the try!

Employment services contract

As you begin to add support services to your agency, the need for a contract to solidify the financial obligations will be important. The employment services contract (Fig. 2-20) is to record the class the client is scheduled to attend, the date, and the fee. Have each client read and sign the contract before the class begins.

Employee contract

Each time you hire an employee to work in your agency, make sure you give them a copy of the employee contract (Fig. 2-21). This valuable form is designed to alleviate any misunderstandings down the road if the employee has any questions about salary, benefits, vacations, etc. It's quite extensive. The feedback was always positive, and it was obviously much appreciated by the people who worked for me over the years.

SETTING UP YOUR OFFICES

Try to visualize your working environment and then, once you've made the list of important factors to look for, begin the process of research.

Office space

In the planning stages of your business start-up, consider how much space you'll need to provide services to your clients. At the barest minimum, look for an office complex that will have at least four individual rooms. The first office will be for the manager, the second one for the receptionist and front office area, the third one is for the employ-

2-18 Job order control sheet.

ORDER #	DATE	COMPANY NAME	PHONE #	CALLER	JOB TITLE	APPLI. SENT	CONTRACT#	EXP. DATE	HIRED Y/N

2-19 Competitive agency employer client list.

DATE	COMPANY NAME	POSITION	PLACEMENT F/T – P/T	SOURCE	MISC

2-20 Employment services contract.

(COMPANY)
1111 First Street, Anytown, USA
(222) 333-4444

Contract/Receipt # _____

Date _____

TOTAL AMOUNT OF FEE $ _____

In consideration of the sum of $ _____ to be paid by

_____ On Date(s) _____

we agree to provide the following services:

Service Description : _____

_____

Commencement Date _____ Completion Date _____

Other Terms and Understandings _____ Payment Upon Receipt of Services _____

This Contract Continues From : _____ 19 ____ to _____ 19 ____

THE AGENCY SHALL REFUND FEES FOR NON-COMPLIANCE WITH THIS CONTRACT AS FOLLOWS :

NO VERBAL OR WRITTEN PROMISE OR GUARANTEE OF ANY JOB OR EMPLOYMENT

IS MADE OR IMPLIED UNDER THE TERMS OF THIS CONTRACT.

<u>YOUR RIGHT TO CANCEL</u>

You may cancel this contract for employment counseling services, without any penalty or obligation, if notice of cancellation is given, in writing, within three (3) business days after you have signed this contract.

To cancel this contract, just mail or deliver a signed and dated copy of the following cancellation notice or any other written notice of cancellation or send a telegram containing a notice of cancellation, to NORTH COAST PERSONNEL SERVICES at 1111 First Street, Anytown, USA, not later than midnight of the third business day after you signed this contract.

<u>CANCELLATION NOTICE</u>

I hereby cancel this contract.

Dated _____ 19 ____ Signature _____

NOTE: The provisions of your RIGHT TO CANCEL shall not apply where time is of the essence and the employment counseling services must be performed at the request and for the convenience of the customer within three (3) days of the date of the contract is entered into, provided that the client furnishes the employment counseling service with a separate dated and signed personal statement in the client's own handwriting, describing the situation requiring immediate services and expressly acknowledging and waiving the right to cancel the contract with three (3) business days. Copy of the customer's statement shall be attached to this contract.

(COMPANY)

BY _____ DATE _____

SIGNATURE OF CLIENT _____

ADDRESS _____ PHONE ( ) _____

This contract is the property of the client
and shall not be taken from the client.

NAME: Susan Ludwig

START DATE: July 18, 1990

POSITION: Employment Counselor/Office Manager

HOURS: 40 Hours per week   Monday - Friday   8:00 am - 5:00 pm

BASE $1,500 Per Month (There will be Bonuses and Profit Sharing after 6
SALARY: months)

PAYDAYS: Paychecks will be distributed on the 1st & 15th of each month.

BENEFITS: After the 90 day training period has passed, Major Medical,
             including Vision and Dental coverage, Profit Sharing and a Life
             Insurance policy will be available to select from. This coverage
             will be determined by the employee, as a maximum $ amount will be
             available per employee.

PERKS: Paid Holidays

             New Years Day
             Memorial Day
             Good Friday (12:00 pm - 5:00 pm)
             Fourth of July
             Labor Day
             Thanksgiving Day
             Christmas Day
             Your Birthday

             Paid Vacations

             Two (2) weeks in the first year. After employment with North Coast
             for five (5) years, then vacations are three (3) weeks.

             Sick Pay

             One half (1/2) day per each month, to be utilized as accrued
             cumulative compensatory time or cash payment only during the
             following calendar year.

REVIEW: Salary shall be reviewed at the end of the first 90 day
             probationary period, within six (6) to nine (9) months of
             employment and annually.

             Performance will be reviewed at the end of the first 90 days and
             then twice yearly from that point forward.

_____   _____
Kristi Mishel   Date

_____   _____
Susan Ludwig   Date

ment counselor (which can easily be partitioned to include an additional counselor at a future date) and, finally, a storage room for inventory, supplies, and inactive files. If at all possible, a fifth room could be used for testing and a small kitchen area.

Look for space between 600–800 square feet with rent ranging from $1.00 to $4.00 per square foot. You can call your local real-estate office and ask to speak with a commercial real-estate salesperson. They are always cordial, and most of them are more than willing to help with your particular needs. Make your wish list, and tell the agent specifically what you're looking for (a general description of area preference and location, the price range you can afford to work within), and then start looking!

Leases

For your first year of business, try to secure the shortest lease contract that is possible. The reason for this is that until you can see where you're going and how fast you'll be expanding, it's always best to plan ahead and not get stuck with offices that are too small. We advise a month-to-month lease if at all possible. If you end up signing a lease for one year you're obligated to pay that amount, regardless of the needs of your agency. What happens if you outgrow your space or need to downsize? Don't get yourself in over your head, especially in the very beginning.

Don't feel pressured when looking at office sites either. When the right one comes along, you'll know it. Just keep at it until you've exhausted all the possibilities. Stay firm, and don't let the real-estate salesperson convince you that what you need is not available. The type of office setup you will be looking for is standard and very easy to find.

Percentage leases

Be extremely careful with this type of setup. These leases require that you pay a portion of your gross revenue, on top of the fixed monthly rent payment. A variation of the percentage lease is a shared office space and personnel, where there is a shared utility expense, reception area, general office/secretary, bookkeeper, and other additional support services. The dollars you can save by not staffing these individuals can sometimes be made up in the percentage lease contract.

Lease terms

Contact legal counsel before signing your business lease. It should be easy to understand and cover such things as responsibilities for liabilities, remodeling, signage, and/or the potential for engaging in support services.

Checklist

- How many restrooms does your city or county health department require if you have both male and female employees?
- Does the city's building and zoning departments allow for your type of business in the building?
- Are there enough electrical outlets?
- Are the air conditioning, heating, and lighting adequate?
- Will the fire department accept your business at the location?

- Who pays the insurance for the plate-glass windows?
- Do you pay a cleaning charge, and is it refundable when you vacate the premises?
- Are the landlords supportive of the changes you request?
- What is the cost of burglary insurance?
- Are all the ceilings free of leak damage?
- Is there sufficient parking space for clients and staff?
- Is there adequate security?
- Are there shared janitorial services?

Furnishings

When selecting the items for your offices, keep in mind the ongoing image you want to portray to the general public. It should always be one of success and profitability. It wouldn't serve the purpose if you put second-hand furniture and worn-down equipment in your offices. All it takes is a little research for the best-buy outlet locations in your vicinity. Since volume discount stores offer new furniture at a lower price, check these places first. Take a look at the "going out of business" ads in the local paper, but be really careful with the condition of the furniture. You want yours to look new and last a long time, so buy with that in mind.

The reception room is usually the first contact the client makes with the physical imaging of your company. This front office should have a business-like atmosphere. Light pastels create the look of grace and dignity, while at the same time giving the space a roomier effect. Since applicants coming to your offices will usually fill out the paperwork in this room, make it comfortable for them. Provide plenty of lighting for filling out the application, and also provide a variety of reading material to occupy time if applicants have to wait for an appointment with an interview counselor.

Don't be meager with the expense in this crucial area, but don't go overboard either. If you want to do some checking on your own, walk into a few business offices and note the decor, color scheme, furniture, and style. Use the style that's most comfortable for you, and don't be afraid to change if healthy criticism comes your way.

The following list is a breakdown of office furniture and accessories. You will not need to buy all of this at once, but keep an eye out for these items, as eventually your offices will be fully stocked:

- Furniture.
  - ~ Desks.
    - – Managers.
    - – Receptionists.
    - – Counselors.
    - – Bookkeepers (can be added later).
    - – Sales (can be added later).
  - ~ Chairs.
    - – One executive swivel.
    - – One reception swivel.
    - – Three reception client.
    - – One or two counselor swivel.

– One steno (for typing tests).
– Eight folding (for classes).
~ Tables.
– Coffee.
– End.
– Conference.
– Typing (stand).
– Computer.
– Lamp.
• Accessories.
~ Filing cabinets.
– One two-drawer.
– One four-drawer.
– Cardboard.
~ Coat rack.
~ Pictures and wall hangings.
~ Plants and plant stands.
~ Chair runners.
~ Lamps.
~ Wastepaper baskets.

Credit

While you are on this shopping spree, fill out several credit applications at the business retailers on your list and begin establishing your long-standing credit relationship with these professional resources. You will be buying from these resources for many, many years.

BUSINESS EQUIPMENT

Shop carefully to get the best deal for all your office equipment. There are a wide variety of resources for you to choose from, whether you decide to buy all new, or some new and some used. You can choose to select credit payments for this equipment or pay cash for all of it.

Research the costs and comparisons initially in the business supply catalogues. Don't forget to add the shipping/handling and tax to each item when you make your calculations. What might have looked to be a great deal at one point loses some of its glitter after all the add-ons.

Weigh very carefully the decision to buy new equipment versus used. We recommend buying all your equipment new because it's extremely difficult to judge just how much wear and tear equipment has had with the previous owner.

When you buy new, you also get the extra advantage of the warranty. Remember to always fill out the warranty information slip and send it to the manufacturer immediately. Be sure to use this added incentive to ensure a better-quality, longer-lasting piece of equipment. Even though it costs a little more in the beginning, it will be far more comforting when you start out with brand new equipment.

You also have another opportunity to establish credit when buying new equipment with this retailer. Take advantage of this, even if you have the cash ready to buy up-front. Pay the account off in 30 days. There won't be any added interest charged to the item, and a strong credit relationship is automatically started.

If you just can't afford to go this route, keep an eye on the Sunday classified sections of large local city newspapers for business equipment for sale. There really are some bargains at substantial savings if you just take the time to carefully look. Sometimes the seller has failed in a venture, merged with another company, or expanded to need larger or more modern equipment. Sometimes you can buy for a fraction of the cost. Just be more careful and ask more questions. Be more judicious!

Sometimes suppliers of new equipment have repossessions or trade-ins that can be purchased for tremendous discounts. Hundreds of dollars can be saved by shopping wisely for secondhand equipment. It just takes more time.

Some companies offer leasing of their equipment. This would work only if you plan to either try out before purchase, or if you temporarily need the equipment. Leases can be costly, so be very careful with this route. One of the only advantages are that your initial dollar outlay is reduced when you buy on an installment contract. Now, let's start with the basics.

Typewriter

Find a good electric typewriter, preferably an IBM Correcting Selectric. This should run you somewhere between $200 and $300. You can buy additional fonts (type styles) at a reasonable cost, so you have the freedom of changing the type style for a variety of typing jobs. You're looking for something that produces crisp, sharp letters with a professional look and has a keyboard that feels natural and is easy to work with. Remember, this is the piece of equipment that will be used for the applicant typing tests, so buy something that can take plenty of wear and tear.

Copier

This is one of the most valuable pieces of equipment you'll ever own. It will get more mileage than any other piece of machinery in your business. Some of the items copied will be résumés, applications, reference letters, correspondence, advertising pieces, etc. Top quality for your copier is essential. Don't cut corners when you start researching this market. You can buy a good copier with add-on capabilities for the future. Things like color print might not be essential in the very beginning, but in the future, as the business expands, you'll find it invaluable for the advertising pieces.

Some business equipment retailers will let you try out the machine for a period of time. This is usually one week or so and is considered for demonstration purposes only. This allows you to test the quality, consistency, and reliability of the equipment. Just don't take advantage of this offer. Some people abuse this by using it to restock their office supplies. Be realistic with your needs and trust the reputable sales outlets through personal referrals or referencing.

Calculators

This piece of equipment is available at almost all the business supply centers. Don't spend the extra cash for fancy calculators when all you really need is a large, easy-to-read print screen. The calculator must have the ability to add, subtract, multiply, and divide. The percentage function is helpful too, but don't waste money on all the other functions that are offered, as you will more than likely never use them.

Buy a calculator for each office. You'll need one for the manager, one for the receptionist, and one for each counselor. Eventually, the bookkeeper and sales staff will also need calculators.

Computer

Back in the early '70s, when I started programming computers, the "state-of-the-art" office computer was a mammoth 360 model that used hand-keypunched cards for data entry and large reels of magnetic tape for storage. Today's desktop and laptop computers are more powerful than those used on board the Apollo spacecraft and the Lunar lander.

The demands of a personnel placement agency require computerization. The questions are, what kind and how many? The answer depends on how big your office will be and what services you will offer.

The elements of computer selection are:

- Speed. Determined by the speed of the CPU. Pentium chips offer 100-MHz speed, with 150-MHz soon to be released and 200-MHz on the drawing board. How much speed do you need? If you are doing CAD (computer-aided design) or similar applications, you need all the speed you can get. For normal office work, a 66-MHz that can be upgraded is more than fast enough. Don't let your desire to have the fastest computer available get in the way of economic reality.
- Memory. This is actually more important than speed. If you don't have the memory to load the applications or related documents they produce, the application must go back and forth between the hard drive and memory. The programs get more sophisticated and eat up more memory with each new release. At present, 16MB of RAM (read-only memory) will provide ample memory for most applications. The motherboard should have room to expand to 64MB.
- Hard drive. There are two types: IDE and SCSI. IDE drives are limited to approximately 600MB, with SCSI able to go more than 2000MB. You can, however, use two hard drives for each type. Two 540MB IDE drives would give you more than 1000MB of usable disk space. As stated earlier, programs get more sophisticated and eat up not only more memory, but also more disk space with each new release. Look at your software needs to determine how big your hard drive capacity should be.
- Motherboard. This should be expandable to 64MB RAM and have VLB expansion slots.
- CD-ROM. If you plan to expand your services to include desktop publishing, seriously look into this option.
- Computer type. This is not turning out to be just a matter of preference. There are die-hard fans of IBM (or compatible) and Apple (Macintosh or Apple II). The specialized nature of each has been narrowed by the competition. My advice is twofold:
  - ~ Look at the computer systems your prospective business clients are using. The people you will be sending them should be literate or at least familiar

with your clients' hardware and software. In order to screen these prospective employees, you should have the ability to, in-house, test their knowledge on these systems.

~ Find the software that provides the most applications for your business and match the computer to that software. We have worked with both IBM's and Apple's (or compatibles) and have found all to be excellent systems. Each has its positive and negative aspects, but both improve with each generation of computers.

• Networking. If you will be sharing files or applications with others in your office, investigate this prospect. Prices have gone way down, making this a viable option for a small business.

• Fax/modem. For communications, this is an essential. The fax is added because of the ease in transmitting documents without having hard copies, and it can also be used as a backup if the stand-alone fax machine breaks.

• Tape backup. This should be mandatory. Set up a regular schedule of backing up your data files. Despite the excellence of hard drives available, they do every once in a while "crash." That is a terrifying word to any computer user and can only be appreciated when it happens to you. If your data files are backed up, the trauma of a "crash" is greatly diminished.

• Service. This is listed last, but it is very important. Purchasing through local, reputable sources provides the opportunity to cure computer problems as soon as possible.

Software

The amount of software on the market is mind-boggling. In order to control expenses, limit your initial choices to the necessities. We recommend the purchase of an "office" software package. The package should include: word processing, spreadsheet, database, telecommunications, and possibly presentation. With this combination of programs, you can do almost anything that is demanded in a normal office situation. The spreadsheet "Cash Flow Projections/Income Statement" to be used in conjunction with a business plan was produced in an "office" package. Prior to buying a specialized program, see if the task can be done with one of these programs. There are many books that will help you do almost anything. Try before you buy.

The big three "office" packages are:

• Microsoft Professional Office. Includes Word (word processing), Excel (spreadsheet), Access (database), PowerPoint (presentation graphics) and Mail (communications).

• Borland Office. Includes Quattro Pro (spreadsheet), WordPerfect (the industry standard in word processing) and Paradox (database). Novell has recently merged with WordPerfect and has signed an agreement with Borland International, Inc. to purchase Quattro Pro. A new package is planned, PerfectOffice 3.0, which includes WordPerfect, Quattro Pro, WP Presentations, InfoCentral, and Paradox.

• Lotus SMARTSUITE. Includes 1-2-3 (the industry standard in spreadsheets), Ami Pro (word processing), Approach (database), Freelance (graphics), and Organizer (information manager).

Of the three packages, we prefer either the Microsoft Professional Office or Borland Office (the new PerfectOffice would be included). Microsoft offers excellent, unlimited technical support of all their products. Borland (Novell and WordPerfect) offers superior products. WordPerfect is the industry standard, and Paradox, with its Object Pal, offers excellence to both the novice and professional programmer.

Accounting software There are too many excellent programs on the market to single out one. Prior to setting up an accounting system, consult an accountant and establish an ongoing relationship with one you get along with and can work with. Let the accountant recommend an accounting package.

Payroll software Our personal favorite and an extremely powerful program is "INSTINCTIVE™ PAYROLL." Instructions in documentation and on screen are in plain English. It operates under Windows and DOS. It handles different types of payroll (hourly and salary, commissions, advances, bonus pay, multiple pay periods and rates, overtime, benefits, deductions), including problem payrolls. It prints checks, forms, and reports, and handles direct deposit and electronic tax filing. It automatically computes taxes, and its files are compatible with most spreadsheets and database programs. There is even a calculator and calendar/diary. If the written documentation, on-screen help, and tutorials don't solve your problem, this offers superior technical support. With this product you will not only be able to do your own payroll, but you will also be able to offer this as a service to other customers.

Fax

Purchase a stand-alone fax machine, but back this up with a fax/modem in a computer.

Printer

A laser printer is a must for any office for its ease of use, quality of print, and speed. Two printers should be used. One for high volume and specialized applications and the other for general purposes. The high-volume machine should be a model 4 or better. Color would be an option for desktop publishing, graphics, etc. The general-use machine can be an earlier version. We have a IIP-compatible model, and it handles everything we throw at it.

Supplies

The amount of miscellaneous supplies needed to stock a busy office can be daunting if you let it. We have developed a simple inventory list for your benefit. Fortunately, you won't need all these materials the very day you open for business, but over time, every bit of this stock will come in handy.

Shop and compare prices at a variety of local stationers and office-discount stores for the inventory materials. Besides getting referrals from friends already in business, check the mail-order catalogues. Quill and The Nation's Leading Supplier of Business Forms for Small Business are two very valuable, extensive sources. Large retail stores like Costco and Office Depot are discount volume stores, and they have many of the products you'll need.

Your primary goal when purchasing these office supplies is to develop a solid base of reliable suppliers for the best prices, regardless of the avenue you select. Create your own set of suppliers that works best for your level of operation, and continually check around for competitive prices and sales. Make sure to send referrals their way and let the new customers know the value of giving your name as the referral.

Begin developing credit relationships with as many of these suppliers as possible. Pay your bills promptly, be clear and concise when ordering, be realistic about the delivery schedules, and don't try to negotiate prices on everything. You can develop a very strong, trusting, and profitable relationship with these professional resources over the years. It will definitely be advantageous when you hit the rough spots. Here's a list for a well-stocked, busy personnel office (not in any specific order of importance):

Desk supplies
- Paper clips and holder (small and large size clips).
- Stapler and staples (for each desk).
- Staple remover.
- Pens (black, red and blue).
- Felt-tip pens (black, red and blue).
- Pencils.
- Rulers.
- Notepads.
- Stamps and stamp holders.
- Drawer organizers.
- Phone message pads.
- Business card holders.
- Drawer organizers.
- Stack trays.
- Yellow stickies (all sizes).
- Glue.
- Erasers.
- Label stickers.
- Calendars (desk and wall).
- Desk name plates.
- Address pop-up.
- Rolodex file.
- Kleenex.
- Wastepaper cans.

Kitchen
- Coffee maker, coffee, cream, etc.
- Coffee stand and cups.
- Windex.
- Paper towels.
- Plastic silverware.
- Glasses, pitcher.
- Ice box.

- Ice cube trays.
- Napkins.
- Ashtray.
- Garbage sacks.
- Paper towels.

Supply room
- Employment applications.
- Job order forms.
- Applicant and employer fee schedule forms.
- Credit application forms.
- Long-distance telephone report forms.
- Help-wanted advertising tracking forms.
- Sales report forms.
- Employee review forms.
- Memorandum forms.
- Placement tally forms.
- Contracts.
- Contract expiration date forms.
- Job order control forms.
- Competitive agency client list forms.
- Employment services contract forms.
- Copy paper, white and colored (8½ × 11 and 9 × 12).
- Toner for the copier.
- Pendaflex files.
- Manila files.
- Tabs for folders.
- Large folders.
- See-through file folders.
- Report folders.
- Plant waterer, fertilizer, and sprayer.
- Paper cutter.
- Three-hole punch.
- Calculator tape.
- Stickpins.
- Poster board for notes.
- Notebook separators.
- Typing tests.
- Clipboards.
- Mouse pads.
- Dictionary, thesaurus.
- Zip code directory.

Miscellaneous
- First-aid kit.
- Radio.
- Fly swatter.
- Room spray.

- No-smoking sign.
- Open/closed sign.
- Briefcase.
- Cassette recorder/tapes.
- Vases/frogs.
- Room deodorizers.

Telephone system

Contact your local phone company's business representative for information about setting up a new phone system. They should have answers for all your questions. It will be to your advantage to be prepared before you call them; otherwise they will waste valuable time trying to sell you services that you don't need.

As you develop, you'll want to have the freedom to expand your existing system, so be sure to purchase a telephone system that gives you that choice. In the beginning, you might start with just yourself as manager/counselor, a reception/secretary, and one additional counselor. If that's the case, you will need at least four incoming lines to start. That way, all three employees can be busy on the phones, and at least one extra line is still available for incoming calls.

In most areas, you can select your own phone number. The phone company usually charges a fee when you pick a specific number, but you can also have an easy-to-remember number, too. When setting up the phone contract, first ask the representative if you can pick your own number, at no additional charge. If the representative says no, he or she will sometimes give you the choice of selecting one of the next five numbers to be assigned through the phone company. They'll read off the numbers to you and help to pick the one that feels and sounds the easiest to remember! This service is free, and many times a great phone number can come your way with little effort.

Be sure to listen carefully to the variety of additional services available in your area. Choose things like Call Waiting, Call Forwarding, and Conference Calling. These services can be added to your monthly service rate at a very reasonable fee.

Long-distance carriers have a major advertising media war going on these days. Look at all the advantages of each carrier and pick the one that's best suited to your particular service. If you decide to change carriers because of better service or better rates down the road, don't worry. It's perfectly acceptable to shop around and get the best deals.

SIGNAGE

You're operating a professional business service, and your sign should reflect that image. The sign should be enticing and welcome the public into your establishment.

This is a perfect opportunity to do a little investigation and see what works for the companies around you. Drive around and check out the different types of businesses in your area. Select a style that's professional, concise, targeted, and easy for the general public to read. Avoid a flashy, slick sign, and, most important of all, make sure it's consistent with all of your other advertising.

When you sign a lease in a large, multilevel office building, there will likely be a posted bulletin board in the lobby that indicates where each company is located in the building. It will identify the name of the firm, the room number, and floor level. There is little choice in style and selection with this type of office complex. Landlords can impose their own restrictions, so be sure to check regulations and secure the written approval of your landlord before you invest in a sign.

If you have a singular dwelling, or office building, you'll get the opportunity to have a sign created for the passing motorist and pedestrian to see your place of business. When discussing this with the sign maker, be sure to calculate the traffic flow speed and have the designer create a sign that's easy to read in the short time allotted. The sign can be erected either on the front of the building or on the lawn out front, and the sign lists the business or businesses inside. Many cities and suburbs have instituted sign ordinances that restrict the size, location, and sometimes the lighting and type of sign used.

Once you've decided on the type of sign you want, do a little more research for a sign maker that can do the job you need at a reasonable rate. Ask your business friends for references, use your trusty Yellow Pages, and call around.

A tip to remember. Sign makers are a rare breed. They are professional artists dealing primarily in the business world. Be patient with their unique personalities, and be very sure to stress the deadline for this project from the very beginning.

EXPANSION

Good business planners take a long-range outlook when developing a new company. They think positive, and they think big. When you're doing your planning, don't just wonder if all the hard work you put yourself through to get this business up and running will give a return. Plan on it! Trust the fact that if you plan the agency start-up effectively and develop the growth carefully, you will automatically expand and eventually outgrow your existing facility.

When your employees are rubbing elbows because of too little office space, the phone capability is at its limit, and the incoming new business is occupying every minute of every hour of every day, these are signs that you are maxing out on your existing systems. The next, most obvious step is to stretch out! This means expanding your firm's capabilities by offering the same established and reputable services in another location.

You might choose to open a satellite office, with your existing facility acting as the home office and providing all administrative functions. This will be considered the branch office. The second location, in the beginning, might only be a singular office for a counselor who is surrounded by several other independent employee businesses using the same receptionist. It's extremely practical to expand with this system, as you will only be paying rent on the space itself, plus the shared cost of an individual to greet the public and answer your phones and utilities. It's amazing how little these additional expenses are, compared to the return on your initial investment.

Just picture it. In all your future advertising, you'll be offering two locations to serve the public, and possibly even more. This shows the general public that your service is successful, and when something works, clients are more likely to be drawn because of this obvious stamp of approval. This type of growth and expansion can be accomplished with a very reasonable dent to your carefully watched bottom line.

When I decided to open my second office, I did exactly what we have just described. I selected a professional office building in a busy section of a much larger city close by, and I opened my new additional office very quickly and with little capital outlay.

Once your decision is made to expand, the steps necessary to accomplish the transition is simple. Select an existing counselor to work in the office, find an appropriate facility, prepare the new advertising campaign to alert the public to the expansion, and then do it! (See Fig. 2-22.)

NORTH COAST PERSONNEL SERVICES
Proudly announces the expansion of our firm.
Now offering two convenient locations to serve you.
Great New City, 1111 5th Street, (222) 333-4444
Other Great City, 6666 10th Street, (222) 555-7777
Effective Job Placement Through Personalized Service

2-22 Card announcing company expansion.

Franchising

If you decide to expand your firm on a large scale, one option to consider is franchising. There are several books available in the marketplace today that can give you all the legal information required to take this step.

Keep in mind that if you do go this route, there are a series of legal requirements placed on the franchiser. They are:

- Take the responsibility to find a new location for the new franchisee.
- Train the entire new staff.
- Develop a workable budget and help with understanding the process.
- Give all the advertising and promotion help you can to ensure success.
- Transfer all the systems and procedures that you've developed to the new business.
- Be available to answer any questions as they arise.

There are several franchise agencies in the permanent placement industry. Examples are Snelling and Snelling, The Personnel Touch, Robert Half International, and Management Recruiters. Each franchise operation is usually privately owned and operates under specific guidelines set down by the franchiser. Although the administrative and operational guidelines are clearly defined, the management style varies from office to office. Some are conducted with the utmost professionalism, while others are poorly run and create a serious image problem in the industry. It all depends on the management style of the owner. Just because the business has a well-known name does not necessarily mean it's reputable.

The temporary division has far more franchises than the permanent. Kelly Services, Western Temporary Services, Manpower, and Olstens are just a few. The cost and training of these franchises vary tremendously, but the blueprints for administration and operation are basically the same. Just as in the permanent franchises, the management style can make or break the company. I've seen poorly run temporary services, even though they carry the well-known names. Famous names might initially obtain the client, but without strong customer service and professional follow-through, they will never generate repeat business.

By offering franchise opportunities to interested entrepreneurs, you will be lending your well-known and established company name and systems. You'll also have the advantage of sharing the grapevine information about the personnel industry and getting involved at the national advertising level.

Set the cost of your franchise offering to one that feels equitable for both the value of the predetermined systems, plus the time that will be given to each new office that's created. The standard rate of payment for franchisees is to make a down payment of one-third to one-half of the value, with the balance due (with interest) over an agreed length of time. Franchisees will also be required to produce a certain rate of revenue each month and will be obligated to pay 5 percent to 10 percent of their gross revenue receipts in royalties each month.

In the long run, good planning and timing are the keys to any successful expansion. Whether you decide to grow gradually or take the leap of a fast-track franchising operation, with all its potential frustrations, it's wise to think out the consequences and go with your instincts.

FEES TO BE BASED ON THE FIRST MONTHS SALARY BEFORE
DEDUCTIONS. (FEE ON WEEKLY SALARY TO BE DETERMINED AT RATE OF
4⅓ WEEKS PER MONTH)

PERMANENT EMPLOYMENT : (LASTING MORE THAN NINETY (90) DAYS)

75% OF THE FIRST MONTHS SALARY ONLY

(ANNUAL PERCENT: 6.25%)

TERMS OF PAYMENT :

* THE FEE WILL BE REDUCED TO 65% IF PAID WITHIN 5 WORKING DAYS
  OF PLACEMENT.

* TOTAL FEE PAYABLE WITH NINETY (90) DAYS.

TEMPORARY EMPLOYMENT : (LASTING LESS THAN NINETY-ONE (91) DAYS)

THE FEE PAYABLE BY THE APPLICANT FOR TEMPORARY EMPLOYMENT
SHALL NOT EXCEED ONE-NINETIETH (1/90) OF THE FEE FOR PERMANENT
EMPLOYMENT FOR EACH CONSECUTIVE CALENDAR DAY DURING THE
PERIOD EMPLOYED. THIS IS NOT TO EXCEED THE FULL FEE FOR
PERMANENT EMPLOYMENT OR EXCEED TOTAL GROSS EARNINGS.
(SECTION 9974.5, BUSINESS AND PROFESSIONS CODE.)

DELINQUENCY CHARGE :

EACH INSTALLMENT PAYMENT IN DEFAULT OVER TEN (10) DAYS IS
SUBJECT TO A DELINQUENCY CHARGE IN AN AMOUNT NOT IN EXCESS
OF FIVE PERCENT (5%) OF SUCH INSTALLMENT OR FIVE DOLLARS ($5.00),
WHICHEVER IS LESS, BUT A MINIMUM CHARGE OF ONE DOLLAR ($1.00)
WILL BE MADE. THE APPLICANT AGREES TO PAY ALL COLLECTION COSTS,
INCLUDING ATTORNEYS FEES, ON ALL DELINQUENT AMOUNTS WHEN SO
ORDERED BY THE COURT.

IF AN APPLICANT MAKING A DEPOSIT ON A FEE FOR PLACEMENT FAILS
TO ACCEPT EMPLOYMENT, THE EMPLOYMENT AGENCY SHALL, UPON
DEMAND THEREOF, REPAY THE AMOUNT OF THE DEPOSIT TO THE
APPLICANT. UNLESS THE DEPOSIT IS RETURNED WITHIN 48 HOURS AFTER
DEMAND, THE EMPLOYMENT AGENCY SHALL PAY TO THE APPLICANT AN
ADDITIONAL SUM EQUAL TO THE AMOUNT OF THE DEPOSIT.
(SECTION 9977, BUSINESS AND PROFESSIONS CODE.)

FEES TO BE BASED ON THE FIRST MONTHS SALARY BEFORE DEDUCTIONS. (FEE ON WEEKLY SALARY TO BE DETERMINED AT RATE OF 4⅓ WEEKS PER MONTH)

PERMANENT EMPLOYMENT : (LASTING MORE THAN NINETY (90) DAYS)

75% OF THE FIRST MONTHS SALARY ONLY

(ANNUAL PERCENT: 6.25%)

TERMS OF PAYMENT :

* THE FEE WILL BE REDUCED TO 65% IF PAID WITHIN 5 WORKING DAYS OF PLACEMENT.

* TOTAL FEE PAYABLE WITH THIRTY (30) DAYS.

TEMPORARY EMPLOYMENT : (LASTING LESS THAN NINETY-ONE (91) DAYS)

THE FEE PAYABLE BY THE APPLICANT FOR TEMPORARY EMPLOYMENT SHALL NOT EXCEED ONE-NINETIETH (¹⁄₉₀) OF THE FEE FOR PERMANENT EMPLOYMENT FOR EACH CONSECUTIVE CALENDAR DAY DURING THE PERIOD EMPLOYED. THIS IS NOT TO EXCEED THE FULL FEE FOR PERMANENT EMPLOYMENT OR EXCEED TOTAL GROSS EARNINGS. (SECTION 9974.5, BUSINESS AND PROFESSIONS CODE.)

DELINQUENCY CHARGE :

EACH INSTALLMENT PAYMENT IN DEFAULT OVER TEN (10) DAYS IS SUBJECT TO A DELINQUENCY CHARGE IN AN AMOUNT NOT IN EXCESS OF FIVE PERCENT (5%) OF SUCH INSTALLMENT OR FIVE DOLLARS ($5.00), WHICHEVER IS LESS, BUT A MINIMUM CHARGE OF ONE DOLLAR ($1.00) WILL BE MADE. THE APPLICANT AGREES TO PAY ALL COLLECTION COSTS, INCLUDING ATTORNEYS FEES, ON ALL DELINQUENT AMOUNTS WHEN SO ORDERED BY THE COURT.

IF AN APPLICANT MAKING A DEPOSIT ON A FEE FOR PLACEMENT FAILS TO ACCEPT EMPLOYMENT, THE EMPLOYMENT AGENCY SHALL, UPON DEMAND THEREOF, REPAY THE AMOUNT OF THE DEPOSIT TO THE APPLICANT. UNLESS THE DEPOSIT IS RETURNED WITHIN 48 HOURS AFTER DEMAND, THE EMPLOYMENT AGENCY SHALL PAY TO THE APPLICANT AN ADDITIONAL SUM EQUAL TO THE AMOUNT OF THE DEPOSIT.
(SECTION 9977, BUSINESS AND PROFESSIONS CODE.)

3
Outside professional support network

In order for you to be totally confident that the decisions you make in business are sound ones, it's essential to have an internal support system in place. This network is created by slowly developing a series of professionals to aid you in your many business decisions. Professionals you choose should be proficient and respected in their individual fields and offer their services to your firm on an as-needed basis. These pros might charge for their services based on an hourly rate, project fee rate, or retainer rate. Regardless of how they charge, it's well worth paying for their proven and time-tested knowledge. We have included the list of professionals needed to assist you.

CERTIFIED PUBLIC ACCOUNTANT (CPA)

This is one of the most important professionals on your list of required support. Your accountant will generally do your year-end taxes, focus on your tax responsibilities, and give liabilities advice. It's not the accountant's practice to berate any of your decisions. He or she is hired to help you understand how to make better decisions and evaluate your current business structure. Not many new business owners understand how to read their balance sheets and profit and loss statements in the beginning of their new ventures. You will rely heavily on your CPA for advice in making sound business decisions. Trust your CPA with all your heart.

ATTORNEY-AT-LAW

Equally important in the decision-making process is the legal advice and support provided by an attorney-at-law. He or she will help with everything from reviewing lease contracts to developing client contracts and keeping you in line with all the laws governing the small business requirements in your state. The laws in California regarding personnel services are incredibly stringent, and my attorney always kept me abreast of changes so I could avoid any legal complications.

COMPUTER HARDWARE AND SOFTWARE CONSULTANT

This might or might not be the same person. Often, computer consultants are specialized and only advise within their specific range, but look for someone who can give you information about both hardware and software. Since upgrades are happening as fast as products hit the shelves, and glitches with your system are as common, it's important to have this person's phone number memorized.

BUSINESS AND MANAGEMENT CONSULTANT

This is the professional who is trained to look at the overview of your business and make system refinement suggestions, as needed. This person looks at the big picture and creates solutions that will alter your existing cash flow. This consultant is capable in all phases of business: staffing, marketing, accounting, operations, etc.

FINANCIAL ADVISER

You also need someone available to guide you through those financial decisions that affect your bottom line. This person generally has a banking background and is proficient in finance, loans, credit lines, and cash flow crises. This person will advise you as to how best direct your revenues and when and where to invest.

INSURANCE AGENT

It's not practical or feasible to run a business without being covered with a variety of insurance coverages. Your insurance agent will always provide you with the current information and best options for your business package. You will be required to have worker's compensation insurance, and you might add other coverage as wanted or needed: liability, life, medical, dental, optical, and others. This valuable support person will help with all the required insurances and give advice on your many options.

PRINTER AND GRAPHICS PROFESSIONAL

Remember that the image you're presenting to the public has to be one of professionalism and class, and these people are the ones to rely on for that imaging. They will not only help in the initial design of your logo and company look, but they will also give specific advice on advertising copy and volume printing rates.

It's extremely important that all of these individuals be reputable, stable, and reliable. One way to find these valuable resources is to first contact your business friends and try to get some referrals firsthand. They are the best resource because they can give you personal examples of professional services rendered. You might also find this support network listed within a business association membership. Their reputation follows them to all levels of business, including trade and service clubs. If they're good, be confident that the names will surface easily, and likely more than once. When someone is not reputable, you'll easily hear that information also. Keep track of what you learn, for it will be helpful in the future. These referrals should all be from a specific individual's experience.

If you can't find someone through a personal referral, then try the Chamber of Commerce Membership Directory, the Yellow Pages in your local phone book, association lists, and trade journals. Take your time and screen carefully.

Be sure to check references. Ask to speak with a few clients and listen carefully for a prepitch sale. We can't stress enough how often you'll need to rely on these people, so make sure they will do what they say they can do!

Over the years I became very good friends with all of the professionals who gave me reliable, consistent advice and direction. My agency also provided services to their firms for their personnel staffing needs. It became a two-way business relationship and satisfied our mutual business needs most adequately for many, many years.

This leads us to the next stage, which is fee structuring and business trades. It's legal in California to trade services with these professionals as long as the services were adequately recorded in your yearly tax returns. My CPA and I traded business for years. His office did our year-end taxes, and our office found his employees. The same relationship existed with our printer and our attorney. It wasn't practical with the insurance agent or business consultant. They either didn't have a need for employee assistance or were not in a position to make the trade because their company was too large.

4
Financial

STARTING CAPITAL AND RESOURCES

What is enough starting capital? Is there a formula that you can rely on to get the business up and going without dipping into savings or scrambling for a capital injection within the first year of operation? Of course there is.

All independent business owners have a different set of qualifications for running a company. Owners might have a strong client history that makes for easier start-up, knowledge of the industry, training, and established business contacts. Or they might be walking into the industry with transferable skills only and no contacts, training, or knowledge of the industry. So, the standard amount of starting capital really varies, based on how much the owner has going in.

The accepted industry-standard starting capital rate is to already have six months of operating capital in the bank before you start your venture. You will be able to calculate this figure when you've completed the business plan, as discussed in chapter 2.

Once you've determined how much capital you need, in what increments and time period necessary, the next step is to figure out where that money is going to come from. There are really only a handful of sources to work with, so make sure to study all your choices and select the one or ones that will give you the most control over your business.

The first source of capital is yourself. Assess your personal assets and cash reserves and consider whether you have the resources to independently finance your operation. If so, you won't have to give up any equity in the business. Because of this, it's obviously the best choice of all. Unfortunately, most of us don't have that kind of easily accessible money, which leads us to the second choice.

Family and friends are the next most obvious choice. It's very important that this type of financing always be treated as a standard loan. Have your attorney draw up the contract and consider this a legally binding relationship. By doing this, you not only protect your family member or friend for repayment of the loan, but you also keep them from ever owning a part of your business. Of course you must realize that if you default on the loan, that last statement is invalid.

The third choice for financing is borrowing from a bank. Banks certainly have ready financing available, and you should already have developed a personal and business relationship with at least one. In working with the banking industry, you will need to have some form of collateral that can be used as security for the loan.

Don't forget about Uncle Sam. The Small Business Administration has a wide array of services and loan programs. Also inquire about "grant" programs. The government always has a program going on for minorities, the disabled, women, and locations in states and cities that are economically disadvantaged, etc.

Each state and several of the large cities have some type of office set up to assist businesses. Such offices provide resources for financing, advice in setting up your business, and information on business licenses and taxes.

5
Legal issues

There are many areas in the personnel industry that require careful attention to detail, and our government regulates the personnel placement business with a thorough hand. Pay close attention to the information in this chapter and take the time necessary to research any additional laws that your local city or county have enforced.

REQUIRED POSTINGS

Contact the closest district of your State Department of Industrial Relations administrative office and request the required legal postings for your new personnel agency. These requirements must be put in a place in your offices where they can be read by all of your clients. They are:
- Industrial Welfare Commission Regulating the Minimum Wage.
- Wages, Hours, and Working Conditions in Professional, Technical, Clerical, Mechanical, and Similar Occupations.
- Wages, Hours, and Working Conditions in the Mercantile Industry.
- Payday Notice.

The United States Department of Labor and the State of California Department of Industrial Relations also provide additional employment-related information in the form of small manuals for your legal files. They are:
- Child Labor Laws in California.
- Laws Relating to Payment of Wages.
- Making EEO and Affirmative Action Work.

HIRING, RETAINING, AND FIRING

There are many legal ramifications to hiring, retaining, and firing your employees. It's wise to consult with your attorney for the laws pertaining to your area and adjust your practices accordingly.

REFERENCE-CHECKING LAWS

Try to get the answers to all of the following questions when conducting a telephone reference check on a potential new employee:
- What were the applicant's dates of employment?
- Why were they released?
- What were their job duties and responsibilities?

- What were their earnings at the time of hire and on leaving?
- Was the person dependable, punctual, seldom absent?
- Would you rehire this person?

Keep a record of all these notations in the employee's personnel file.

APPLICATION REVISIONS

The employment laws regarding the screening and selection of employees changed so often in California, I was forced to reprint my agency application several times in 10 years! Be sure to request an update of the new revisions as they occur. This will allow you to keep your application questionnaire current and not worry about you or your counselor's asking questions that have become outdated, or illegal. This information can also be shared with your employer clients for their application updates. They will appreciate this thoughtful and professional assistance.

SMALL-CLAIMS COURT

Make a visit to your local small-claims court offices and request the entire packet of information regarding small-claims actions. There will be detailed information about the steps to follow and the laws regarding this form of collection. Your attorney might also have this material available for you. The more familiar you become with and understand this system, the more effective it will be in collecting your agency fees.

6
Insurance

The small business owner faces a potential myriad of insurance policies for covering a wide range of potential problems. The following is a sampling of the most frequently considered coverages:
- General liability.
- Automotive liability.
- Worker's compensation.
- Fire and theft.
- Medical/dental/optical.
- Retirement.
- Life.

The best combination of general liability insurance for your brand-new business can be broken into three components: comprehensive general liability, auto liability, and required worker's compensation policy.

GENERAL LIABILITY POLICY

These are a few of the insurable risks that might be presented to your business:
- Personal injury to employees and/or the general public.
- Loss to the business caused by the death or disability of the owner or key employees.
- Loss of income resulting from interruption of business caused by damage to the firm's operating capital.
- Loss or damage of property, including building, supplies, fixtures, and merchandise.

This type of policy also covers any kind of bodily injury to nonemployees. The only exception to this coverage is the injury caused by professional malpractice and automobiles. You might also be liable for the bodily injuries to pedestrians, clients, delivery persons, and other types of outsiders.

AUTOMOBILE LIABILITY POLICY

A business can be liable for injuries and property damage caused by employees operating their own or someone else's car while on company business. Even though their personal automotive insurance policy might cover a portion of the liability, it might not be nearly adequate. Therefore, you should also add nonownership liability insurance to your general liability insurance.

WORKER'S COMPENSATION INSURANCE

In every state, employers are liable for injury to employees at work caused by an employer's failure to provide safe equipment and working conditions. They are also held liable for hiring competent employees and warning employees of an existing danger. The extent of coverage per employee and the employer's liability vary from state to state.

FIRE INSURANCE POLICY

This policy is for losses due to fire at your business. There are indirect losses also. They are considered consequential losses and might be even more important to your business's well-being. This is called business interruption insurance. Consequential losses are:

- Extra expenses of obtaining temporary quarters.
- Loss of use of a facility.
- Continuing expenses after a fire (salaries, rents paid in advance, interest obligations, etc.)
- As a landlord, the loss of rental income on buildings damaged or destroyed by fire.

MEDICAL/DENTAL/OPTICAL

You might be able to offer a comprehensive health and life insurance program for your employees and their families. Group insurance can be provided for about $75 per month per employee. You need to decide whether or not to offer the insurance on hire or have the policy coverage begin at the end of the employee's 90-day review period.

The benefits package could cover:

- Group term life insurance.
- Accidental death and dismemberment insurance.
- Major medical and surgical coverage.
- Dental care coverage.
- Vision care coverage.
- Medical health care coverage.
- Dependent health care coverage.

If you choose insurance coverage for your employees, the insurance company you select provides a booklet describing the benefits package. A copy of the policy should be given to an employee when he or she joins the program. There are several different policy payment choices available to most employers:

- You will pay for the full cost of the program for each employee. You will pay 100 percent of the premiums for insurance coverage of eligible dependents.
- You will pay 100 percent of the premiums for insurance coverage on the employee, an employee makes a (XX-percent) contribution for eligible dependents, the balance of which is deducted from his or her paycheck by a payroll deduction.
- You will pay 100 percent of the premium for insurance coverage on your employee. You will also pay 100 percent of the premium for insurance coverage for eligible dependents through payroll deductions.

- You will pay 50 percent of the premiums for insurance coverage on your employee. Your employee will pay 50 percent of the insurance premiums for his or her own coverage, plus 100 percent of the premiums for insurance coverage of eligible dependents through payroll deductions.

As an employer, you have the right to offer employees an extension of insurance coverage after discontinuing employment with your firm. They will be covered under your group health insurance program, and they and their dependents can have the right to continue coverage under your health insurance program for a limited period of time, at your expense or theirs.

Insurance can be purchased to cover a tremendous list of potential risks. Decide how much of a loss you can bear yourself, and weigh this against the insurance company's premium for assuming the risk.

Search for an insurance firm that specializes in business insurance policies. Look for a package insurance at discounted rates, and ask at least two insurance company agents to give you their premium rate estimates. The development of the right insurance for your business is a time-consuming activity in the beginning, but in the long run, the return in peace of mind will be worth it.

7
Agency structuring

Some agencies focus their time and attention on one specific industry or on providing only one type of service. Others offer a wide range of choices for their clientele. We have covered all the choices available to you as a new agency owner, and we hope that within this chapter you'll find the one that fits your style.

SCHEDULE OF FEES

When you begin pricing your services, be sure to get all the information about the local competitors' fees. Your fee structuring method should depend entirely on the local market and your concentrated specialization. You can find out these rates by polling the local marketplace. Ask what the other agencies are charging for services rendered and what additional services they are offering. If you plan to provide something that isn't currently being offered, charge what you think the market will bear.

If you price your services too low in the beginning, you'll eventually end up failing. This will happen because your markup for labor and materials costs doesn't cover the overhead expenses or generate sufficient profit.

I felt comfortable setting my initial agency fees right in the middle of what was currently being charged by my competitors. It seemed to me that some were exorbitantly high and some were ridiculously low, so going for the middle was easy. It also kept me safe with new clients inquiring about the fees before they decided to work with the new service. Some people only made the most-expensive choices, and others made only the least-expensive choices, but those people were few and far between. Most wanted a comparable fee and quality service, and they were comfortable with the midrange rates.

If someone is interested in your services, but you can't agree on the price, you need to stop and make the evaluation as to whether the money you make or lose will be worth the adjustment. In the beginning of the business, you might want to be flexible and do the work for any price. Remember, since this field requires genuine expertise, your qualifications should be the highest consideration.

After many, many years in the permanent agency field, I had an opportunity to see what worked and what didn't work for my competitors, and I finally selected a fee structure and repayment plan that I found both fair and equitable for all parties. For a complete example of this fee structure and payment plan, refer to "COMPETITIVE FEE STRUCTURE" later in this chapter.

PERMANENT VERSUS TEMPORARY PLACEMENT SERVICES

One major decision in the creation of your services is deciding whether or not to offer a temporary or permanent placement firm to the general public. Many companies offer both services and, given the choice, we recommend that you consider the
advantages of providing a full-range agency, both temporary and permanent. First,
let's consider the pros and cons of a permanent versus a temporary offering.

Permanent agency only—Pros

One real benefit for operating solely as a permanent agency is in the initial start-up
phase. The capital investment for a temporary agency is considerable because of the
payrolling expense the agency requires. Without the cost of covering the temporary
payroll, the start-up cost for both fields is exactly the same. So are the initial advertising, printing, legal, and administrative expenses.

Another benefit for selecting one or the other type of service is the concentrated
effort it takes to refine your policies and image. You might choose to focus specifically on management positions. There are few agencies that concentrate on this
level of placement alone: in other words, assistant managers, administrators, directors, CEOs, CFOs, supervisors, and any other positions that require management
skills.

The last benefit can be put into the classification of return on investment for
time spent working on filling orders. Once you build your applicant pool, the job
orders that come from the employer can be filled without advertising and without
prescreening the ad response. You can eventually select from your open files the
three most qualified applicants, contact them by phone, discuss and describe the positions, schedule interviews, assist with negotiating the final hiring, and collect the
fees. The time it takes you to accomplish these tasks is minimal, and the fee is high.
Not too bad, considering all the variables.

Permanent agency only—Cons

Most of the competitive agencies will be offering full-range services. Sometimes you
might lose accounts because the clients would rather have alternative choices in
their hiring policies. This is understandable, considering that you will have a lifelong
relationship with these clients, and their needs over the years will vary.

The temporary agency competition will offer a temp-to-perm choice to the competing client. This means they can select an employee for a review period, charging
a fee for the temporary service, and also charge a placement fee when the employer
decides to bring the employee on to the permanent payroll. You'll only have one
choice, and that's to charge fees for permanent placement.

Temporary agency only—Pros

We're back to the concentrated effort strategy. This type of firm can be financially
successful with the right policies, advertising, and staff to run it smoothly. It's a busy
business, with a nonstop cycle and activity happening almost all the time. Some
businesspeople prefer this kind of deadline stress and some don't.

Considerably more national advertising is printed about temporary agencies than permanent agencies. This alone will help in the development of your services. Another positive addition to the temp-only firm is the network of competitive agency assistance. Refer to chapter 12 on Competition. It describes the advantages of working with your opposition for guaranteed placements.

Temporary agency only—Cons

As previously stated in the section on perm-only cons, your local competition might be giving full-range service in your area, and the employers might want to take advantage of the thoroughness of a permanent search firm. Reference checking and selection go a long way in the long-term relationship with each employer.

The start-up cost for temp agencies is high because of the payroll expense incurred. Since you would be acting as the employer for your applicants, payrolling, insuring, and bonding them, you pay them first and then bill the employer client for services rendered. So the up-front cost to cover the payroll expense is quite high. Once your business is established, and the bank account has increased substantially, the initial outlay for payroll will not be a consideration, but in the beginning, it's a huge responsibility. Note: There are companies available that offer the payroll expense only to any start-up temporary agency.

Combined temporary and permanent agency benefits

Every client, whether it's the employer or the employee, has a variety of different needs over the lifetime relationship with your agency. It's realistic, therefore, to have a wide range of services to accommodate those needs as they arise.

AREAS OF CONCENTRATION

As discussed earlier, it's perfectly acceptable to offer agency services that concentrate in specific fields or industries. By that we mean letting the general public know, through your agency advertising program, that you will only be providing placement in certain areas. These might be:

Management positions

Administrators, directors, supervisors, CEOs, CFOs, managers, assistant managers, office managers, etc.

Accounting positions

Controllers, staff accountants, full-charge bookkeepers, bookkeepers, account clerks, payroll clerks, accounts receivable bookkeepers, accounts payable bookkeepers, etc.

Sales positions

Public relations, outside sales, inside sales, customer service, sales clerks, counter sales, telemarketing, sales and service reps, route sales, etc.

Clerical positions

Secretaries, receptionists, administrative assistants, switchboard operators, etc.

Blue-collar positions

Warehouse persons, driver delivery persons, janitors, building maintenance workers, electricians, plumbers, carpenters, sheetrockers, etc.

Technical positions

Computer technicians, programmers, data entry, software or hardware sales and service, etc.

Miscellaneous fields

Restaurant, medical, automotive, banking, insurance, legal, graphics, printing, computer, manufacturing, wholesale, retail, hotel/motel, entertainment industry, educational facilities, etc.

A full-range agency offers both permanent and temporary placement services in all fields, all industries, and for all clients.

FEE REPAYMENT STRUCTURE

After many, many years in the permanent agency field, I had an opportunity to see what worked and what didn't work for my competitors, and I finally selected a fee structure and repayment plan that I found both fair and equitable for all parties.

North Coast's fees were a flat 75 percent of the employee's first month's salary. This fee was payable by both the applicant and the employer, on a split 50/50 basis. For example, if the monthly salary was $1,500, then the fee, calculated at the 75 percent rate, equaled $1,125. The employer paid $562.50 and so did the applicant. Since both parties were charged with one-half of the agency fee, each had an initial investment in one another. Later on, the employer was required to reimburse the applicant one-half of his or her portion, after six months on the job, and the final one-half at the end of the year.

Believe me, this fee split/reimburse policy worked better than anything I'd ever seen. Not only did I get tremendous feedback from lots of satisfied clients, but I also received input from my competitive agencies when they slowly switched their fee policies to match mine. Everyone was satisfied. My agency got paid for services rendered, the cost was shared, and finally, the applicant got reimbursed after proving value to the company.

North Coast offered a 10 percent discount (up front) on payments made within the first five working days from the start of the hire, and almost all employers, and many applicants, took this credit savings.

In the standard account receivable cycle, applicants were required to pay 10 percent of the fee on acceptance of the job and then the balance in three equal payments over a 90-day period. Since we always knew when the paydays were, their payments were due on their payday. Then they could work a month, pay a third, work a month, pay a third, and so on. So, if their monthly salary was $1,500, the three monthly payments were only $168.75. It was a plan that made it extremely easy for the new workers to budget payments, and they knew they were going to be reimbursed in six months and again in one year. That gave them the extra incentive to work longer than the 90-day review.

OPERATING SCHEDULE

Decide what hours you want to work and what days your agency will be open to the general public. The standard business schedule is: Monday through Friday, 8:00 a.m. to 5:00 p.m.

Evenings

It would be advisable to remain open one evening during the week to accommodate those working in jobs that conflict with your weekly hours. Thursday evening is always a good choice because the retail stores are generally open that evening, and the public has grown accustomed to reaching places on that evening of the week. Your office could remain open until 8:00 p.m. Be very careful about the security for yourself or your employee when working alone in that evening shift.

Saturdays

It's also helpful to the public if you remain open on Saturday, one weekend per month. You could set up a monthly repeat schedule, possibly the first Saturday of every month. It could also be every first and third, or second and fourth Saturday of the month. The hours might be shorter, 9:00 a.m. to 4:00 p.m. or maybe even 10:00 a.m. to 3:00 p.m.

Holidays

North Coast Services was generally closed on the days that the banks were closed. That meant the usual holidays: Christmas, Thanksgiving, New Year's Day, Easter, Good Friday (12:00 p.m.), Labor Day, Memorial Day, Independence Day, etc.

TERRITORY PARAMETERS

Define the distance criteria for serving your clientele. Are your services for placement going to affect businesses in your city only? How about countywide? Statewide?

When you advertise your currently available positions in the newspaper, the draw from the applicant pool will be quite vast. This is because there will be responses from unemployed workers and dissatisfied workers, and you'll always get the relocation responses to the help-wanted advertising, too.

We concentrated on countywide placement, which included a population base of about 200,000. But we were more than willing to help a company find an employee if they were outside of the county, too. Most jobs we recruited for were primarily in the county seat, but the outlying communities were serviced as well. It's important to let the public know your targeted area in your advertising program. This way they can see the consistency and reliability as part of your company image.

SUPPORT SERVICES

Support services include secretarial service and workshops.

Secretarial service

Offering this additional service is a great way to increase your cash flow on a daily basis. Your secretary can occupy his or her lax time with these projects, or you might choose to hire a part-time college student or retired person to come in and work on these projects in the evenings when the office is closed. The agency activity comes to a halt after the workday has ended, but your payment to the landlord is for 24 hours a day. Remember, the office space and equipment sit idle during the nights and evenings, and most weekends.

Workshops

It's only natural to offer personnel-related classes for your applicant pool. This helps them in packaging themselves and gives them the valuable tools they need to present themselves at their very best for the interviews you set up. These workshops could be a two-hour class held once a week. The charges would vary accordingly.

- Resourcing (how to develop employer contact lists).
- Interviewing skills (trap questions, preparation, close).
- Dress codes.

Listed in the following are a variety of services your firm could offer in addition to the agency placement services:

- Secretarial service.
- Résumé preparation.
- Cover letters.
- Typing and word processing.
- Faxing.
- Mail-receiving services.
- Copy service.
- Message service.
- Audiotape editing.
- Transcribing services.
- Laser printing.
- Graphic design.
- Typesetting.
- Newsletter preparation.
- Brochures.
- Mailing lists.
- Label making.
- Collating.
- Editing.
- Notary public.
- Computer tutorial.

8
Develop an administrative structure

ACCOUNTING SYSTEM

We strongly suggest registering for an Accounting I class at your local junior college and getting a basic, all-around understanding of the accounting cycle if this is your first business. Unless you understand the money-in and money-out concept, it will be very difficult to keep a basic set of accurate books and, as your business expands, it will be more difficult to keep track of the records. Many businesses fail for lack of planning an exact system for tracking the expenses (outlay) versus revenue (income).

Just be sure to keep simplified but accurate business records from the very first dollar spent and earned. After you have consulted with an accountant and received the recommendations for an accounting program, go to a software business such as Egghead software and see if you can preview the program. This software program is very important, not only for accurate records but also to limit the involvement and expense of an accountant. Don't misunderstand. An accountant is essential. He or she provides an important year-end check against your record keeping and also keeps abreast of the changes in the tax codes. But why pay for bookkeeping services when you can do it yourself? Most programs automatically make the double entry and at the same time enter that amount in the proper tax form and schedule. At the end of the year, you buy the tax program that's compatible with your software and, in a matter of minutes, all that year's data is placed on your state and federal tax form. Many programs print out an exact replica of the tax forms and schedules, and some offer the option of electronic filing. After you feel confident with this accounting software, you can also offer an accounting service as an adjunct to your agency.

Schedule specific hours to work on the data entry and posting to accounts. Buy a receipt book for payments made in your office in person or in cash. Set up a petty cash drawer so you always have cash available as needed for change or emergencies.

Finally, by taking the Accounting I course in your local junior college, you will learn how to effectively read and work with your monthly financial statements. These are the profit and loss statements and balance sheets, which give you a snapshot of the daily money-in and money-out cycle and help you make crucial decisions for marketing and expansion.

When a position is offered and a bill is sent for services rendered, there should be no surprises. Applicants who come into your office to register for employment will be given a fee schedule at the same time they are given the application to fill out. They will be required to sign their name at the bottom of the application, indicating their understanding of the fee structure before they even go on any interviews. They will also sign a contract explaining the terms of the fee before each individual interview.

Accounts receivable system: Money in

When you or your counselor fill a job order, the client is going to be responsible for paying your company a fee for services rendered. This is called an accounts receivable account because you're willing to extend the debtor credit. Payments will be received over a period of time. The applicant will have 90 days to pay his or her portion of the fee, and the employer will have 30 days to pay its share. Both parties are given discounts for early payments on the account, as well as timely payments, as indicated on your fee schedule.

Closing a job order

Let's walk through the entire process of closing a job order. This means shifting all the job order paperwork from the recruiting stage to the billing stage. This is the part in the business cycle where all your hard work pays off! Be sure to remember to contact the remaining applicants who were sent for interviews on this job, and let them know the placement has been filled.

Step one The first step is confirmation from the employer and applicant on the agreement to hire and acceptance of the position. This generally comes in a telephone call from the employer giving you the selection choice. You will then need to contact the chosen applicant and make the job offer. This was always one of the most satisfying parts of the placement business for me. Then call the company back immediately and confirm the hire, start date, and start salary.

Step two After the congratulations on the new hire are given to both parties, a reminder should be made that the policy of your firm is to offer a 10-percent discount on the entire fee if the full amount is paid within five working days from start date of the position. Calculate this beforehand and be ready to give the figures to both the applicant and employer when making your congratulations phone call.

Step three Prepare and mail congratulations policy letters to both employer and employee. (See the letters at the end of this chapter.)

Step four Prepare and mail congratulations/billing letters to both employer and employee. (Refer to the example Congratulations/billing letter later in this chapter.)

Step five Record a reminder message on your calendar to trigger the follow-up call with the employer in two weeks from the start date. This is to make sure that the placement is working out satisfactorily. You can even call the applicant to check with him or her also, but don't make the call during working hours.

Step six Set up payment due dates on your calendar for these collection purposes.

- Date payment is due.
- Date for reminder letter (five days before payment is due).
- Date for phone call on late payment, etc.

Step seven Create a ledger card for each account and file it in an open accounts receivable file (see Tables 8-1 and 8-2).

Table 8-1
Example ledger card heading (applicant)

John Smith	Warehouse Person	Start: 6/1/95
333 4th Street	ABC Company	Salary: $1500/mo
Newton, U.S.A.	1234 10th, Newtown	Fee: $1125
(111) 111-1111	(222) 222-2222	Split: $562.50

Payment Dates and Amounts

June 5, 1995	$ 56.20	<$506.30> if paid in full
July 1, 1995	168.77	
August 1, 1995	168.77	
September 1, 1995	168.76	<$160.32> if paid on time

Table 8-2
Example ledger card heading (employer)

ABC Company	John Smith	Start: 6/1/95
1234 10th, Newtown	Warehouse Person	Salary: $1500/mo
(222) 222-2222	(111) 111-1111	Fee: $1125 Split/Reimburse

Payment Dates and Amounts

| June 5, 1995 | $ 506.30 | (with 10% Discount) |
| July 1, 1995 | 562.50 | |

Step eight Put the application, résumé, job order, and any other notes together in a separate file. Also, put all correspondence into this file, i.e., a copy of the congratulations letters, reminder letters, etc.

Step nine Enter all the job order close information into your computer and create an invoice that will accompany the congratulations letter.

Step ten Enter the contract expiration date from the placement contract in the appropriate tracking binder for follow-up.

Step eleven Prepare to announce the placement in the next staff meeting.

One final note about client accounts. It's extremely important to keep all the records current. Make your postings daily and never let this crucial accounting phase fall behind or get out of hand.

Bank deposits

After you set up your bank account, there will be deposit slips and a stamp to endorse each check that's to be deposited. When a payment is made on the account, follow these steps:

1. Record the payment received on the client ledger card.
2. Complete the bank deposit slip.

3. Stamp the back of the check to endorse the payment.
4. Enter the deposit amount into the check register.
5. Deposit the check and file the deposit receipt.

Each month you will receive a bank reconciliation statement for your business account. Always balance the statement right away and be sure to keep the check register accurate. Remember to add and subtract the monthly interest payments and bank charges.

Monthly billing statements

When I first started in the personnel placement business, it was my responsibility to collect all the moneys due. I learned all about the accounts receivable, bank deposits, and billing from being in this job. The one thing I learned about the most was collections! Keep in mind that new applicants searching for work are not usually earning any income before coming into your agency. Their personal bills are stacking up, and they might be getting behind. When that's the case, clients will automatically feel that the rent and gas and electric bills are definitely a priority over your fee!

In order to circumvent this frustrating cycle, over the years I refined a billing schedule to fit this exact problem. First, it's essential to let clients feel that you have honestly earned and deserve your fee. Always be professional, helpful, honest, and consistent with all your business dealings. Keep the clients aware, from the very beginning of the business relationship, that there is a fee charged for services rendered and a payment plan to allow for extended credit. Give excellent incentives to reduce the cost and, finally, provide a structured accounting cycle to support the revenues. If you choose the split-fee/reimbursement structure, keep reminding clients of the shared cost with the employer and the reimbursement of their paid portion after six months and one year.

First you'll need to define your billing cycle. Will you be sending statements out on the 1st, the 15th, or on the 30th? We chose to send the statements on the last day of each month, since most employers paid their employees on the 1st and the 15th. We wanted them to have a reminder of their agency payment responsibility when they got their paycheck.

Although each individual client has a payment schedule tailored to his or her individual paydays, clients need to receive a monthly billing statement. This is designed to trigger their memory and allow them to set up their budget for payment. A reminder is always helpful. Actually, in this business, several reminders are even better.

Late payments

The client should be made aware of your late payment policy in several ways. First, it's printed on the initial statement sent with the congratulations letter. Second, it will appear again on each billing statement mailed for the monthly payments. Third, provide a gentle verbal reminder when discussing the agency fee repayment plan. As long as you remain consistent with your billing policies, there should be no problem.

There will be certain circumstances when you might decide to adjust the payment structure to fit the applicant's needs. Just don't go overboard with your kind heart and lose in the end.

Adjustments to final bill

The adjustments to certain accounts happen when a person doesn't work out for some reason. You obviously can't charge an applicant for finding them a permanent job when he or she doesn't keep the position. The law in California states that any job lasting longer than 90 days is considered to be a permanent job. Anything lasting less than 90 days is temporary.

The adjusted fee therefore is as follows: $\frac{1}{90}$ of the permanent fee for each calendar day employed. Payments for temporary positions are to be made as paychecks are received. So, in short, work a month, pay $\frac{1}{3}$, work a month, pay $\frac{1}{3}$, etc. If the applicant stays the full 90 days, he or she owes the full fee.

Collections

When your company policy is to provide a quality service, then generally there will be fewer collection headaches. But there's always going to be some bad debt problems in every business. Research your local collection agencies and select the one you feel most comfortable using. The collection agencies charge a standard fee for collecting these aged accounts receivables for you. They usually keep 50 percent of any revenue gathered from these accounts, and once a month they write a check back to the agency for work performed. Before releasing any accounts to the collection agency, learn all the legal procedures available in the small-claims court process.

The following is a list of steps to follow to help ensure smoother collection policies.

1. Take the time to learn all of the collection laws in your state. It's important that you follow the guidelines designated by your local authorities. You can pick up this valuable information at your local courthouse for small-claims actions. If you don't follow these specific laws to the letter, you might not only lose the revenues due you, but you might also end up with a suit of your own.
2. Use your bank to collect for you. The banking industry now charges a modest fee ($10.00) to collect your bounced checks. Present the insufficient-fund check to your bank with a written request for collection. Your bank will then present the check to your customer's bank, where it will be held until sufficient funds become available. Contact your bank and make arrangements with them to act as your collection agent.
3. Continue to add late charges and interest payments each month, whether a payment is made or not.
4. Prepare a collection policy letter warning of legal action if payment is not received with 10 days. (Refer to examples of policy collection letters at the end of this chapter.)
5. Set the fee payment dates on client paydays to ensure timely payments.
6. Send a reminder-of-payment-due letter five days prior to payment.
7. Make the follow-up call two days after the payment due date.
8. Do what you say you're going to do.
9. Give a credit application to every applicant you send on an interview.
10. Be aware of when it's time to bring in your attorney.
11. When making the collection reminder calls, make the boss the heavy. (Unless, of course, you're the boss!)

12. Negotiate with the employer on the applicant fee.
13. Learn about bad check laws. Post the bad-check-policy-statement notice in your reception office.
14. Be flexible in extending payments.
15. Get creative with your collections. I once had a client pay his fee with a bad check. Every day I called the bank to see if the check would clear, and every day I was told no. I finally asked the clerk to at least give me a clue as to how far off the balance was. She said within $25. The next day I took a $25 check from my business account and deposited it into the client's bank account. The day after that, I redeposited the client bad check into the business account, and it cleared! Needless to say, the client was shocked when the account was reduced to pennies, but the bill was cleared and the law was on my side. My only risk was losing the $25, but it was worth every penny!
16. Learn all about the collection agency business and screen several companies before selecting the one you feel most confident in. These businesses do all of the collection of your aged accounts receivable for you. However, they do charge a healthy fee for this service. Usually, the rate is 50 percent of all revenues collected. They will pay for filing small-claims fees, and they'll even show up in court for you, win the judgment, and collect the fees.
17. Deadbeats! These are the bad debts that will be written off at the end of your fiscal year. They are the accounts that have gone through every stage of your thorough collection process and been with the collection agency for at least two years. At that point, I usually write this account off the books as a bad debt.

Accounts payable: Money out

The reason I call the business revenues "money in" and the payables "money out" is that my accounting manager told me it was the easiest way to think of the income and expenses of doing daily business. In the last chapter, we covered the "money in" or accounts receivable information. In this section, the "money out" or accounts payable will be explained.

Just as in the receivables, there are bills that have to be paid to remain in business. Monthly rent/lease, payroll, advertising, postage, supplies, and monthly dues, to name just a few. These are called the payables because they come due each and every month and have to be paid. Almost all of your accounts payable will be set up on a monthly payment schedule.

Try to set up credit accounts with as many of the companies that you buy goods and services from as possible. By doing this you will be able to set up a monthly payment plan, plus receive the benefits for payments made on time or early.

Most business payables are set up on a "net ten days." There are benefits to paying them on time, or even early. Some companies will give a reduction in the cost when your payment is done within certain time periods. It's very similar to when you deduct a percentage from your clients' fees when they pay their bills on time (or early).

It's always a good idea to keep your word with your creditors. They need to be able to trust you. Also, if and when there's ever a temporary cash flow problem, they'll be more inclined to be patient with the overdue payment. When you know that a payment is going to be late, a timely phone call will work wonders. Call ahead of the scheduled due date and let them know what's going on. Don't wait until the payment is past due to talk with them. And don't be afraid to share your rough times with these business associates. They've all had their fair share of cash flow crunches themselves.

You might eventually learn how to rob Peter to pay Paul. This means holding the payment due on one credit account while using those designated funds to cover another account that is more crucial or would incur a higher late fee. Make very sure to keep the check register current at all times and record each payment made on the correct invoice by posting the date the payment was made and the check number.

Don't forget the tax benefits derived from your interest payments. At the end of each fiscal year, you should receive a statement from your creditor with an indication of interest paid to date on the account. Since you're given tax deductions for all interest paid each year, record this valuable information and remember to take the deduction earned.

Finally, try to set up a working budget that will allow for moneys available in the peak advertising seasons, cost-saving advertising specialties, and emergencies. A lot can be said for preplanning the expenditures of your business. Be careful, though. Don't overspend, and always keep an eye out for the best deals possible!

Payroll accounts

When you open payroll for your very first employee, getting the correct information for setting up the payroll account is crucial. You'll need to have the new employee fill out a W4 Form that designates his or her filing status. This information has to correspond with the government regulations for withholdings. If the employee claims no deductions, he or she will receive a larger refund at the end of the year. Likewise, if the employee claims one or more deductions, the moneys due will be relegated in each paycheck and spread out over a much longer period of time.

The W-2 that's issued to the employee at the end of the year (no later than January 31st), will identify all income earned (the gross amount), and all deductions taken during the fiscal year. This leaves the final figure, which is called the net amount. That's actual moneys received by the employee.

Payroll records

As the employer, you must maintain all records pertaining to payroll taxes (Income-tax Withholding, Social Security, and Federal Unemployment Tax) for at least four years after the tax becomes due or is paid, whichever is later.

There are several different kinds of employment records that must be maintained to satisfy federal requirements:
- Income-tax withholding records:
  - ~ Name, address, and Social Security number of each employee.
  - ~ Amount and date of each payment of compensation.
  - ~ Amount of wages subject to withholding in each payment.
  - ~ Amount of withholding tax collected from each payment.
  - ~ Reason that the taxable amount is less than the total payment.
  - ~ Statements relating to employees' nonresident alien status.

~ Information about payments made under sick-pay plans.

~ Withholding exemption certificate.

- Social Security (FICA) tax records:

~ Amount of each payment subject to FICA tax.

~ Amount and date of FICA tax collected from each payment.

~ Explanation for the difference, if any.

- Federal Unemployment Tax (FUTA) records:

~ Total amount paid during calendar year.

~ Amount subject to unemployment tax.

~ Amount of contributions paid into the state unemployment fund.

~ Any other information requested on the unemployment tax return.

Since the information and reporting laws vary for each state, find the correct legal requirements at your local Employment Development Department or ask your attorney to supply you with the correct information. Be extra careful when doing the payroll, as it can sometimes be tedious and hard to understand. Find someone who can help you understand the steps. We have listed a few of the details for your consideration, but they are by no means thorough and complete. The states each have different requirements.

Hourly salary

There are pros and cons for paying employees in this method. If they are paid hourly, each and every hour they work is recorded and, at the end of each week, or two weeks, a time card is submitted for payment of hours worked. They will expect to be paid overtime if they work over 8 hours in one day or 40 hours in one week. Overtime pay is calculated at the employee's regular hourly rate, plus 50 percent. This is called time and a half. For example: the hourly rate is $6.00/hour, and the overtime rate is $9.00/hour. The taxes you pay are the same, whether you choose hourly payments or a salaried structure. Most support staff positions are set up on an hourly basis (secretaries, bookkeepers, etc.)

Monthly salary

Again, there are benefits to paying your employees a set payment for each month. There is never any question about the hours worked. They might work longer than 8 hours in one day or 40 hours in one week and still receive the pay for the set amount. Most management positions and sales representative positions are paid on a monthly salary basis.

Paydays

Select the days of the month that your company will be issuing paychecks, and make it the policy to distribute these checks on the same days each month. Some companies pay weekly, on the same day each week. Some choose to pay every other week, again on the same day. Others will pick the 1st and the 15th, and again, another will choose the 16th and the 30th or 31st. As you can see, there doesn't seem to be any rhyme or reason for the selection process. It's simply based on personal preference.

I've always paid my staff on the 1st and the 15th. I chose these days for several reasons. First, it was less expensive to have my bookkeeper calculating the salaries only twice a month. Second, most companies set up their credit payment plans on the 1st and the 15th. This pay structure enabled my employees to meet their personal financial obligations much easier. And finally, it was the way I was always paid as an employee! Funny how the 1st and the 15th took on a whole new meaning for me, once it lost the payday excitement and became the payroll ordeal!

Since you, as the employer, are required to submit matching funds to the Internal Revenue Service for federal withholding tax, you'll need to set up a hold account with your bank to keep the monthly payments until they are due to the IRS. You pay this tax only on a quarterly basis, but always deposit your moneys due monthly. That way, when the payment date arrives, you'll have the necessary funds to meet your legal obligation. The IRS is not patient when you don't send them their quarterly tax payments! The following are the legal deductions you will withhold from each paycheck, as well as the additional special withholding categories:

Legal
- Federal Income Tax Withholding (FICA).
- State Tax Withholding.
- Social Security Insurance Tax (SSI).
- State Disability Insurance (SDI).

Optional
- Stock options.
- Vacations, etc.

Contracting employees

Be extremely careful with the concept of avoiding the payroll expense by hiring contract people. The laws are well-defined for the responsibilities of individuals being paid by you in this manner. First, they cannot be required to work any set hours. They make their own schedule. Second, they cannot be trained in any way. They have to come right into the job and begin producing without any supervision whatsoever.

Contract employees are required at the end of the year to pay their own taxes. You're not responsible for their tax liability. The best example of a contract employee is the salesperson in your firm. Think about the different ways to bring someone in and pay them a set base salary, with incentives for commissions and bonuses. Detailed contract employee requirements are covered in chapter 10.

INTEROFFICE COMMUNICATION

For the ability to make your thoughts known and keep abreast of any and all changes that happen in a normal office structure, it's necessary to put into place a strong communication system.

Staff meetings

Plan to have daily, weekly, monthly, and annual staff meetings. This is a great time to share news about the business community, update the status of each current job opening, bring up problems, and give out compliments. It's also the time to put your collective heads together and refine any glitches in the existing operating systems. I always encouraged my staff to give me their ideas for solutions to business problems and, of course, any new ideas for marketing, etc.

The daily meetings can be held from 8:30 a.m. to 9:00 a.m. Make the time productive, and you'll see a much smoother operation. Lack of communication is the basis of almost all business upheavals.

Chain of command and complaints

Whenever I hired a new employee, I put the person that was previously doing those tasks in charge of the new person. So, if there were ever any questions about the job or minor problems, the new employee communicated directly with his or her immediate supervisor, not me. If there was a serious problem, the supervisor came to me and discussed it, and a solution was searched for that would be equitable for all concerned.

This saved me a tremendous amount of time. Instead of being required to constantly put out fires, I spent my valuable time exploring, building, and creating new avenues for the business. This is one of the values of delegating. Although I was the boss and always had the final say, I found that this system was much smoother.

Of course, you have to hire with this in mind. Even though new employees are not supervising anyone when you hire them, they will have the supervising responsibility as they advance within your firm.

Memorandums

Some people think of the memo as time-consuming and unnecessary. I don't. When things get busy, as they often do, memories and issues that were discussed a week ago or a month ago seem to fade. If it's written down, dated and signed, there's always a paper trail to support the idea. Keep that bit of information in mind. Always keep notes, write every idea down that you, or your employees, come up with, and look at them from time to time. An example memo form is in chapter 2.

Protocol

Protocol is actually a concept. Each person within your firm needs to have a basic understanding of what's appropriate and what's not. This might mean something as slight as who goes first through the door or who speaks first in the meetings. Respect and consideration is the key. It's really no different from the manners taught to children.

One of the primary areas of protocol in business is privacy. When your door is closed, it means you're not to be disturbed for any reason. Teach your staff these signs, and allow for some learning time to become familiar with your idiosyncrasies and requirements of protocol.

Wasted time

Whenever I saw someone on my staff doing something that looked like a waste of time, I realized it was my responsibility to keep this person actively producing for each eight-hour day of work. You don't want to pay for anyone to read a personal book, take a long personal call, or visit with a friend who stops by unannounced. You shouldn't feel like that's asking too much of any employee.

In order to keep this from happening, the rules about productivity have to be explained from the very beginning of employment and kept consistent throughout the years. Also, be the one to set the example. Don't play at work yourself and then expect employees to keep busy all the time.

Have a list of projects, and prioritize them so that when employees do hit some lag time, they'll know where to go to find the next productive function. Some of the chores are tedious, some are fun, and some are long and drawn out. Make sure there are a variety of down-time projects for each employee, and keep an eye on them to ensure they follow your instruction.

Monthly reviews

Monthly reviews will be covered in detail in chapter 10 under "SALARY AND PERFORMANCE EVALUATION POLICIES." It's as important as any other form of communication within your office structure. Never allow the review to pass without listening to your employee's problems and ideas also. Give them encouragement and strokes, and you'll be surprised at how much you get back in return. We all need strokes in life. Just don't ever forget how much you needed it when you were an employee.

FILING SYSTEMS

Efficiently run businesses have effective filing systems. There's nothing worse than searching for something that's been lost or misfiled. It's not only frustrating, but it's also a waste of the company's payroll time.

We've all heard about the applicant who is checking in to update his or her file and is told, after a frustrating search, that the file has been lost! What an embarrassing problem. Don't ever let this happen in your office. Set up your filing systems in the very beginning and always keep them updated and current. The following are the categories required for files:

Active applications

Counselors should keep new applicants' applications in their deep desk drawers. Pendaflex files will separate the required categories. For example: permanent, part-time, clerical, bookkeeping, computer, sales, general labor, management, etc.

Keep these files active for about a three-month period. If the applicant has not found work within that period of time, it's more than likely that he or she is going to be difficult to place. Many times you'll see the applicant register with your service and then not call in to check on his or her file. If there are no notes on the paperwork of a contact within the last 60 days, put the file on inactive.

Inactive applications

This paperwork builds up quickly and should be kept in a large four-drawer filing cabinet in the receptionist's office, storage room, or testing room. Plan to keep these files alphabetically and make them easily accessible. Some states have laws that require you to keep the application for a certain period of years. Check with your local state authorities for this data.

Active job orders

You and your staff will be working with these files all day long: in the morning, during the staff meeting, and periodically during the day as the interviews are being conducted. Each counselor will keep active job orders all in one file folder and file them at the very front of all the open applications.

Inactive job orders

Inactive job orders are filed in the same four-drawer filing cabinet as the inactive application, but in numerical order. Many times over the years, the same companies would give us a job order that had been worked on in the past through North Coast. Instead of requiring the caller to repeat all the job description information, we just pulled the inactive order from the file and filled out a current one with all of the updated information. This was a much quicker system than having employers repeat themselves, and it saved a lot of time when things got busy.

Placement contracts

Placement contracts need to be printed, and they are the legal binding forms that secure payment for services rendered. They will be numbered and bound, with two copies for each contract. That's so the original can be given to the client and the yellow copy stays in the book. All the contracts in each binder stay in one place, and each counselor simply works with the contract book in sequence until it's depleted.

Inactive contract books

Inactive contract books can be filed in your store room along with the inactive applications and job orders. Keep them handy for reference, and file them in numerical order.

Legals

This is all the information you can gather about the current employment laws, legal postings, etc. We kept information about changes in the personnel laws, updates from the state department of employment, suits filed against other agencies, and anything else we felt belonged in the legal file. Review this file once a year and update it as necessary.

Policy letters

Keep a file of all the example policy letters in a binder, and show them to employees during training. The binder is much easier to review and far more functional when the letters are categorized and easy to find. We have included samples of numerous policy letters at the end of this chapter.

Competition

There is tremendous value in keeping track of all the news about your competitors. You will want to have a copy of their application, fee schedule, contract, and any other news about the company that you feel is valid.

Applicants generally register with more than one agency and are more than willing to share the good and the bad about the other companies. You can learn a lot, avoid mistakes, and refine your own systems with this valuable news. (There is more information about competition in chapter 12.)

Associations

There are many, many organizations in each community that can be beneficial to you and your business. When you attend meetings and become a member, organizations will send you much data pertaining to their specific group: membership lists, company news, member bios, etc. Keep all this information in a handy place for referral. (There is more information on business associations in chapter 11.)

Newspaper advertising forms

Newspaper advertising forms identify which job orders are being currently advertised in your local newspaper. Keep all of these advertising forms in one place.

Bookkeeping files

Several files will be created in the accounting department. They are:
- Current accounts receivable client files.
- Receipts from payments made.
- Invoices.
- Internal Revenue Service information.
- Employment development department information.
- Ledger cards.

FEE SPLITTING WITH A COMPETITOR

Sometimes a job order might be difficult to fulfill. This happens for one of several reasons: the applicant pool for this particular job request is low, meaning the qualifications are so specific that applicants are hard to locate in your area; the salary for the position might be set at too low a rate; you're not getting the attention of the applicants who are reading your advertising.

When the job order comes in, try scanning the open file first. If you don't have any current applicants qualified for the position, then you'll have to advertise the opening. If, after doing this, the right person doesn't come forward, the next step is to possibly change the advertisement just a little bit to draw a different client. The last thing we did before sharing the fee with a competitor was call the employer and tell them that the salary listed for the opening might not be high enough to draw any qualified applicants. When the employer is willing to increase the salary, that alone can draw the correct applicant response.

When all else fails, rather than call the employer client back and give him or her the news that you were unable to fill the order, call one of your favorite competitors and release the job description information for recruitment through the competitor's agency. The agency will be happy to share a fee with you! You don't have to give the company name, just the job order information. This split-fee relationship obviously has to be developed early on, or competitors won't respond in such a positive and helpful manner when you do call. The fee is paid to the competitive agency only after the placement is made, and the fee is paid.

I found this fee-split arrangement very helpful several times. Another benefit is that other agencies will contact your firm when they have problems filling a client order, too. Remember, the fee is always calculated at the original agency fee structure, and it's paid only after the revenue is collected for the placement.

TESTING

If you're going to provide clerical or bookkeeping employees for placement, it's helpful to also provide test results prior to each interview. Employers like to see the preliminary test scores and will often make their decision based partially on the speed and accuracy of the individual test results, as well as the applicant's experience and personality.

When setting up the testing facility, provide good lighting, a comfortable work station, and some semblance of privacy. It's nerve-wracking enough for these clients to be looking for work. It would be unkind to put an applicant in a room with several other applicants with noise and distractions during the testing period.

For clerical employees (secretaries, general office clerks, data entry clerks, receptionists, etc.) there are typing tests, spelling tests, grammar tests, and any others you might desire.

For bookkeeping and accounting employees, the most obvious test is the bookkeeping test. The other important one is the ten-key adding machine test. This is primarily done for speed and accuracy. (Tests can be purchased at a business supply center.)

INVESTIGATING EMPLOYERS

It would be disastrous to begin working relationships with employer clients who have serious problems of their own. You want to be very sure that their reputation, financial solvency, and management style are worthy of your placement services. Can you imagine the problems if an applicant is placed within the firm and learns that the company is bordering on bankruptcy or operating under shady management? Most people quit their jobs due to just a few of these standard problems.

These obstacles can be avoided if an investigation of the company and its policies is carried out before the working relationship begins. The categories for preliminary investigation are the following:

Management style

If the company has developed strong personnel policies, employees produce more without being asked. When policies are not solid, the employee might adopt an attitude early on of "eight hours of work for eight hours of pay."

Strong management style looks like this:

- Flexible time, allowing for a convenient eight-hour schedule. Some arrive at 7:00 a.m. and work until 4:00 p.m., while others might choose to arrive at

9:00 a.m. and work until 6:00 p.m. This conforms to the employee's personal lifestyle and promotes employee morale.
- Regular meetings to air differences and suggest improvements.
- Benefits packages for employees, providing medical, dental, optical, profit sharing, continuing education, etc.
- Standard raises and bonuses that are automatically built into the payroll system.
- Group activities such as baseball, bowling, picnics, Christmas party, etc. are available to all employees.
- Standardized performance evaluations that allow opportunities to improve and advance within the company.
- Clear and concise job descriptions with a specific chain of command.
- Policy manuals and employee handbooks that provide clear definitions of company standards and policies.
- A clean and healthy work environment.
- Adequate parking facilities.

Financial solvency

You should evaluate the financial stability of small-to-medium businesses. This can make the difference between your placement receiving a guaranteed paycheck or not. This is not as necessary for large, well-known companies, since almost everything about them is public knowledge.

Strong financial stability looks like this. The company:
- Has a good credit rating, which means it pays its bills on time.
- Has a strong capital base allowing for growth and expansion, even during difficult economic times.
- Shows consistent profit.

Reputation (within the industry)

A good reputation in a business is essential, despite the size, product, service, or location of the firm. Employees need to feel proud of the company they represent, and they should speak highly of their coworkers.

An excellent reputation could look like this. The company:
- Produces a quality product or service.
- Has a strong customer service division.
- Has a strong repeat customer base. This reveals solid, honest relationships.
- Generates new business by referrals.
- Pays its financial obligations on time.
- Is respected by competitors.
- Is fair in all business situations.
- Participates in community activities.
- Might sponsor a nonprofit organization.
- Is well-represented in business associations and in the community.
- Shows repeated and constant growth by modernizing to keep up with an ever-changing economy.

Start-up and on-site information

The information gathered for the start-up phase of the investigation is: how the company began, who started it, and when it was started?

The on-site investigation includes such things as:

- Parking for customers, guests, and employees is adequate, easy, and protected.
- There is a friendly feeling in the reception area. The interior design is bright and cheery, not dark and depressing.
- The phone lines are busy, and the receptionist is qualified to handle the incoming calls and client traffic.
- The reception area is clean, neat, and stocked with adequate reading material and coffee.
- The employees are dressed cleanly and neatly.
- When the company has good management policies, communication between staff and management is nonverbal, easy to perceive, and comfortable.
- The interviewer shakes your hand with a friendly handshake.
- The interviewer appears prepared to conduct professional interviews.

Listed in the following are a few simple steps to take when checking out the new client:

1. Call the Better Business Bureau and ask if any complaints have been registered against this firm.
2. Contact the Dunn and Bradstreet Company and request a report on the new client's financial status. Dunn and Bradstreet also publishes a book reporting companies' financial ability to meet the accounts payable. This can be found in the public library. The accuracy of the information is not guaranteed, as Dunn and Bradstreet must rely on data supplied by the company itself. Usually this is correct, due to competitive sources, etc.
3. Make it a policy of your firm to schedule an immediate appointment with the employers you begin working relationships with. They will not only be pleased to see your enthusiasm and professionalism, but they will also give you the information you need to describe the internal operation to each applicant you send for interview. You can learn a lot by walking through the plant or offices and getting a general feel for the place.

Once you've satisfied yourself that the business is stable and sound, you'll be comforted by knowing that worrisome part of the relationship will never raise its ugly head. Not only are you ensuring the long-term placement for your applicant client, but you can also look forward to repeat business with this employer.

INVENTORY CONTROL

Set up an adequate and expandable system for all your inventory. Schedule time once a month for yourself or one of your employees to assess the stock at hand and reorder as needed. Whoever is responsible for the inventory needs to do this review on a consistent basis.

Pay close attention to the sales promotions that your suppliers offer, and always continue to shop around so that you're consistently getting the best buys. The inventory suppliers will not always be consistent.

When you purchase these supplies, try to buy at a reasonable volume. This is very important because you don't want to have any unused stock sitting around for very long. Some of the products you buy will not satisfy your needs once you try them out. Remember, your needs will be changing constantly just to keep up with refining your existing operating system. Keep an open mind about this crucial business rule. If you overbuy on any one item, it can be a waste of your valuable capital and can quickly drain the supplies budget.

Have all the supplies in a stockroom and labeled so that the stockroom is easy to access by all employees. Teach them how to alert the inventory control person when a certain item is running low. It's a team effort to keep things running smoothly in any size business, so make the inventory control a part of the operation policies.

INACTIVATING APPLICATIONS

There are several reasons for closing an application:
- The applicant doesn't meet your agency requirements for experience, personality, and/or appearance.
- The applicant calls to say he or she is working and no longer needs your services, and you can pull his or her file.
- The applicant has paid the agency a placement fee, and all of the job order paperwork is filed.
- The applicant is obnoxious.
- Three months after the applicant registers with your agency, you don't hear from him or her asking to keep his or her file current.
- Dishonesty.
- Bad reference.

Be sure to keep these files in order, as many, many times applicants will call and ask you to reactivate their personnel file. When an applicant makes this request, all you need to do is request the current information (new address, new phone number, most recent position) and put the file back into the active drawer.

SCREENING AND SELECTION

It took many years of placement experience and losses to the competition to develop a system for screening the job applicants and making selections that beat the competition at their own game.

Screening

In a very short time, you'll see the pattern of interviews and learn how to work with each job seeker according to your current needs. Applicant interviews fall into three basic categories.
- Response to specific want ad.
- Cursory.
- Referral.

We'll go into further detail about how to interview these three categories in chapter 9.

Selection

Sometimes you'll take the new job order and learn, at that time, that the company is also calling other services for help in the placement. Companies occasionally do this so they can generate as many interviews as possible. If this is the case, ask the hiring source to give your agency the first three available interview times in their schedule. Then take the open application file home with you that evening. Scan the current résumés and applications for the correct matches, and call the job seekers at their homes to describe and discuss the potential job. Set up the interviews in the selected time slots and call the employer first thing the next morning with the applicant names and interview times! By the time the other agency even begins working the job order, you've not only done the work before them, you've very likely made the placement.

Be sure to only select qualified applicants for each job order. Don't ever try to pull the wool over anyone's eyes. If you learn anything during your interview that could be considered a weak point, be sure to share it. Clients don't need surprises later on down the road, especially if they think you withheld information just to make a match! This applies to clients, employers, and applicants. Give out as much information as you have and also give any tips that you think might help them in the interview.

Schedule only three appointments for the employer. Make sure these are your very best people. Many times you'll have more qualified applicants to choose from, but the manager doesn't need to be overwhelmed with choices. If you have two great choices, then don't fill the empty slot with someone that's not quite as qualified. Just send the two that you do have, and let the employer know that there are other choices, but not as perfect. The employer will appreciate your honesty.

When you call the company in the morning to discuss the interview choices, let the manager know your order of preference for whom you would select for hiring. Managers always appreciate this supportive information. During the selection process, you'll be able to inactivate several applications because as you call these people, many of them will no longer be available.

TRACKING COMPETITION

Set up individual files for your competitive agency firms and develop an ongoing system for recording as much information about them as possible. Keep the files current. It will be valuable reference material over the years. You can learn all kinds of helpful hints and clues by keeping alert when you overhear something in a meeting, or when an applicant shares his or her experiences. You might not think it's important when you hear it, but no matter how insignificant, record the data. There are various resources for gathering this data:

Applicant interviews

This is where you will likely hear the most freely given information. It's through the eye of the job seeker. An applicant that has recently been interviewed by another agency, or been scheduled for an employer interview, willingly shares his or her feelings of satisfaction or dissatisfaction with the other services. It rarely takes prompting to have a flood of input come your way, especially if it's less than desirable.

Employer feedback

Company clients who have had exposure to your competitors will also share their professional input and personal feelings when asked. Some are satisfied and plan to continue to use the resource. If that's the case, find out what it is about the competitive service that they appreciate the most. Others have had a bad experience and don't ever expect to return. Take it all in, make notes, and build the competitor file with this valuable information.

Again, this method of learning how to avoid costly mistakes saves your agency considerable time and expense. All it really takes is knowing the people to ask, what to say, and where to put the information to good use.

Association contacts

All industries have their own special organizations for group membership in their specific fields. Personnel associations are citywide, countywide, and statewide. There will be a rep from your competition who will be attending these monthly meetings. The competition will also send representatives to several other associations. Pay attention to the people companies send to represent their firm, how involved they get in the group activities, how much input they share with others, and how hard they are pushing for sales contacts.

Marketing contacts

When you or your salesperson are out in the field making those all-important sales calls, listen carefully to the feedback from the potential clients. Learn from their comments about the frustrations with the other agencies, so you can learn how to improve the working relationship with your firm. Never repeat the same mistakes that turned them away from the competition in the first place!

Advertisements in the media

We could always tell how well the competition was doing by the dollars they spent to advertise their services. When reading these ads, check within the advertisement itself to see if there are new services being added or new people on board. Scan the trade magazines and newspapers for this crucial input.

Employee grapevine

Most of the employees who work in competitive fields have a comfortable relationship with each other. Since they have so much in common, they discuss their personal feelings about their jobs. The topics covered are many: employers (personality), management style, salaries, benefits, etc. Pay attention to this resource. It's the inside information that's most valuable.

Spotters

Spotters are the people you individually select to go to the competitive agencies for review purposes. Spotters will walk through the systems as either an employee or employer. This way, you'll have a direct report back on all operating systems and procedures. Be very careful when you choose a person to perform this task for you. The confidentiality and professionalism is very important. Keep an ear open for the following kind of information:

- Placement fee and payment structure.
- Expansion details.
- Employee cutbacks (layoffs).
- Management style.
- Business reputation.
- Financial solvency.
- Pending company sale.
- Pending close.
- Office location and parking facilities.
- Office equipment.
- Activity (busy phones, full reception area, etc.).
- Timeliness.
- Basic business honesty, integrity, morals, and ethics.

We all know that bad advertising spreads faster than any other kind of paid advertising. People have no problem sharing how they feel about poor business policies, pushy salespeople, or frustrating experiences. By listening carefully, you can learn from the mistakes of your competitors at their expense, not yours!

POLICY LETTERS

The following are policy letters that you can use in your business.

LETTER TO A SALES PROSPECT WHO IS DIFFICULT TO SEE

[DATE]

[NAME]
[COMPANY]
[ADDRESS]
[CITY, STATE, ZIP]

Dear [NAME]:

   I have tried to call you several times during this past month, but have had no success in reaching you. I can appreciate how busy you must be this time of year.

   [SENDER'S COMPANY] is keenly aware of the heightened competition in [INDUSTRY] and is committed to responding with more creative and attentive servicing to corporate customers such as you. We combine the personal touch and convenience of a local personnel firm with all of the sophistication of the major companies in our city.

   I will call you in the near future to try to schedule a visit at your convenience. I look forward to meeting with you.

                    Sincerely,

                    [SENDER'S NAME]
                    [SENDER'S TITLE]

[ID LINE/INITIALS]

SALES LETTER TO RENEW CONTACT

[DATE]

[NAME]
[TITLE]
[COMPANY]
[ADDRESS]
[CITY, STATE, ZIP]

Dear [NAME]:

I was pleased to hear that you have become a [TITLE] at [COMPANY]. Please accept best wishes from all of us at [SENDER'S COMPANY].

You may remember that we had several phone conversations when you were [FORMER TITLE] at [FORMER COMPANY]. It is my hope that we can work together once again, continuing to provide you with the quality of service you have come to expect from us.

Please let me know if I can be of assistance to you or help you better serve your clients. We at [SENDER'S COMPANY] are committed to providing the quality personnel services required to run a successful business.

Again, I wish you continued success.

Kindest regards,

[SENDER'S NAME]
[SENDER'S TITLE]

[ID LINE/INITIALS]

LETTER WELCOMING NEW CLIENT

[DATE]

[NAME]
[COMPANY]
[ADDRESS]
[CITY, STATE, ZIP]

Dear [NAME]:

We're pleased to welcome you as a new client and want to take this opportunity to thank you for your selection of [SENDER'S COMPANY] to handle all of your personnel needs. You have chosen a firm that is committed to providing you with excellent service and superior professional support.

We have assigned [NAME OF REP] as your personal sales representative. Of course, [FIRST NAME OF REP] will work closely with our entire staff of specialists to ensure that you receive the best guidance on all matters.

Our firm specializes in personnel placement to help you and your company prosper. We address your future potential, as well as assess your past performance. What's more, we provide ancillary services that can be vital to your success, such as [EXAMPLES].

As a client of [SENDER'S COMPANY], you will receive [LIST BENEFITS].

[NAME OF REP] will be calling on you shortly to arrange an initial appointment. Should you have any further questions on any or all of our services, please do not hesitate to call me.

Again, welcome to [SENDER'S COMPANY].

Sincerely,

[SENDER'S NAME]
[SENDER'S TITLE]

[ID LINE/INITIALS]

LETTER ASKING FOR A REFERRAL

[DATE]

[NAME]
[COMPANY]
[ADDRESS]
[CITY, STATE, ZIP]

Dear [NAME]:

It was great meeting you at [LOCATION] last week. I appreciate the opportunity to fill your personnel needs. I trust you'll be as pleased with this product as you have been with the products you have purchased through me in the past.

At our meeting you mentioned that you run into a good number of small-business owners in your business dealings. If you think it is appropriate, I would welcome the opportunity to furnish these people with the same quality of service that my colleagues and I at [SENDER'S COMPANY] have supplied you.

As I mentioned to you, [SENDER'S COMPANY] has been getting more and more into the area of [SPECIALTY]. Would you consider thinking of a few business owners you know who could use my services?

I'll call you next week to see if you'd be willing to refer me to these people. A referral from you would go a long way in opening new doors for me and my colleagues.

I look forward to talking to you next week.

Best regards,

[SENDER'S NAME]

[ID LINE/INITIALS]

LETTER RESPONDING TO COMPANY INQUIRY

[DATE]

[COMPANY NAME]
[ADDRESS]
[CITY, STATE, ZIP]

Dear [NAME]:

Thank you for your inquiry about [SENDER'S COMPANY]. The enclosed material should give you a better understanding of our company and the services that we offer.

We are proud of our reputation for putting the customer first in every area of our operations. We feel that this attitude is one of the most important contributors to our success and to the success of the customers we serve.

I will be contacting you within the next two weeks to see if you have any questions or need any additional information. Again, thank you for your interest.

Sincerely,

[SENDER'S NAME]
[SENDER'S COMPANY]

[ID LINE/INITIALS]
Enclosure

LETTER SELLING SERVICE TO BUSINESS

[DATE]

[NAME]
[ADDRESS]
[CITY, STATE, ZIP]

Dear [NAME]:

Have you ever wondered why every time you need personnel services, your placement service company's phone is busy or your contact can't get to your business for at least a week?

If your company is like most, every lost day of your [SERVICE] capabilities can spell headaches, delays, and increased expenses.

Rest easy. [SENDER'S COMPANY] guarantees you that when you use us as your personnel placement service company, we'll be there when you need us with the solutions to your staffing problems. Our trained staff has years of experience in the industry, experience that gets your operation back into A-1 condition.

[SENDER'S COMPANY] specializes in servicing small businesses like yours. I've enclosed a partial list of our current clients. Feel free to check our reputation with any of them. I think you'll find the response is unanimous praise.

As a special offer to new customers, we are offering [OFFER]. But the offer's only good if you sign up by [DATE]. Simply fill out the enclosed postage-paid card, mail it back to us, and we'll get you started on worry-free personnel placement service.

Act now to get the special introductory offer.

Sincerely,

[SENDER'S NAME]

[ID LINE/INITIALS]
Enclosure

LETTER REQUESTING AN APPOINTMENT AFTER INITIAL DISCUSSION

[DATE]

[NAME]
[COMPANY]
[ADDRESS]
[CITY, STATE, ZIP]

Dear [NAME]:

Thank you for taking the time to talk to me on [DAY].

[PERSON REFERRING] suggested that I meet with you to discuss the personnel placement needs of [COMPANY]. I have enclosed information about the types of staffing we have been able to secure for one of our clients, [NAME OF CLIENT]. Building your business through [SERVICE] is one part of the services we can offer [COMPANY].

At your earliest convenience, I would like to meet with you to learn about your company and its [SERVICE] goals. I will call at the end of next week to see when a meeting might be possible.

Congratulations and best of luck. I know your company will be well received in the [CITY] community.

Yours sincerely,

[SENDER'S NAME]

[ID LINE/INITIALS]
Enclosures

[DATE]

[NAME]
[COMPANY]
[ADDRESS]
[CITY, STATE, ZIP]

Dear [NAME]:

[PERSON REFERRING] recommended I meet with [PERSON] to discuss the personnel placement needs of [COMPANY]. In a recent discussion, they told me that you are handling the review process. I understand that the materials I had sent to [PERSON] were passed along to you.

At your earliest possible convenience, I would like to meet with you to learn about your company and its staffing goals. Enclosed are some recent examples of the sort of service our clients have received.

I will call you at the beginning of next week to check your schedule. Thank you, in advance, for your consideration.

Cordially,

[SENDER'S NAME]

[ID LINE/INITIALS]
Enclosures

LETTER CONFIRMING PROPOSAL FOR SERVICES

[DATE]

[NAME]
[COMPANY]
[ADDRESS]
[CITY, STATE, ZIP]

Dear [NAME]:

I just wanted to send you a brief note to tell you that I truly enjoyed speaking with you and look forward to advising you in the area of personnel placement. [PERSON REFERRING] spoke very highly of you.

I've enclosed a proposal and application for [SENDER'S COMPANY] for the following services:

[SERVICE 1]
[SERVICE 2]
[SERVICE 3, ETC.]

I feel very comfortable with our proposal and recommend that we take matters to the next step. Please sign where indicated on the enclosed application and mail it back to me in the envelope provided with a check payable to [SENDER'S COMPANY] for [COST].

Thanks in advance for your business. I hope to meet with you in person soon.

Cordially,

[SENDER'S NAME]
[SENDER'S TITLE]

[ID LINE/INITIALS]
Enclosures

FOLLOW-UP LETTER TO MEETING

[DATE]

[NAME]
[COMPANY]
[ADDRESS]
[CITY, STATE, ZIP]

Dear [NAME]:

Thank you for taking time out of your schedule to meet with me at [LOCATION] on [DAY]. It was a pleasure to meet with you and discuss your company's personnel placement needs. I hope this is just the beginning of a solid relationship between our two companies.

As I told you at our meeting, our company specializes in servicing the [SERVICE] needs of companies like yours. Please feel free to call on me at any time to discuss those needs. I would be glad to meet with you to review any of them.

Thank you again for the meeting. I hope to be able to work with you in the not too distant future.

Sincerely,

[SENDER'S NAME]
[SENDER'S TITLE]

[ID LINE/INITIALS]

SHORT FOLLOW-UP LETTER TO PHONE CONVERSATION

[DATE]

[NAME]
[COMPANY]
[ADDRESS]
[CITY, STATE, ZIP]

Dear [NAME]:

I've enclosed a copy of our personnel placement kit, which you requested when we spoke on the telephone yesterday. Among other things, the kit contains [CONTENTS] and a client list.

I look forward to meeting you on [DATE]. Thank you very much for your interest in [SENDER'S COMPANY]. I'll speak with you soon.

Yours truly,

[SENDER'S NAME]

[ID LINE/INITIALS]
Enclosure

FOLLOW-UP LETTER ON LOST SALE

[DATE]

[NAME]
[COMPANY]
[ADDRESS]
[CITY, STATE, ZIP]

Dear [NAME]:

Checking through my records, I noticed that you were no longer an active customer of [SENDER'S COMPANY]. When I called your office, I was informed that your company is now using one of our competitors. Your office manager, [OFFICE MANAGER], was refreshingly forthright in telling me how [SENDER'S COMPANY] fell short of the mark in keeping your business.

I'm pleased to tell you that we have set up a whole new system of personnel placement, which [OFFICE MANAGER] expressed a desperate need for. We feature a wide array of services.

[OFFICE MANAGER] told me that you make all staffing decisions at [COMPANY]. If you need additional information from me, [NAME], please feel free to call. I welcome the opportunity to serve your company once again. I will do my best to ensure your satisfaction.

Sincerely,

[SENDER'S NAME]

[ID LINE/INITIALS]

LETTER ANNOUNCING THE FORMATION OF NEW BUSINESS

[DATE]

[NAME]
[ADDRESS]
[CITY, STATE, ZIP]

Dear [NAME]:

In [MONTH] I left my position as [FORMER TITLE] at [FORMER COMPANY] to establish my own personnel placement business. I would like to take this opportunity to pass along my business card and to tell you a little bit about my business.

My practice will deal with [DESCRIPTION]. My services will focus on three primary areas:

* [AREA 1]

* [AREA 2]

* [AREA 3]

If you are in [CITY] and would like to get together, please call.

Sincerely,

[SENDER'S NAME]
[SENDER'S TITLE]

[ID LINE/INITIALS]

LETTER THANKING CUSTOMER FOR A REFERRAL

[DATE]

[NAME]
[COMPANY]
[ADDRESS]
[CITY, STATE, ZIP]

Dear [NAME]:

Thanks for referring me to [PERSON'S NAME], who you thought might be in need of personnel placement services. I called on [PERSON'S FIRST NAME] on [DAY] and enjoyed meeting with her at [PERSON'S COMPANY].

You were quite correct in assessing [PERSON'S NAME]'s staffing needs. I am sure my firm can meet her full-range personnel needs and help her plan for the future.

Thank you for calling [PERSON'S NAME] ahead of time to let her know I'd be calling on her. She told me how positive you were about my services. That endorsement from you was an incredible boost to my credibility before I even walked in the door.

Thanks again for the referral and your kind words.

Sincerely,

[SENDER'S NAME]
[SENDER'S TITLE]

[ID LINE/INITIALS]

LETTER EXPRESSING APPRECIATION FOR SUPPORT

[DATE]

[NAME]
[COMPANY]
[ADDRESS]
[CITY, STATE, ZIP]

Dear [NAME]:

The time has simply flown by, but on [DATE], [SENDER'S COMPANY] will celebrate [NUMBER] years in business. We're proud of the personnel services we have provided and the reception we have received in the marketplace, all in [NUMBER] short years.

Much of the credit for our success has resulted from the support of loyal customers like you who have consistently come back to us to place orders. It's friends like you who have put [SENDER'S COMPANY] on the map as the supplier of personnel placement services to businesses throughout the [AREA] area.

Thank you for your support over the last [NUMBER] years. We plan to continue to provide the excellent services that have satisfied you in the past. We look forward to a prosperous future made possible by customers who've stuck with [SENDER'S COMPANY] since its humble beginnings.

Thanks again.

Best regards,

[SENDER'S NAME]
[SENDER'S TITLE]

[ID LINE/INITIALS]

LETTER THANKING CUSTOMER FOR REPEAT BUSINESS

[DATE]

[NAME]
[ADDRESS]
[CITY, STATE, ZIP]

Dear [NAME]:

I wanted to take the time to thank you for the way you have handled your business dealings with us. This note is written just to make sure that you know how high a value we at [SENDER'S COMPANY] place on our relationship.

We are trying to do a good job for you and will always welcome your suggestions. If you like our service and the way we do business, we hope you will recommend us to your friends and acquaintances. If not, we hope that you will tell us why.

Please feel free to call upon us whenever we can be of service. We want you to feel that [SENDER'S COMPANY] is always responsive and eager to give you the best personnel placement services in the business.

Yours very truly,

[SENDER'S NAME]
[SENDER'S TITLE]

[ID LINE/INITIALS]

LETTER SUSPENDING FURTHER CREDIT

[DATE]

[NAME]
[COMPANY]
[ADDRESS]
[CITY, STATE, ZIP]

Dear [NAME]:

We regret to inform you that [SENDER'S COMPANY] has found it necessary to turn your account over to [AGENCY NAME] for collection of the [AMOUNT] you have owed since [DATE].

We must further inform you that all of your credit privileges [SENDER'S COMPANY] have been revoked as of the date of this letter.

Please resolve this matter immediately so that we may reinstate your credit privileges and continue our business relationship.

Cordially,

[SENDER'S NAME]
[SENDER'S TITLE]

[ID LINE/INITIALS]

<u>LETTER THANKING CLIENT FOR CLEARING BACK INVOICES</u>

[DATE]

[NAME]
[COMPANY]
[ADDRESS]
[CITY, STATE, ZIP]

Dear [NAME]:

I received payment for all of the past invoices. Thank you very much.

We have [NUMBER] months left on our initial contract. Beginning with [MONTH], I will bill you at the end of each month. That way, I'll be able to adjust our fee to the work performed. The figure will not exceed the [AMOUNT] we agreed upon earlier. Let me know if this meets with your approval.

Sincerely,

[SENDER'S NAME]

[ID LINE/INITIALS]

118

LETTER REQUESTING COMMERCIAL CREDIT

[DATE]

[NAME]
[COMPANY]
[ADDRESS]
[CITY, STATE, ZIP]

Dear [NAME]:

After an extensive market survey, we have determined that your company's [PRODUCT OR SERVICE] best meets the specifications required by our company. But before we begin placing orders—which we anticipate will occur on a quarterly basis—I am writing to inquire about your terms for granting commercial credit.

Since there is probably specific information that you require before establishing a credit account, perhaps it makes the most sense at this juncture for you to send me the necessary forms that we should fill out.

I look forward to hearing from you, and to establishing a credit relationship with your company.

Sincerely,

[SENDER'S NAME]
[SENDER'S TITLE]

[ID LINE/INITIALS]

LETTER TO CREDITOR ABOUT RETURNED CHECK

[DATE]

[NAME]
[COMPANY]
[ADDRESS]
[CITY, STATE, ZIP]

NOTIFICATION OF RETURNED CHECK

[NAME], we were just notified that the check we made out to you on [DATE] (check number [NUMBER] for [AMOUNT]) was returned by our bank for insufficient funds.

We are terribly sorry for the inconvenience this has caused you, and would like to reimburse you for any penalties you have incurred because of the returned check. We have subsequently made a deposit to our account sufficient to cover this draft.

Please be assured this will never happen again.

[SENDER'S NAME]
[SENDER'S TITLE]

[ID LINE/INITIALS]

INSUFFICIENT FUNDS - APPLICANT LETTER

[DATE]

[NAME]
[ADDRESS]
[CITY, STATE, ZIP]

Dear [NAME]:

We are again contacting you about your check number 9999 for $120.69, which was returned to us because of insufficient funds. We wrote to you once before about this matter, but you have not responded.

Within 10 working days from the date of this letter, we expect to receive a cashier's check or money order for $120.69, plus a fee in the amount of $20.00 for _____, for a total of $140.69. If you are unable to send payment for the entire amount, please call me to explain the circumstances and work out a payment solution.

You have been a good client and we do not want to lose you. Please respond today.

Sincerely,

[SENDER'S NAME]
[SENDER'S TITLE]

[ID LINE/INITIALS]

P.S. If your payment is already in the mail, please accept our thanks and disregard this notice.

LETTER SERVING AS FIRST REMINDER AFTER STATEMENT

[DATE]

[NAME]
[COMPANY]
[ADDRESS]
[CITY, STATE, ZIP]

Dear [NAME]:

This is to inform you that we have not received the payment of [AMOUNT] that appeared on our billing statement of [DATE]. If you have already made the payment, please disregard this notice.

If there is any question about your bill, please call my office immediately.

Thank you for giving your prompt attention to this matter.

Sincerely,

[SENDER'S NAME]
[SENDER'S TITLE]

[ID LINE/INITIALS]

<u>30-DAYS-PAST-DUE LETTER</u>

[DATE]

[NAME]
[ADDRESS]
[CITY, STATE, ZIP]

Dear [NAME]:

This is a reminder about invoice number 9999 for $6,500.99, which is now over 30 days past due. If there is a problem with this invoice, please call me at once so we can correct it.

Thank you for your business and for your prompt attention to this matter.

Sincerely,

[SENDER'S NAME]
[SENDER'S TITLE]

[ID LINE/INITIALS]

P.S. If your payment is already in the mail, please accept our thanks and disregard this notice.

LETTER SERVING AS SECOND OVERDUE NOTICE

[DATE]

[NAME]
[COMPANY]
[ADDRESS]
[CITY, STATE, ZIP]

Dear [NAME]:

We are still waiting for the payment of [AMOUNT] due since [DATE].

Failure to resolve this matter may result in the suspension of your credit privileges and can jeopardize your credit rating.

Sincerely,

[SENDER'S NAME]
[SENDER'S TITLE]

[ID LINE/INITIALS]

LETTER SERVING AS THIRD OVERDUE NOTICE

[DATE]

[NAME]
[COMPANY]
[ADDRESS]
[CITY, STATE, ZIP]

Dear [NAME]:

Your account is overdue for [AMOUNT], as we previously noted in our correspondence of [DATE]. We have had a long and pleasant business relationship in the past and hope to continue this relationship in the future.

If there is any reason you cannot make full payment on this account, please call my office immediately to discuss a new payment schedule.

Unless we hear from you, we will be forced to take other steps to remedy this problem. You will thereby be jeopardizing your credit rating.

I look forward to hearing from you this week.

Sincerely,

[SENDER'S NAME]
[SENDER'S TITLE]

[ID LINE/INITIALS]

LETTER SERVING AS FOURTH OVERDUE NOTICE

[DATE]

[NAME]
[COMPANY]
[ADDRESS]
[CITY, STATE, ZIP]

Dear [NAME]:

Despite three previous reminders about the [AMOUNT] overdue on your account since [DATE], we have received no response from you.

As previously noted, we will be pleased to discuss a revised payment schedule in order to help you resolve this matter. Unless we have heard from you within 5 days, however, we will find it necessary to turn your account over to a collection agency.

We thank you for turning your attention to this matter immediately.

Sincerely,

[SENDER'S NAME]
[SENDER'S TITLE]

[ID LINE/INITIALS]

LETTER SERVING AS FINAL OVERDUE NOTICE

[DATE]

[NAME]
[COMPANY]
[ADDRESS]
[CITY, STATE, ZIP]

Dear [NAME]:

As of this writing, we have received no response to correspondence about payment of [AMOUNT] due since [DATE].

Therefore, we must send this final notice to inform you that your account will be turned over to a collection agency if full payment is not received by [DATE].

We urge you to give your prompt attention to this matter.

Cordially,

[SENDER'S NAME]
[SENDER'S TITLE]

[ID LINE/INITIALS]

LETTER SERVING AS SECOND NOTICE ON CHARGES DUE

[DATE]

[NAME]
[COMPANY]
[ADDRESS]
[CITY, STATE, ZIP]

Subject: Credit Charges Due

Dear [NAME]:

Is something wrong? A few weeks ago we sent you a notice that your charge account payment was past due for [AMOUNT]. In spite of this notice, we have received no payment from you. You should be acting now to preserve your good credit rating.

We will be understanding if there is a reason why you have not been able to make the payment. Call me to explain the circumstances. We always make every effort to accommodate our customers who are encountering financial difficulties, as long as they cooperate with us.

If you fail to either bring your account up to date or contact us to make some new arrangements, however, we will be forced to turn the matter over to our collection department and instruct them to inform the various credit-reporting bureaus about your delinquent status.

Sincerely,

[SENDER'S NAME]
[SENDER'S TITLE]

[ID LINE/INITIALS]

FOLLOW-UP TO RESPONSE TO SECOND NOTICE COLLECTION LETTER

[DATE]

[NAME]
[ADDRESS]
[CITY, STATE, ZIP]

Subject: Credit Charges Due

Dear [NAME]:

The payments on your account have become seriously delinquent. The credit manager of [COMPANY] has turned your account over to us for collection.

You have already been sent a late payment notice, followed by a letter from our credit department requesting payment. Both of these moderate requests have remained unanswered by you. We have also attempted to reach you by telephone, but have had no success in reaching you.

Because you have been unresponsive to those efforts to bring your account up to date and to preserve your good credit rating, we have notified various consumer credit-reporting agencies of your present delinquent status. We now intend to take every legal recourse we can to collect from you the entire amount you owe, plus whatever late charges and legal fees may be incurred.

It is still not too late to clear up this matter. You can still pay the amount you owe and start restoring your credit rating at [COMPANY] by coming in personally, calling us, or using the enclosed postage paid reply card to make arrangements for payment.

You must respond immediately or we will have to take corrective action against you.

Sincerely,

[SENDER'S NAME]
[SENDER'S TITLE]

[ID LINE/INITIALS]
enc.

LETTER ACCEPTING PARTIAL PAYMENT

[DATE]

[NAME]
[COMPANY]
[ADDRESS]
[CITY, STATE, ZIP]

Dear [NAME]:

Thank you for partial payment of the [AMOUNT] owed on your account. Please note that your balance is now [AMOUNT REMAINING], overdue from [DATE].

While we appreciate this partial payment, it is essential that complete payment be received by [DATE] in order for us to reinstate your credit privileges and continue our business relationship.

Sincerely,

[SENDER'S NAME]
[SENDER'S TITLE]

[ID LINE/INITIALS]

ALTERNATIVE LETTER ACCEPTING PARTIAL PAYMENT

[DATE]

[NAME]
[COMPANY]
[ADDRESS]
[CITY, STATE, ZIP]

Dear [NAME]:

    We received partial payment of [AMOUNT] after you called us about your account and arranged a new payment schedule. We trust that this mutually agreed-upon schedule will result in complete and timely payment of the [AMOUNT REMAINING] still due on your account.

    Thank you for the partial payment. Please call my office if you have any questions about your account.

                Sincerely,

                [SENDER'S NAME]
                [SENDER'S TITLE]

[ID LINE/INITIALS]

LETTER ACKNOWLEDGING PARTIAL PAYMENT

[DATE]

[NAME]
[ADDRESS]
[CITY, STATE, ZIP]

Dear [NAME]:

You have responded to our request to bring your account up to date by making a partial payment of the amount due. To protect your good credit rating, we ask that you pay the entire past due payment of [AMOUNT].

Please pay this amount immediately.

Cordially,

[SENDER'S NAME]
[SENDER'S TITLE]

[ID LINE/INITIALS]

LETTER COMPLAINING ABOUT SALES REPRESENTATIVE

[DATE]

[NAME]
[COMPANY]
[ADDRESS]
[CITY, STATE, ZIP]

Dear [NAME]:

As you are probably aware, [SENDER'S COMPANY] orders a significant amount of merchandise from your company. We are pleased with the quality of the products, but I am writing you because of difficulty I am having with your sales representative assigned to our territory, [NAME OF REPRESENTATIVE].

While we do make frequent purchases from your company, we have time and time again requested that [NAME OF REPRESENTATIVE] deal directly with our office manager for product ordering. We have asked that he call to set up an appointment before arriving on the scene. On many occasions, [NAME OF REPRESENTATIVE] has simply shown up at our offices. Often, even when he has already met with the office manager, he approaches other staff members directly to encourage them to buy your products or have them ordered.

I must ask that [NAME OF REPRESENTATIVE] follow the procedure we have clearly outlined for him to use in approaching us for orders. His method of "cutting through the red tape" results in time away from work that our staff members need to get done. By having our office manager handle the ordering, we have centralized that function. I am sure you can understand why this procedure is important to us.

While we let [NAME OF REPRESENTATIVE] know about the appropriate procedure when he first took on this sales territory, he has continued to fail to follow it. Many of our staff members are up in arms about the disruption and continue to complain to me about his direct sales approaches.

As I mentioned, we are very pleased with your products. We are also pleased with the speed and efficiency with which you handle orders. We are not looking to make life difficult for [NAME OF REPRESENTATIVE]. We simply ask that you speak to him about following the procedure that we have established here.

Cordially,

[SENDER'S NAME]

[ID LINE/INITIALS]

133

LETTER WELCOMING NEW EMPLOYEE

[DATE]

[NAME]
[ADDRESS]
[CITY, STATE, ZIP]

Dear [NAME]:

   We are looking forward to your arrival here in [LOCATION] and having you as part of [SENDER'S COMPANY]. We were very pleased when you accepted our offer of employment and are sure that you will be a valuable employee.

   As you know, the company has plans for growth in many areas. In your new position as [TITLE], your experience and knowledge will help fuel that growth.

   Please let me know if there is anything I can do to make your move easier. We are looking forward to having you in the office on [DATE].

                    Sincerely,

                    [SENDER'S NAME]
                    [SENDER'S TITLE]

[ID LINE/INITIALS]

NEW EMPLOYEE ANNOUNCEMENT

[DATE]

[NAME]
[COMPANY]
[ADDRESS]
[CITY, STATE, ZIP]

Dear [NAME]:

    [SENDER'S COMPANY] is pleased to officially announce the appointment of [NEW EMPLOYEE] as [TITLE].

    [NEW EMPLOYEE] has worked for the past [NUMBER] years as [TITLE AND DESCRIPTION]. He or she will bring a keen understanding of the [INDUSTRY] and is anxious to work with each of you to define and meet your objectives.

    This new appointment brings additional strength to [SENDER'S COMPANY]. I encourage you to call [NEW EMPLOYEE] at [PHONE NO.] for your [SERVICE] needs.

                Sincerely,

                [SENDER'S NAME]
                [SENDER'S TITLE]

[ID LINE/INITIALS]

LETTER ACKNOWLEDGING APPLICATION FOR POSITION

[DATE]

[NAME]
[ADDRESS]
[CITY, STATE, ZIP]

Subject: [POSITION] Position

Dear [NAME]:

Thank you very much for applying for the [POSITION] position at [SENDER'S COMPANY]. Please be assured that your application will be reviewed along with others that have been received. If your qualifications are considered appropriate for this position, you will be contacted again for the purpose of setting an appointment date.

In any event, please accept the appreciation of [SENDER'S COMPANY] for your wishing to include us in your future professional plans.

Sincerely yours,

[SENDER'S NAME]
[SENDER'S TITLE]

[ID LINE/INITIALS]

LETTER RESPONDING TO QUALIFIED APPLICANT

[DATE]

[NAME]
[ADDRESS]
[CITY, STATE, ZIP]

Dear [NAME]:

Thank you for your application for the position of [POSITION].

We have had an overwhelming response to our ad for this position and expect to select a qualified applicant by [DATE]. If you have not heard from us by then, please feel free to call and inquire about the status of the position.

Thank you for your interest in the company. Best wishes for the future.

Cordially,

[SENDER'S NAME]
[SENDER'S TITLE]

[ID LINE/INITIALS]

LETTER INVITING APPLICANT TO SECOND INTERVIEW

[DATE]

[NAME]
[ADDRESS]
[CITY, STATE, ZIP]

Dear [NAME]:

Thank you very much for taking the time to meet with me during my recruiting trip to [CITY]. I was most favorably impressed with you, and our recruiting committee has concurred in my recommendation that we invite you to meet more members of our company.

If you continue to be interested in our company, I would appreciate it if you would call our recruiting coordinator, [NAME], to arrange a mutually convenient time to visit us.

We look forward to hearing from you. Again, thank you for your interest in our organization and for having taken the time to talk with me.

Best regards,

[SENDER'S NAME]

[ID LINE/INITIALS]

LETTER TO APPLICANT WHO DID NOT QUALIFY FOR POSITION

[DATE]

[NAME]
[ADDRESS]
[CITY, STATE, ZIP]

Dear [NAME]:

Thank you for your interest in the position of [TITLE] at [SENDER'S COMPANY]. I have carefully reviewed your application and regret to tell you that I do not feel you have the qualifications necessary to fulfill the responsibilities of this job.

Good luck in your job search. I feel certain that you will find a position where you can use your talents and experience to good advantage.

Sincerely,

[SENDER'S NAME]
[SENDER'S TITLE]

[ID LINE/INITIALS]

LETTER RESPONDING TO QUALIFIED CANDIDATE WHO DID NOT MATCH POSITION EXACTLY

[DATE]

[NAME]
[ADDRESS]
[CITY, STATE, ZIP]

Dear [NAME]:

[TITLE] POSITION AT [SENDER'S COMPANY]

[NAME], thank you for your interest in a [TITLE] position at [SENDER'S COMPANY]. We received many responses from very highly qualified candidates like you.

With so many superbly qualified candidates, we looked finally for the one whose background and qualifications gave us just the right "fit" for our exact needs. I'm sorry to have to say that the position is being offered to one of the other candidates.

This does not mean, however, that we were unimpressed with the credentials of the other candidates. Perhaps in the future we will have another opening that will better fit your qualifications. I wish you well in your pursuit of the right position.

[SENDER'S NAME ALL CAPS]
[SENDER'S TITLE   ALL CAPS]

[ID LINE/INITIALS]

LETTER INFORMING APPLICANT THAT SOMEONE ELSE GOT THE JOB

[DATE]

[NAME]
[ADDRESS]
[CITY, STATE, ZIP]

Dear [NAME]:

Thank you for the time you took to come in and talk with us about the [TITLE] position. We cannot place you now because we have chosen another candidate whose background, we feel, is more closely suited to our current needs. We will keep your resume in our active file, however, should a more suitable position open up.

Thank you again for your interest in [SENDER'S COMPANY]. Best wishes for success in your career endeavors.

Cordially,

[SENDER'S NAME]
[SENDER'S TITLE]

[ID LINE/INITIALS]

LETTER RESPONDING TO APPLICANT WHO IS PARTIALLY QUALIFIED

[DATE]

[NAME]
[ADDRESS]
[CITY, STATE, ZIP]

Dear [NAME]:

Thank you for your application and for your interest in [SENDER'S COMPANY].

We had a very large number of applicants for the position of [TITLE] and gave all the applications serious consideration. Although we were impressed with your application, we feel that the job requires someone with more experience than you currently have. With your qualifications, however, I am sure you will find a suitable position very soon.

I wish you the best for your future success.

Best regards,

[SENDER'S NAME]
[SENDER'S TITLE]

[ID LINE/INITIALS]

LETTER INFORMING APPLICANTS THAT THERE ARE NO POSITIONS MATCHING THEIR TRAINING OR EXPERIENCE

[DATE]

[NAME]
[ADDRESS]
[CITY, STATE, ZIP]

Dear [NAME]:

Thank you for inquiring about employment possibilities at [SENDER'S COMPANY]. We appreciated the opportunity to review your qualifications in relation to our current job openings.

At this time, however, we do not have a position open that would properly use your training and experience. We would like to keep a record of your qualifications in our active file, however, so we may consider you for any appropriate future openings.

Although we are currently unable to offer you a position, we do wish you success in your career.

Cordially,

[SENDER'S NAME]
[SENDER'S TITLE]

[ID LINE/INITIALS]

LETTER REJECTING PERSON RECOMMENDED FOR JOB

[DATE]

[NAME]
[ADDRESS]
[CITY, STATE, ZIP]

Dear [NAME]:

Thank you for applying for the position of [TITLE] at our organization. While you were recommended by [RECOMMENDED], and your education and experience appear to be exceptional, the response that we received from the few inquiries that we made was overwhelming. I regret to inform you that a candidate was chosen shortly before your letter of interest arrived.

Best wishes for success in your career search.

Best regards,

[SENDER'S NAME]
[SENDER'S TITLE]

[ID LINE/INITIALS]

cc: [RECOMMENDED]

LETTER MAKING JOB OFFER

[DATE]

[NAME]
[ADDRESS]
[CITY, STATE, ZIP]

Dear [NAME]:

We at [SENDER'S COMPANY] are pleased to offer you the position of [TITLE] at the monthly salary of [SALARY]. In addition, you will receive two weeks' paid vacation in [YEAR] if you start on or before [DATE]. [SENDER'S COMPANY] will also reimburse you for family medical insurance coverage until you are picked up on our plan. I hope this letter will assist you in making your decision.

[SENDER'S COMPANY] hopes you will be able to join its family. We look forward to hearing from you on or before [DATE].

If you have any questions about [SENDER'S COMPANY], please call me.

Sincerely,

[SENDER'S NAME]
[SENDER'S TITLE]

[ID LINE/INITIALS]

enc.

cc: [PERSONNEL CONTACT]
Personnel file

LETTER CONFIRMING JOB OFFER

[DATE]

[NAME]
[ADDRESS]
[CITY, STATE, ZIP]

Dear [NAME]:

It gives me great pleasure to confirm our verbal offer and your acceptance to join [COMPANY] as a [TITLE].

Your compensation will include your monthly salary of [SALARY], plus the benefits outlined in the enclosed summary. After three months of employment, you will be eligible for nine days of vacation in the calendar year [YEAR]. According to the terms of our current policy, your salary and performance will be reviewed in [MONTH & YEAR].

Our regular working hours are from [TIME] to [TIME], Monday through Friday. On your first day, please report directly to [PERSONNEL CONTACT] in the personnel department to arrange orientation and to initiate the administrative procedures. We believe that you will make a significant contribution to [SENDER'S COMPANY] and, at the same time, will realize both the personal and professional growth you seek.

As soon as possible, please acknowledge your acceptance of this job offer by signing the enclosed copy of this letter and returning it to me. We very much look forward to your joining the company on [DATE].

Best regards,

[SENDER'S NAME]
[SENDER'S TITLE]

[ID LINE/INITIALS]

Enclosures

cc: [PERSONNEL CONTACT]
Personnel file

146

LETTER TO APPLICANT WHO HAS ACCEPTED OFFER

[DATE]

[NAME]
[ADDRESS]
[CITY, STATE, ZIP]

Dear [NAME]:

   We are very pleased that you have accepted the position of [TITLE] at the monthly salary of [SALARY], with one week's paid vacation in [YEAR]. We hope that this will be a mutually rewarding and long-lasting relationship.

   I hope that you can start work on [DATE] at [TIME], at which time you can sign up for our benefits plan and I can orient you to our company. Once again, it is a pleasure to have you in the [SENDER'S COMPANY] family.

   If you have any questions, please call me.

                              Best regards,

                              [SENDER'S NAME]
                              [SENDER'S TITLE]

[ID LINE/INITIALS]

cc: [PERSONNEL CONTACT]
Personnel file

LETTER OF RECOMMENDATION

[DATE]

[NAME]
[TITLE]
[COMPANY]
[ADDRESS]
[CITY, STATE, ZIP]

Subject: [CANDIDATE]

Dear [NAME]:

I have been privileged to know [CANDIDATE] for [NUMBER] years in my role as [TITLE] at [SENDER'S COMPANY]. I am currently [TITLE].

While [CANDIDATE] reported to me [SENDER'S COMPANY], I found her management abilities to be invaluable in helping me to establish [SENDER'S COMPANY] as a leader in the [INDUSTRY] market. The conscientious effort and cooperation in doing professional, high-quality work were appreciated.

As a [TITLE], [CANDIDATE] was efficient, innovative, and responsive. The subordinates were motivated with challenge and the opportunity for personal growth.

If you find that [CANDIDATE]'s career objectives match your position description, I know of no reason you would be disappointed by the employment performance. Please let me know if you require further information.

Sincerely,

[SENDER'S NAME]

[ID LINE/INITIALS]

QUALIFIED LETTER OF RECOMMENDATION

[DATE]

[NAME]
[TITLE]
[COMPANY]
[ADDRESS]
[CITY, STATE, ZIP]

RECOMMENDATION FOR [CANDIDATE]

   [NAME], I am writing to you in response to your request for a recommendation of [CANDIDATE], who worked for me in the [DEPARTMENT] department of [SENDER'S COMPANY]. This person was not a [POSITION SOUGHT] when he worked for me, however, but rather a [TITLE]. I am not qualified to comment on the capabilities as a [POSITION SOUGHT].

   Bill was an average [TITLE]. He is a pleasant person who got along well with his fellow employees.

   He also seemed enthusiastic about his job in the [DEPARTMENT] department. His attitude toward his work and his cooperation were above average.

   If you need any further information from me, please let me know.

                              [SENDER'S NAME - ALL CAPS]
                              [SENDER'S TITLE - ALL CAPS]

[ID LINE/INITIALS]

LETTER ASKING FOR EMPLOYEE REFERENCE

[DATE]

[NAME]
[TITLE]
[COMPANY]
[ADDRESS]
[CITY, STATE, ZIP]

Dear [NAME]:

[CANDIDATE] has applied for the position of [TITLE] at our company. On his résumé, [CANDIDATE] has listed your company as a former employer.

Could you please send us verification of [CANDIDATE]'s employment, including his job description, dates of employment, performance rating, and the reason for his departure? We will, of course, consider this information to be confidential.

Thank you for your assistance.

Sincerely,

[SENDER'S NAME]
[SENDER'S TITLE]

[ID LINE/INITIALS]

LETTER COMMENDING EMPLOYEE ON JOB WELL DONE

[DATE]

[NAME]
[TITLE]
[COMPANY]
[ADDRESS]
[CITY, STATE, ZIP]

Dear [NAME]:

   Congratulations on your outstanding performance during [YEAR]. Adding [NUMBER] new clients with an average gross profit of [AMOUNT] each is truly commendable.

   Please accept my sincerest congratulations on a job well done.

                              Very truly yours,

                              [SENDER'S NAME]
                              [SENDER'S TITLE]

[ID LINE/INITIALS]

cc: Personnel file

LETTER TERMINATING EMPLOYEE. FOLLOW-UP TO NO RESPONSE LETTER

[DATE]

[NAME]
[ADDRESS]
[CITY, STATE, ZIP]

Dear [NAME]:

Your employment with [COMPANY] has been terminated effective [DATE], because of your failure to comply with personnel policy #[NUMBER], and your failure to respond to my letter of [DATE].

Please contact [PERSONNEL CONTACT] in the personnel department to discuss severance pay and pension plan disbursements.

Cordially,

[SENDER'S NAME]
[SENDER'S TITLE]

LETTER INVITING SOMEONE TO AN OPEN HOUSE

[DATE]

[NAME]
[TITLE]
[COMPANY]
[ADDRESS]
[CITY, STATE, ZIP]

Dear [NAME]:

We are having an open house to celebrate our opening in [CITY]. Please join us on [DATE] at [TIME]. Directions are enclosed.

We hope you and your staff will be able to attend!

Best regards,

[SENDER'S NAME]
[SENDERS TITLE]

[ID LINE/INITIALS]

LETTER FOR RENEWAL OF OFFICE RENTAL LEASE CONTRACT

[DATE]

[NAME]
[COMPANY NAME]
[ADDRESS]
[CITY, STATE, ZIP]

Dear [NAME]:

As you know, your lease for office #200 in the West Coast Sales building will expire on July 31, 1993. Enclosed you will find a contract to extend your tenancy for an additional three years.

The contract includes a rental rate of $495.00 per month. This rate reflects
_____.

Please sign both copies of the contract. In order to assist our planning, we would appreciate your returning them to our office at least 30 days before the lease expiration date. A signed copy will be returned to you for your records.

I trust that your tenancy in our building has been satisfactory. If you have any questions or suggestions for improvement, please do not hesitate to call me.

Sincerely,

[SENDER'S NAME]
[SENDER'S COMPANY]

[ID LINE/INITIALS]

154

CONGRATULATIONS/BILLING LETTER FOR APPLICANT

[DATE]

[NAME]
[ADDRESS]
[CITY, STATE, ZIP]

Dear [NAME]:

Congratulations on your new job with (Company) as their (Job Title) starting June 1, 1995. Your starting salary is $1,500 per month. The total fee for this position is $1,125.00. The employer is paying ½ of this fee, totaling $562.50 and reimbursing your share ½ in six months ($281.25), and ½ in one year ($281.25). Detailed below are your payment dates and amounts of your account.

TOTAL FEE	$ 562.50	
June 5, 1995	$ 56.20	<$506.30> if paid in full
July 1, 1995	168.77	
August 1, 1995	168.77	
September 1, 1995	168.76	<$160.32> if paid on time

As you can see, we offer a 10% discount of the total fee if paid within the first 5 working days. We also offer a 5% discount of the final payment if all the payments are made on time. We accept Mastercard and Visa for your convenience.

If you have any questions regarding this billing, please contact us as soon as possible.

Good luck with your new job!

Sincerely,

[SENDER'S NAME]
[SENDER'S TITLE]

[ID LINE/INITIALS]

CONGRATULATIONS/BILLING LETTER FOR EMPLOYER

[DATE]

[NAME]
[COMPANY NAME]
[ADDRESS]
[CITY, STATE, ZIP]

Dear [NAME]:

Congratulations on hiring your new employee (NAME). Since the starting salary is $1,500 per month, the total fee for this position is $1,125.00 (NAME) is responsible for ½ of this fee, totaling $562.50 so your share will also be $562.50. As agreed, (NAME'S) fee portion will be reimbursed back to them in two equal payments—½ in six months ($281.25), and ½ in one year ($281.25).

Detailed below are your payment dates and amounts of your account.

TOTAL FEE	$ 562.50	
June 5, 1995	$ 506.30	(with 10% Discount)
	or	
July 1, 1995	562.50	(30 days from date of hire)

As you can see, we offer a 10% discount of the total fee if paid within the first 5 working days. We accept Mastercard and Visa for your convenience.

If you have any questions regarding this billing, please contact our bookkeeper as soon as possible.

Good luck with your new employee! We look forward to working with (COMPANY NAME) again in the future.

Sincerely,

[SENDER'S NAME]
[SENDER'S TITLE]

[ID LINE/INITIALS]

9
Operations

There are several functions that need to be performed in the personnel business to make it run as a smooth operation. We have included each task description in detail.

INTERVIEWING
The applicant interviews

Most applicants are a little uncomfortable in the very beginning of the interview. It's obvious by the signs of nervousness through their body language and eye contact. Thus we always tried to break the ice by talking about something that was typically not employment related.

There are several topics to choose from:
- You might find something of interest on the employment application to discuss.
- The uniqueness of the current weather (hot, cold, snow, rain).
- The frustration of having to wait before the interview.
- Compliments on the style of clothing worn by the applicant.
- Anything else you can find to take the edge off.

I never started out with, "So you're looking for a job, huh?" That was pretty obvious. Once the ice was broken, it was much easier to move into the interview phase without making them nervous.

My personal business office was also decorated to put them at ease. There were family pictures on the walls and desk, plants and flowers around, and, most important of all, a casual but professional atmosphere. This helped to make the pending employment interview and screening process much more relaxing for both the applicant and myself. It was always much easier to gather more information when the applicant was comfortable and relaxed.

An average interview should last somewhere between 15 minutes to ½ hour. In it, you want to cover all the details that are necessary to effectively make the appropriate matches with an employer job order.

As discussed in chapter 8, three types of interviews are:
- Response to want ad.
- Cursory.
- Referral.

Response to advertised job order
Responses to advertised jobs are the interviews that will generate the quickest revenues for your company. Schedule them for initial screening with the counselor

working on the job order. This needs to happen as quickly as possible so that activity can begin right away. The sooner employers are recontacted after placing a job order, the happier they are.

We call this the revenue-generator client. Without these valuable clients, all the job orders in the world sitting in your files mean nothing and will earn you even less! These are the clients who will potentially make the fees for you. Be selective with your screening, and ask as many of the legal questions as possible to prescreen for the employer. When your receptionist is setting up appointments and pre-screening calls from ads, be sure to schedule these key people immediately, and schedule the cursory and referral interviews later.

Be extremely confidential when talking about the advertised position. Don't let the name of the firm be known until you feel absolutely sure the selection is a good one. Unfortunately, I've found that too many people want something for nothing. They've even gone so far as to read the name of the employer upside down on my desk and leave my office to meet the company on their own without the agency as a liaison. Sometimes they even got me to go so far as to set up the interview and then back out for some reason before signing the contract. Then they went to the employer on their own. Be very careful. Once you get burned (and believe me, you'll get burned at least once), you'll always be more cautious.

The cursory interview (data gathering only)
The cursory is the quick-in, quick-out interview. It should only last approximately 15 minutes. This is assuming, of course, that there are no current job openings to discuss. These applicants are registering with your agency in a series of stops along their job-searching path. They are very likely registering with all the agencies, responding to several ads, knocking on many doors, and telling everyone they know that they are looking for work.

These are what we call the how-far, how-much, how-soon, and how-low interviews. They don't qualify for any job orders available at the time they register with the agency, so the notes you'll be taking and the basic questions you want to ask are:

- Why are you looking to make a job change?
- What have you done so far in your search?
- How far are you willing to travel for a job?
- How much salary do you need/want to make?
- How soon can you start a new job?
- How low (starting salary) can you afford to go?

With this information, you can put them in your open files, coupled with the 1, 2, and 3 rating codes as described in this chapter under "The close."

These notes are crucial because they trigger your memory of the individual conversation, personality, and skill when a new job order does come in for them.

Be sure to remind them that if any of the information on their application changes, or if they happen to secure a position on their own, they need to call and let your office know. After asking the key questions, you can then file them in the appropriate category of skill. When a new job order comes in that fits their qualifications, you won't waste any valuable time by calling them for something that's not enough money or happens to be further than their commute distance choice.

Referrals

Usually these applicants are coming to your agency because of a positive reference from either a client, business associate, school, or friend. Again, don't spend too much time with them if they are not qualified for any current job orders. Treat them as you would a cursory interview. This interview should take just a little bit longer than the cursory. These are the referral interview questions:

- Who referred you to the agency?
- When did the referral happen?
- Why are you looking to make a job change?
- What have you done so far in your search?
- How far are you willing to travel for a job?
- How much salary to you need/want to make?
- How soon can you start a new job?
- How low (start salary) can you afford to go?

It's always a nice gesture to send a thank-you card to the individual who referred this client to you. (See the referral policy letter at the end of chapter 8.)

Additional questions

There are many other things you might want to ask in the conversation, if you feel you have the time.

- Why did you choose this field?
- Which of your previous jobs did you like the best? The least?
- Why did you leave your last job?
- What kind of people annoy you?
- Why did you move to this area?
- What did you like the most about your previous job?
- What has been the most interesting job so far in your experience?
- Do you have any long-term ambitions or goals in life?
- What are they, in priority order?
- How soon can you start a new position?
- Have you worked with any other agencies?
- Were you satisfied with their services?
- Is there anything else about yourself you think might be helpful for us to know?
- Do you feel there are any weaknesses or problems we should be aware of?
- If you could do anything and be anything, what would that be?

These are some special questions to ask in the screening interview of your sales applicants:

- What would you say if a customer said your prices are too high?
- What would you say if a customer said, "We don't need that high a quality?"
- Who has been the most interesting client or customer so far in your sales career?
- What would you say if a customer said, "I'm satisfied with my current supplier?"

Try to keep these interviews moving along, and don't get lost or wrapped up in a social conversation that isn't making you any money. It's pretty easy to get emotionally involved with these clients, as some of their personal stories can be very heart wrenching and their particular search processes extremely depressing.

Almost all applicants are inclined to tell you just how serious or difficult their situation is, so that you will be motivated to work harder for them than your other clients. Make as many notes as you can on the employment application. We always used a red pen so the notes were easier to read at a later date.

The close

As you can see on the application form in chapter 2, there's a section for rating applicants in three basic categories. These ratings are the last notes made, at the very end of the interview, before you file the paperwork. This is an extremely easy way to recall the details of the interview long after the in-person meeting. The categories are:

- Appearance (how do they present themselves?)
- Personality (how polite and professional are they?)
- Experience (do they have the work or educational experience to support what they want to do?)

We rated on a scale of one to three. One is the highest, and three is the weakest. It's okay to rate a + or a − along with the rating number.

An example rating might have the Appearance 1+ (they looked great!), Personality 2 (nice, but really nervous), and Experience 2+ (degree, but no hands-on experience). Applications with these notes will go into your open files, and any one of your staff can pick this information up easily. Even if the staff person didn't conduct the initial interview, he or she can trust your professional evaluation. Be sure to rate all the people you see. Eventually, as the numbers of clientele increase, the rating will come in very handy.

Note: Don't mark the application form in any other way as you go through this preliminary reading! The application form has been deemed to be, by civil rights rulings, an item that could be called forth as evidence in the event of a discrimination claim. Notes on the form might be used to signify prejudicial preferences on the part of the counselor. If you have any notes to make other than the Appearance, Personality, and Experience, we suggest you write these on a separate sheet and attach it to the application.

The employer interviews (employer to applicant)

In the state of California, the laws for legal interviews are extremely specific. Each category, and the series of questions within each category, are defined clearly, leaving no room for error. The questions are specific and written to keep companies from discriminatory hiring. Most job applicants are aware, to some degree, of the legal and illegal discriminatory questions for employers. They seem to have no problem bringing it to your attention if you happen to slip up.

Since most employers are not aware of all of the helpful points, we have listed the California Legal Interviewing Guidelines in Table 9-1. These are the categories and questions that can and cannot be asked in the prescreening or interviewing of any applicant.

Table 9-1 California Legal Interviewing Guidelines

NAME	(Yes)	Have you ever used another name? or Do we need any additional information about your name to check your work and record?
	(No)	Maiden Name?
RESIDENCE	(Yes)	Place of residence?
	(No)	Do you own or rent your home?
AGE	(Yes)	Request for proof that applicant meets legal age requirements. Are you over eighteen years of age? or If under eighteen can you, after hired, submit a work permit?
BIRTHPLACE, CITIZENSHIP	(Yes)	Can you, after hiring, produce proof of your legal right to work in the U.S.?
	(No)	Direct questions about birthplace or citizenship of applicant or parents.
NATIONAL ORIGIN	(Yes)	Please list all the languages that you read, speak or write.
	(No)	Any question about nationality, ancestry, origin or native tongue of applicant or parents.
SEX, MARITAL STATUS, FAMILY	(Yes)	Name/address of parent or guardian if applicant is a minor. Statement of company policy about employees who are related.
	(No)	Any questions about applicant's sex, marital status, number/age of children, child-care control, childbearing or pregnancy. With whom do you reside? or Do you live with your parents?
RACE, COLOR	(Yes)	NONE
	(No)	Any question about race, color, or color of skin, eyes, or hair.
PHYSICAL DESCRIPTION, PHOTOGRAPH	(Yes)	Statement that a photo may be required for employment.
	(No)	Questions about height or weight, or requirements for a photograph before employment.
RELIGION	(Yes)	Statement by employer of regular days, hours, or shifts to be worked.
	(No)	Questions regarding applicants religion, religious days observed or Does your religion prevent you from working weekends or holidays?
ARREST OR CRIMINAL RECORD	(Yes)	Have you ever been convicted of a felony, or within the last (time period), a misdemeanor resulting in imprisonment? Such a conviction will not necessarily disqualify you from employment.
	(No)	Arrest record or Have you ever been arrested?
BONDING	(Yes)	Statement that bonding is a condition of hire.
	(No)	Questions about refusal or cancellation of prior bonding.
MILITARY SERVICE	(Yes)	List relevant skills acquired during U.S. military service.
	(No)	General questions such as service dates, type of discharge, or foreign military service.
ECONOMIC STATUS	(Yes)	NONE
	(No)	Any questions concerning present or past assets, liabilities, credit rating, bankruptcy or garnishment.

ORGANIZATIONS ACTIVITIES	(Yes)	Please list memberships in job-related associations, organizations, or professional societies. Omit any which indicate race, religious creed, color, sex, national origin, ancestry or age.
	(No)	List all organizations, club, lodge and society Memberships.
REFERENCES	(Yes)	Who referred you for a position here? or Names of persons willing to provide professional/character references.
	(No)	Any questions about former employers or acquaintances which elicit information about applicants race, color or any other legally restricted information.
NOTICE IN CASE OF EMERGENCY	(Yes)	Name and address of person to be notified in case of emergency.
	(No)	Name and address of relative to be notified in case of emergency.

As you can see, the list of categories and particular questions is quite extensive and covers all areas of interest. Be sure to acquire your own state's legal guidelines for interview questions. This information should be available to you through your own state department of personnel, listed under state offices.

Employer interviews (agency to employer)

This type of interview is done a little bit differently. First of all, there are no laws governing the legalities of this conversation. You can ask, pretty much within reason and certainly within the law, the things you would like to know.

Refer to the job order form in chapter 2 for an example. This will describe, in detail, the questions you need to ask the employer when taking the job order. It covers all areas you will ever need to know, including the growth potential of the position.

REFERENCE CHECKING

Each state has its own laws regarding legal and illegal reference checking. The State of California laws are as specific as the Legal Guidelines for Interviewing. We could only ask these questions:
- Did you employ (applicant name)?
- When did they begin their employment?
- When did they end their employment?
- Why were they released (or) why did they leave?
- What were their earnings at the time of hire and on leaving?
- Were they dependable, punctual, and seldom absent?
- Are they eligible for rehire?

Many times, when you call the company, you find that if it was a satisfactory employee, the manager or personnel person will give accolades for their previous worker. And, if the employee was unsatisfactory, the employer will intone the disappointment. This gives you the legal reference and is meaningful in judging the applicant without jeopardizing the laws. Again, in California, you can only ask the questions as previously stated. Ask your attorney to give you the current reference-checking requirements for your area.

We did notice one thing whenever we called employers for references. They tended to give only the basic, legal responses. This was because we were not going to be the one to employ this person ourselves. If the potential new employer were to call the previous employer, the responses were always much more detailed. Because of this, we often recommended that the company make the final reference call. The company never seemed to mind, once we explained the situation.

Some employers would rather have you do all the preliminary screening, and that includes the reference call, no matter how brief it might be. Just be flexible, and work with each company on an individual basis.

SCHEDULING APPOINTMENTS

Try to set up a schedule that is convenient to you as well as your clients. We always started the first daily interview at 9:00 a.m. and had the appointments set up until the noon break. Then we started again at 1:30 p.m. and interviewed until 4:00 p.m. This gave us time to make phone calls, do paperwork, and accomplish any other daily activities that were necessary.

It was best to interview most of the applicants toward the first of the week. By the end of the week, we began wrapping up the details of the work orders and planning the next week's schedule.

You will eventually find a system that works best for you and your staff. As we stated earlier, it's advisable to have someone available to interview during the lunch hour, one evening a week, and one Saturday per month to accommodate the applicants who are working and can't get away during regular business hours. We certainly had our fair share of cancellations and no shows to contend with, but eventually we were able to get a sense of how the scheduling could adapt to the daily business.

If there is a mistake in appointment scheduling, such as when two people are set up for the same time slot, just relax. It's not the end of the world, so don't panic. Most people understand simple errors in scheduling and will help ease the frustration by offering to reschedule for a more convenient time. Just be sure to try to give the cursory and referral interviewees the rescheduled date and keep the response-to-the-ads interview more immediate.

NEGOTIATING THE HIRE

Negotiation means adjusting, sacrificing, and working towards an acceptable solution that's satisfying for both parties. In order to be as effective as possible in the negotiating stage of the hiring process, you'll need to stay actively involved with the placement throughout the entire process. Ask the employer and the applicant to report back to you, for their feedback, after each and every interview you or your counselors schedule. This might seem like a tedious or time-consuming process in the beginning. You'll learn quickly that the more information you have about what's transpired between the two individuals, the better you'll be at securing the match.

The applicant needs to let you know because he or she might or might not be interested. The employer needs to let you know for the very same reason. Many times, the company wants the person who has been interviewed, and the person selected might not choose this particular job, for one of any number of reasons.

Once the feedback has come in and been recorded, the job offer is announced to you regarding one of your candidates. You get the benefit of calling this person and making the job offer. I personally found this particular function to be one of the most satisfying in the entire business. I just wish I could have done it far more often. Cherish the good feeling because for every offer you get to make, a rejection comes right behind it to the other applicants sent on the interview.

The employer might want your client to start the new position at a certain salary, but the applicant has already indicated to you the level of base income that is the prerequisite to accepting a job. Let the applicant know of the pay raise policies, and let the employer know of the person's willingness to work towards a salary increase as soon as possible. Try to get the two to meet halfway on their salary positions.

If the applicant absolutely cannot meet at the halfway point, try looking at other areas that might affect the level of income. The benefits package could be the area that can be adjusted. Instead of the company offering $X base, plus full benefits, consider offering $X+, with less benefits.

There are many areas that might need discussing in the hire. These will be the start date, dress code, start salary, raise potential, whom they report to, parking, etc. Keep a fair and open mind when trying to achieve a solid, long-term placement. Your clients will thank you for this professional attitude time and time again.

DESCRIBING CURRENT ORDERS

Many situations required careful attention to detail when selling an idea or concept to an applicant. Also, there are many types of people requesting the same information again and again. You will not be giving the same "pat" response each time.

Call-ins

Whenever we advertised for a position that would generate a strong reaction, we called it the onslaught response. Our phones would ring anywhere from 50 to 200 times for each position advertised in the Sunday paper.

Many of the individuals calling were obviously not qualified for the jobs advertised, but they were more than willing to learn. Many others were more than willing to put their more qualified skills on hold to do the current job. The terms we used for these overqualified and underqualified applicants were the wannabees and the overqualifieds.

Never discount these individuals simply because they don't fit the specific job order they call about. Give them a brief overview of the opening, ask about their specific qualifications, and, if appropriate, schedule them for an interview.

Be very careful when describing the new job over the phone. You should indicate which industry, i.e., retail, real estate, manufacturing, service, automotive, etc. Sometimes the person calling will make screening much easier by simply saying he or she is not interested in working in the banking industry.

If the opening is an exclusive, be sure to let the caller know that. When you do this, the caller gets the impression that most of your job orders are exclusive. Some might want to register with you some time in the near future and wait for an opening.

Don't give away the baby. This means saying so much about the opening that the caller can figure out who the company is. The caller will go directly there, not pass go, and certainly not tell the company where he or she heard about the position.

Make the description brief. These onslaught calls can take up a lot of valuable time. Eventually you'll develop a comfortable system of your own to screen these calls.

Interviews

Be very careful about where you have the open job order on your desk. Don't ever let it just lie around for prying eyes.

If it's a confidential order, say so. This means the employer is replacing a non-productive employee without their knowledge. The applicant needs to know how important it is to keep this information confidential.

Over 30 percent of the job orders that came to North Coast Personnel were confidential in nature. It's not as unusual as it sounds. And at least 25 percent of the applicants who registered with the agency were currently employed and dissatisfied with their positions. See how much secrecy goes on in the personnel field? We always found it to be amazing.

The last thing to remember when describing the job in the interview is to be complete with your information. Don't hold back something you've learned that might be a detriment for the job seeker if he or she is hired. Mark Twain said, "If you tell the truth all the time, you never have to remember anything." This is a good idiom to remember when conducting business.

TAKING JOB ORDERS

Taking a job order simply means recording all the information on a job order report form when an employer requests a new employee. Be thorough when asking all the questions on the order form. When the employer responds, write down everything he or she tells you. An example of the job order form is in chapter 2.

Listed in the following are all the questions to ask when taking an order:

- Date: Date the job order was received.
- Company name: Name of the firm requesting the employee.
- Type of business: Indicate what industry this company is connected with. Is it automotive, computer, retail, insurance, etc.?
- Address: This is usually where the applicants will be interviewed and eventually work. Be sure to include the street name and number, suite number, city, state, and zip code. (If there is a separate interview address, indicate the difference and explain why.)
- Cross street: This will help the applicants find the interview location faster so they won't be late.
- Mailing address: Always ask for an address for sending résumés, business correspondence, etc. This will probably be in the form of a post office box number.

- Phone number: Get the number of the company, the fax number, if applicable, and any extension number that gives you a direct line to the hiring source.
- Job title: Find out what the employer calls this position. If the company hasn't come up with a title yet, offer to help select an appropriate one, based on the job description information.
- Company size: How many employees does the company have? Is it a sole proprietorship, corporation, national firm, or franchise operation? Are there seasonal increases?
- Confidential: Find out if the company is replacing a nonproductive employee. If so, you should be very careful when you call about giving the receptionist your company name. Find out if the interviews are going to be scheduled on a Saturday, so no one is in the building, or after hours during the week.
- Preferred start date: When does the company want someone to begin working? Not all companies need someone yesterday. Just 90 percent!
- Growth potential: Find out if there is room for growth within this new job, and how soon will it happen. Not all applicants want or require a job that keeps changing. Most do, however, so be sure to get this crucial information and share it with the potential applicant as a screening tool.
- Duties: A complete description of what the person will be expected to perform. Be sure to list all the responsibilities and explain them carefully and in detail to your applicant. Sometimes the company has this information already prepared in the personnel files. You might ask them to fax or mail you a copy of this data. Occasionally the job description is not reasonable. By this we mean there are not enough hours in the day to accomplish all that they're asking. If you recognize this, gently speak up.
- Qualifications: Find out what it will take to do the job. What kind and how much work experience, education, special skills, and background have to be confirmed before an interview can be scheduled?
- Rate of wages: This information is sometimes given to you in the form of a range of salary, depending on the skill level of the applicant hired. Several companies have a preselected start salary and then another figure that indicates the training period increase. Spend enough time on this question to feel confident about discussing it with your clients. If it's unreasonable, as in too much work for too little pay, say so. Companies respect the fact that you understand industry rates for similar positions.
- Work schedule: Indicate the standard work schedule required for the employee. Monday through Friday? 8:00 a.m. to 5:00 p.m.? Evening work? Weekends? Overtime?
- Paydays: All companies have a different payday selection. Most pay their employees on the 1st and 15th of each month, and others on a weekly basis.
- Benefits: Find out what the benefits package consists of and when the benefits start. Some companies choose to begin the benefits on hire, and some wait until the 90-day probationary period has passed. Ask if they offer medical, dental, optical, and any other.
- New position: Find out if this is a newly developed job within the firm because of an expansion, or is the employer simply replacing someone who is leaving or moving up the ladder? Find out the reason for the phone call, and you'll also find out how quickly the problem needs to be solved.

- Preferred interview times: This question is more in consideration for the busy schedule of the hiring source. Find out if the company plans to do all the interviewing in one day, or if the company prefers mornings or afternoons, (or Saturdays and after hours for confidential job orders). Earlier we discussed some of the tips for working towards developing an exclusive account. This is one area that means a great deal to the company. Find out when their first three interview times are available, and then fill those time slots right away.
- Order placed by: Most often, the job order comes over the telephone, but sometimes it's in person (over lunch or in a meeting), or through the mail.
- Exclusive?: Hopefully, you'll be marking this with a resounding yes after a short time in business!
- Given by: Indicate the name and title of the person listing the order with you. (Make sure to ask for the spelling of the person's name.)
- Interviewed by: This is not always the same person who gave the job order to you. Get the person's name and correct spelling.
- Sales call date: The date the contact was made to generate this account and who made the connection.
- Person hired: Record the name of the applicant chosen for the job. You will also want to write the information down if this is a shared order and one of your competitors fills the order. Be sure to indicate which agency made the placement and the fee structure of the agency.
- Start date: The applicant's first date of employment is recorded on this line.
- Start salary: Since your fees are based on a percentage of the salary, it's important for your bookkeeper to have this for billing purposes. Since our fees were based on 75 percent of the first month's salary, we only charged on the start pay, not the increase after the 90-day training program.

The box graph at the bottom of the job order form is for recording the specifics of each applicant sent to the company for interview. This is where you indicate the date the applicant is scheduled to meet with the interviewer, the name of the applicant sent, his or her contract number, and the results (feedback) of the meeting.

SCREENING APPLICANTS

One of the primary reasons a business uses a placement service is to guarantee the cost savings in screening potential employees. It's not only frustrating, but also extremely expensive when a company recruits (advertising and interviewing), hires, and trains, only to find out that the new employee has a serious personality problem, drinking or drug problem, high previous job turnover rate, or poor references, etc.

A professional placement agency should have the skill, background, and capability to help their clients avoid these costly mistakes. Occasionally, it's really easy to get snowed when interviewing. But, when it's the primary function of your day, and interviewing is what you do for a living, very rarely can an individual pull any wool over your eyes. Screening involves many steps:

Scheduling the initial appointment

The very first contact you have with the applicant prior to an interview is to discuss his or her match of qualifications versus skill for a specific opening in your agency.

An interview with you or your counselor will only happen when the crucial questions asked by the counselor are answered in a clear, concise, and positive way. In other words, specific points will be covered about the job and the background of the applicant to see if the match and interest are there.

Overall assessment

This evaluation is for personality traits, personal appearance, responsiveness, alertness, confidence, desire, enthusiasm, etc.

Contacting previous employers

Contact the previous employer so you can get a clear and concise employment reference of the applicant's work history. This is done prior to setting up an interview with the new employer.

There are several factors that will alert you to a poor applicant referral choice:

- Timeliness. Being late for the initial interview with the counselor.
- Honesty. Answering each question with hesitation, or getting caught outright in a lie.
- Appearance. A unkempt or unclean look. Inappropriate dress.
- Reference. A poor reference from any previous employer.
- Testing. Failure to achieve an acceptable level of a required test result.
- Body language. A nervous client, eyes shifting, squirming in the chair, sweating profusely, fidgeting, no eye contact, etc.

Red flag

Sometimes a bad feeling comes over you as you're talking with an applicant, and there really isn't any identifiable reason or source for this discomfort. We call this the red-flag feeling. It's more of an intuitive response to the interview than anything. I never, ever went against this sixth sense, and I was always glad that I relied on it so heavily.

The applicant might sound good, look good, have the right skill, be right on time, say the right things, have the right amount of enthusiasm, and have great references. And yet, there is something wrong, something that you can't quite put your finger on.

Don't ignore this feeling, ever. It saved us from embarrassment countless times, and on several occasions it allowed the employer to see how strong our screening skills were and how high our ethics and moral code were.

Don't let the company pay for your mistakes. Do your job, and the employees you place will stay, advance, and might eventually become the hiring source within the client firm. What a great long-time relationship you can develop with each company when you stick by your moral code.

CREDIT CHECKING

Applicants are given the option to pay their placement fees to your firm on a monthly payment plan, extended over a three-month period. To avoid costly and frustrating collection problems down the road, it makes good sense to have the applicant fill out a credit application at the same time he or she fills out the contract. Set this valuable policy in motion from the very beginning.

By doing this, there will be far fewer problems collecting your fees for services rendered. This is because you and your staff will have exactly the same information that collection agencies use when they go after aged accounts receivables for their clients.

The credit information requested is relatively brief, but quite thorough. It will assist you in your collection process, and it also alerts your potential clients that they will have extreme difficulty if they try avoiding their financial responsibility to you. In my agencies, just presenting the credit application frightened off several of the takers from the very beginning. We were always grateful for this and never felt badly when they backed out. They realized we had all the information necessary to find the resources for the financial investigation, plus a contract that would hold up in court.

Be sure to back up what you say you're going to do with action. Don't go to all the effort of having them fill out the credit forms and then not put every bit of effort you can into collecting your fees. For more information on collections, refer to chapter 2, where you'll also find a copy of the credit application.

RECRUITING

Recruiting means searching for qualified applicants for the position available in your firm. This can be done in several ways.

Newspaper advertising

Before placing the ad in the local newspaper, make a trip to the newspaper's business offices and set up a corporate account, with contract rates. This will give your agency the ability to secure the lowest ad rate for the largest ad possible. You'll be required to run a minimum number of lines on a consistent basis. Develop a good working relationship with these people, and your ad costs will be much lower.

Select the newspaper in your target area that consistently runs the largest list of want ads. By doing this, your ads will draw the maximum response. Fortunately, you don't have to pay for any typos in your want ads. Be sure to call the newspaper as soon as you see the error, and get a credit when a mistake has been made. Finally, learn how to abbreviate so that the maximum applicant response comes from the smallest cost!

You might also choose to place these ads in trade journals. Almost all industries have them. Since it's advertising for a more focused industry, you'll get responses from a client pool that has experience within that particular field. Unfortunately, trade journals are usually published on a monthly basis. Anxious employers generally prefer a quicker advertising campaign.

Scatter ads

A scatter ad is a small, four- to five-line help-wanted advertisement that's designed to target only the applicant pool for the one specific job opening. Write up a short ad and place it in your local newspaper using as much abbreviation as possible.

It's not necessary to pay for costly advertising when you can get the job done with a one-day ad. We only ran the scatter ads on Sunday. We put the ads in for one day, screened the response, and almost always found the person that we needed from this response, plus many more who registered because they saw the ad.

We placed several (10 to 20) scatter ads on each Sunday (see Fig. 9-1). The main bulk of the advertising budget was spent on these scatter ads because the revenues earned from the applicant responses were extremely profitable.

Consider how you want applicants to respond when you run these scatter ads. If written communication skills are important for the position, you might want the applicant to mail or fax a cover letter and a résumé first. If verbal communication skills are more important for the opening, you might choose to have the applicants call in so you can conduct a telephone screening before deciding to schedule the interview.

ADMINISTRATIVE ASST. 1 pers.
ofc. Employee Bnfts exp prfd.
Will train right person. Excl
Growth potential. FEE SPLIT
North Coast, (111) 222-3333

SALES REPS (2), territory,
major corp, microcomputers.
Ext. training. Sales exp reqd.
Sal+comm. 1st yr est. $35K
North Coast, (111) 222-3333

OFFICE MGR, F/C Bkkpr, busy
ofc. Supervisory bkgd, excl
bnft pkg. To $24K, FEE PAID
North Coast, (111) 222-3333

SERVICE MGR, electrical bkgd
clean DMV, strong back. Excl
bnfts. Strng Cust. Svc. Skll.
To $15/hr st. FEE NEGOTIABLE
North Coast, (111) 222-3333

RECEPTIONISTS, (2) 60 wpm
exl bnfts, growth potent.
PR skills. To $10/hr. FEE SPLIT
North Coast, (111) 222-3333

9-1
Examples of scatter ads.

Laundry lists

The laundry list is a long list of all the openings available in your company at any given time. This list is posted by job title and salary. Usually the highest-salaried positions are listed first, then progressively reduced to the lowest-salaried positions in the end. If you can, run this laundry list once a month, on Sunday or Wednesday, so the general public can see that you have many more openings than listed in the scatter ads they see on Sundays.

As you can see on the laundry list in Fig. 9-2, 41 jobs are currently available, but you only need 20 lines of type. You do this by indicating, with parentheses, how many openings there are with that job title. The laundry list is one of the strongest recruiting tools available to the personnel agency owner. It draws far more applicants to the agency pool than most other one-shot advertising resources.

Keep copies of all the newspaper advertisements that are run each time. Set up a three-ring binder and have the secretary cut out the ads and tape them in the binder. Next to each ad, make a note of how many phone calls were received. This gives you a good reference point for designing future ads. Work with the ad copy that drew a strong applicant reply, and redesign the ads that only drew a minimal response.

Chief Financial Officer	$60K
General Manager/Mfg	$55K
Operations Analyst	$40K
Sales & Marketing Mgr	$35K
F/C Bookkeepers (2)	$35K
Registered Nurse	$33K
Office Manager	$30K
Computer Technician	$28K
Warehouse Manager	$26K
Restaurant Manager	$24K
Public Relations Rep	$22K
Administrative Asst	$22K
Secretaries (4)	$18K
Warehouse Workers (3)	$18K
Driver Delivery (2)	$15K
Receptionists (5)	$15K
General Office (2)	$12K
LVN	$11K
Assembly Workers (8)	$10K
P/T Retail Clerks (3)	$ 8K

9-2
Example of laundry list.

Display ads

Display ads attract the attention of job seekers who are currently working and not reading the want ads daily. If you place the ad in the business, sports, or women's wear section of the paper, you might pull someone who is simply scanning the newspaper for news or any interesting ads. This form of recruiting is a little less specific, unless you design an ad that has your company name, logo, address, and phone number, with space to change the job line for each insert. That way, readers will become familiar with seeing the ad, and they will always look to see if there's anything that might interest them.

Be creative with your advertising campaign. The ability to research your competition and watch their advertising will pay off. Be willing to change your ads, and always listen and record honest criticism from your clients and business associates and friends.

Radio

If you decide to advertise for a position on the radio, do your homework first! Find out what the target area for the station is, meaning how far the signal will be broadcast. Ask for the number of people it will reach. And finally, try to find out what the percentage of successful ads are that have run in the past. You can ask for referrals of some of their satisfied clients. This form of recruiting can be a bit frustrating because you might draw far more unqualified applicants to your business than you ever wanted. You really only want to open the window a little bit and let a select group of qualified applicants through. With radio advertising, your target range is very wide, and you get a varied range of applicant skill responses. You might choose this form of advertising when you first open your agency in order to build your applicant pool.

Word of mouth

When you can't find the appropriate person through advertising in the newspaper, try asking around. This is also called networking. It means calling a few associates and friends to see if they know of anyone with the specific skills you're looking for. If they can't help personally, ask them if they can suggest an idea of where else to look. Don't always rely on just your own resources. Keep the network active, and it will always pay off in the long run.

Head hunting

Head hunting means contacting employees who are currently working in exactly the same jobs within the same industry. These people might be dissatisfied with their work and ready to make a change. If the people are not interested themselves, they might have a friend who is. Always ask for a suggestion for the next step in your search process.

High schools, colleges, and trade schools

High schools, colleges, and trade schools are often great resources for available applicant pools. They often have career days and encourage business owners and managers to attend. These students might start as part-time employees and gradually work into a full-time job. Fortunately, the schools might also have a referral service. Unfortunately, the schools can only be used for an opening in your firm when the employer is willing to train someone into the position. Think of the schools each time a training position comes in. The students are primed and ready to apply their newly learned tools to a new job.

Personnel directors

Contact your business associates in the personnel departments of large firms and let them know of your search. Many times they have a large pool of qualified unemployed applicants in their files. They also might be aware of a company that's cutting back on its staff.

Clubs, organizations, and trade associations

Many members of the social and civic groups (Rotary, Kiwanis, Professional Business Women, Jaycees, Kiwanis, Lions, Professional Association, or Leads Groups, etc.) almost always know someone who is looking for work or a job change. These members, as well as trade group executives, are in a position to refer people.

Suppliers and vendors

The supplier personnel and vendor representatives are a great source of people to keep informed about your recruitment need. They are also in a prime position to spread the information to their many clients.

TIME MANAGEMENT

As the owner of your firm, it's your responsibility to ensure that your agency is running smoothly at all times. This simply means making sure there is no valuable time wasted every day. Time is expensive. It costs you money to have all the daily, weekly, and monthly tasks completed. If you weren't doing it, you would have to pay someone to do it for you. And, although you will work for free in the development of your business, eventually you will not want to work for free at all!

When I first opened North Coast, I did it all: secretarial, bookkeeping, reception, general office, sales, and management. I performed all these functions on top of, and in addition to, all the employment counseling and job placement. In reality, the last two functions were the bread and butter of the business.

Once I began to realize that I alone was the primary revenue generator, it became abundantly clear that it wasn't cost effective for me to do all the other chores. Since I generated the income for the firm and knew the most within the industry, my salary was at the highest level. This meant my time was at a premium. If I found myself doing business functions that were just as easily done by a lesser-salaried employee, then I was wasting my time.

If you have someone who can file, let them do it, instead of doing it yourself! If you find yourself making bank deposits, keeping records, or photocopying, and there's a staff member who makes considerably less than you do, have them do it!

Simply be aware of the tasks that are being performed that are costly, time-consuming, and nonproductive, and do something about it.

My very first employee was my daughter, Sandy. She was a sophomore in high school at the time and came into the agency three afternoons a week for a couple of hours to do the filing, copying, and errands. She earned an hourly salary, and it freed me up to do the things that were more financially productive for the business. It was helpful for us both, and we enjoyed working together.

Then, as the business got even busier, I hired a full-time reception secretary, in addition to my daughter. This employee took over North Coast secretarial service duties, screened all my calls, set up my applicant appointments, and handled all the general office responsibilities.

From there, the business grew because I was able to devote so much more of my time to interviewing, placement, marketing, building the employer client base, refining the existing systems, and solving problems as they arose.

In chapter 10, we'll go into detail about all of the job descriptions and responsibilities of staff members. Keep on top of who does what, and get the best use of time as possible, including yourself. Don't do tasks that a six-dollar-an-hour person can do. Even though you feel you can do it in half the time, remember, it took you time to learn, and it will also take the new person time to get up to speed.

It might look like you're losing money up front and very possibly you are, but in the long run you'll be glad you took this route because it will save you money in the end. This is called time management!

Another form of time management is list making. All good executives, managers, CEOs, and directors are list makers. They do it by nature, and it carries over into their private lives. My friends and family kid me all the time about my list-making propensity. By creating lists, you can prioritize your tasks and function more smoothly on a daily basis with some semblance of order. It can happen!

Instead of making a list that's one- or two-pages long and crossing off as you go, try to keep the daily task list to six items only. The reason for this is simple. You need to create a confidence builder for yourself, and most people can accomplish six tasks in a day. Actually, most managers can do considerably more each day and in reality always do. That's why there's only six tasks on the list. You know that each day, new and exciting challenges will be presented to you. As a business owner, there will always be daily problems to solve, new clients to see, places to go, things to do. Don't overtax yourself by setting up a list that will never get smaller. It's important that you get the internal strokes that crossing off each task gives you.

Goal setting

It's very satisfying to complete your business goals. Also, it's much easier to accomplish tasks if you're working toward a specific goal. (Your daily task-list goal might simply be to complete the list.)

You might choose to set up a weekly task list, monthly task list, and yearly task list. Write down the goals you want to achieve, and then build the task list. Prioritizing the tasks in the correct order will make it easier to achieve the goal. Work on setting up goals that are reachable, and stay on them until you're done.

I've always said that the primary reason I was so successful in my business was that I learned the two crucial factors for business success from my parents. My mother, who was a teacher, is an inordinate list maker. My father was a career military officer and a natural disciplinarian. So, with this combination, she taught me how to make the lists, and he taught me how to finish them! What a great combination for guaranteed success!

CRISIS MANAGEMENT

Crisis management is pretty self-explanatory. It's a new business term that literally means solving problems as they arise. If you break down the two words, crisis and management, you'll see what we mean.

CRISIS = THE PROBLEM
MANAGEMENT = SOLUTION TO PROBLEM

The crisis could be just about anything. It might be something as minor and easy to solve as faulty advertising copy, an employee personal problem, a client misunderstanding from a lack of communication, or possibly a scheduling mishap. These problems happen all the time, and solving them is rarely difficult. A major crisis could be illness, death of a staff member or family member, theft, fire, earthquake, or being low on cash, etc.

No matter what the crisis is, just don't lose sight of your goals. Use your gut to make the decisions, not your head. Always have a plan A, plan B, and plan C for the solutions to the problems (in case plan A and B don't work). Crisis management is the new-age terminology for solving the daily, weekly, and monthly business problems that arise in any and all companies!

10
Staffing

As soon as possible, sit down and design employee job descriptions. Unfortunately, I was working 70 hours per week when I finally forced myself to stop and develop some position descriptions.

Once you've established what background is necessary for the people you hire, the training time for these individuals will be much shorter. When you hire, take into consideration how much time it takes to teach systems and procedures, terminology, and style. Usually an employee is up and running in about three months. This means that he or she has no further questions and can be 100 percent productive.

The experience-versus-education standard is a personal one in this field. In some of the positions, such as the office manager, sales person, and full-charge bookkeeper, it's necessary to hire individuals with hands-on training.

For the secretary, receptionist, general office clerk, and employment counselor, be willing to train an applicant who has minimal experience.

Hiring a friend can be disastrous. It's rare to find a situation with this working relationship that turns out well. More often than not, personality issues rear their ugly heads. Many times, hurt feelings and misunderstanding get in the way. Just remember, if you do decide to hire a friend, know going in that your friend might not remain your friend when all is said and done. Be prepared to take that risk.

One of the best idioms in life, as well as business, is: learn from your mistakes. It's okay to take a risk, and it's okay to fail. Just don't ever make the same mistake twice, and never, ever repeat the failure!

There are only five labor function categories in almost all businesses, and the personnel agency is no different. We have listed these categories for you:

LABOR

Job description

This person will be running errands for you and your staff, making the daily bank deposits, doing all the photocopying, filing, picking up business supplies, making daily coffee, cleaning the cups every day, watering the plants, emptying the wastebaskets, and any other nontrained responsibilities you can think of. We're sure you'll find many more things for this person to do. Your main concern should be whether or not someone can do the job with minimal instruction.

Qualifications

This is the position that requires the least amount of experience. But personality, honesty, appearance, motivation, enthusiasm, and integrity are the key. You can hire someone who is still in school. Contact your local high school and talk with the work experience counselors. They'll try to find someone for you who has all the qualities we've listed, plus the willingness to work part time during the school year and full time during holidays and the summer.

When I worked for the permanent and temporary agency, before opening North Coast Personnel, we hired a young lady who was only 17 years old and still a senior in high school. She worked with us part time for five years, and this helped put her through college. Her work schedule was readjusted each semester to coincide with her school hours, and she was available to work full time during the summer and regular school vacations.

Salary

This is the lowest-salaried employee in your firm. He or she is paid the least because he or she has the least amount of experience. If you hire someone through your local high school, you should pay the person minimum wage. You can pay less, according to the Fair Employment Practices Law, but it would be better to pay the going rate. You'll have a happier and more productive employee.

CLERICAL

Job description

This is the secretary/reception position. The job responsibilities will include, but not be limited to, data entry, answering phones, scheduling appointments, describing advertised positions, greeting new clients, processing daily mail, handling policy letter correspondence, writing contracts, screening calls, making coffee, opening the offices, doing inventory control (ordering supplies), etc.

Qualifications

When recruiting for this key individual, try to select someone who has growth potential, in addition to the skills listed previously. This person has to have a right-hand mentality. By this we mean the understanding that his or her primary responsibility is to ensure that you, the manager, are freed up to do all that you're capable of doing. This means taking responsibility for all the tasks that would be a waste of your time. Understanding this crucial business concept takes a bright, motivated, caring, sensitive, and confident individual.

Make sure that this person has sound decision-making capabilities, flexibility, and an ability to meet deadlines. In the interviewing and selection process, let the applicant know that this is a starting position only, and that the person selected will advance within the firm. Tell the applicant that once he or she has had the opportunity to learn the required job and studied all the other positions with the company, he or she will be able to pick and choose which job he or she wants to be groomed for. Many wise managers know that the secretary/receptionist position in any company is the most responsible job. This employee has to know all that's going on. Many secretaries have a hand on, or finger in, almost everything the company is doing. Most important of all, the secretary/receptionist represents you and your company image to the general public. This employee is the first contact, the first vision, the first voice. Make sure the employee is someone you feel proud of.

Salary

This person should be paid an hourly rate, depending on the amount of experience he or she brings to the job. If the person has at least three to five years of experience in another office, with all the typing speed, 10-key-by-touch skill, and computer knowledge, the going rate is between $8.00 and $12.00 per hour.

BOOKKEEPER

Job description

This employee is responsible for tracking the business receivables and expenses, (money-in and money-out). He or she will be responsible for all of the daily record keeping, accounts receivable, accounts payable, billing, payroll, quarterly tax reports, reconciliation of the monthly bank statement, budgeting, credit and collections, and preparing bank deposits. Since you'll be using an accounting program that will aid in the creation of your monthly accounting reports, the bookkeeper will also produce the general ledger, balance sheet, and profit and loss statements for your monthly review.

Qualifications

There's such a wide range of skill levels for the bookkeeper that we recommend you recruit for a full-charge bookkeeper with computer experience. In today's business environment, it's more likely that all bookkeepers have computer knowledge, but be sure to find one with the specific software experience selected by your firm. When you advertise in the paper, include the type of accounting software you plan to use in your business, so the response to the ad will have a more narrow focus.

Salary

The bookkeeper is also paid relative to how much experience he or she offers. A full-charge bookkeeper earns $12.00 to $18.00 per hour.

SALES

Job description

Each business has a different requirement for a sales position. Listed in the following are the sales job descriptions. Select the one that's most useful for your business and consider adding the others as your company expands. You might also decide to combine the job duties of several of the positions listed. Just remember, if you choose to do this, make sure the compensation is adequate.

Telemarketer

You might want to hire someone whose primary function is to talk on the phone each day and introduce your business services to the employer marketplace. The telemarketer will be calling primarily to generate job orders that are currently available. An extensive record is kept by this person, and callbacks are part of the job.

When I hired the telemarketer for my firm, it was only after several years in business. This was because I felt that I needed to establish a well-known name in the industry first, with sound business practices and honest relationships. Then, when my salesperson called the potential client, there was a much stronger response, rather than a quick no. Sometimes the telemarketer was able to trigger the employer to begin a search that was only formulating prior to the phone call. This employee was paid on a commission basis only. He or she was paid a set amount for job orders developed and a percentage figure of the placements made and revenues received from that job order.

Outside sales representative

In the early stages of the development of your company, you'll be the one to call on the new companies for client development. Eventually, you'll want to hire someone to do this job instead of you. This person will also be making cold contacts while out in the field. There are example policy letters in chapter 8 that are extremely helpful for the salesperson. The salesperson will be responsible for all of his or her correspondence.

Each company that's visited should receive a standard packet of your company sales information. In this packet is a description of your company services, business cards of the salesperson and yourself, employer fee schedule, a brochure, and a copy of the legal guideline for interviewing. It's also very important for the salesperson to keep an accurate log of every contact made each day, week, and month. An example copy of the sales report form is in chapter 2.

Public relations representative

This individual does exactly what the job title indicates. He or she represents your company to the public. This includes creating advertising copy, attending association meetings, grand openings, civic occasions, and anything else that would be appropriate.

Marketing representative

The difference between a sales representative and a marketing representative is simple. The salesperson makes the contact with the potential client, sells the service, and closes the sale. The marketing person designs the method in which this contact is made. Will it be through a personal meeting, a follow-up to a target mailing, association contacts, cold calls, print media, radio, or television? As you can see, the avenues for contact resources is quite extensive. The marketing representative should know the correct return on the investment of your dollars for each avenue.

The marketing person decides and then implements the avenue that the sales follow. How does the word get to the public? This is the most creative side of sales, and it takes quite an industrious mind to work all the angles and come up with the one that's best for your company.

Qualifications

Experience is the most important factor in hiring this employee. A track record of sales growth and productivity is essential. References will give you this key data, so don't forget to make those calls. A salesperson is the one person, of all employees you hire, who can pull the wool over your eyes. Be extra careful with this personality type. Some of them are very good at snow jobs and telling lies. We've seen too many company owners get taken by a greedy salesperson. Be very cautious with this recruitment requirement.

Salary

The salesperson will earn a base salary, plus a commission on sales.

He or she should also be part of your bonus plan policies. The salary for a salesperson varies in every area. Talk with other agency owners, or other service industry owners, and get a line on what the going rate is in your particular area.

If you hire your salesperson as an independent contractor, you'll be required to file an annual information return (Form 1099). You have to have paid this person $600 or more in the course of the calendar year, and you'll be subject to penalties if you don't file this necessary paperwork.

Here are some factors that the IRS uses to determine if your independent contractor qualifies for this method of payment for services rendered. Does the contractor:
- Have his or her own business license?
- Have cards, stationery, and a real business address?
- Have a business bank account?
- Sell his or her services regularly to various customers?

OFFICE MANAGER
Job description

The office manager is responsible for the smooth operation of the administrative division of your company. This means overseeing all personnel procedures, accounting practices, inventory control, and daily problem solving. Most often, this is not a full-time job, but it can be joined with the duties of the employment counselor or the bookkeeper. During one phase of the business, my office manager was also the full-charge bookkeeper. During another period, the office manager was also an employment counselor. Both times, it worked smoothly because I had hired someone who was multifaceted and responsible for overseeing the daily operations.

Qualifications

This person should have a sense of maturity and several years of business experience under his or her belt. The office manager must know how to solve personality conflicts, minor catastrophes, and the daily ups and downs of running a busy business. Some owners prefer to hire an older person so he or she can command a certain level of respect from subordinates. Common sense, a strong commitment to honesty, business ethics, and company loyalty are some of the personality traits to look for when recruiting.

Salary

Depending on the length of prior experience, this person will be paid between $15.00 and $22.00 per hour.

EMPLOYMENT COUNSELOR

Job description

An innately curious person is perfect for the role of the employment counselor. There's a tremendous amount of information to learn in this position. The person needs to be able to gather as much as he or she can in a short period of time and assimilate it quickly. Applicants have a tendency to forget about time when they sit with a counselor. Each applicant thinks his or her story is the most important one, and telling it with emphasis is crucial to the applicant. The counselor cannot get wrapped up in each situation and lose track of time.

The counselor needs to be able to spot dishonest people and not get taken with the liars. Once the initial data is exchanged, the rest of the time spent with clients should be productive, without making the job seekers feel like they're in an assembly-line operation.

My mentor taught me that the only way to keep productive and functional as an employment counselor was to maintain a steady balance in my personal life and not take any work home. She always said it was important to separate my work time (listening to so many sad stories) and my personal time. Her advice was that if I couldn't learn this valuable lesson early, I'd never last in the industry. She was right. During the first 10 years, most of the time I mentally shut down from employment at 5:00 p.m., went home, and lived a full life with my husband and child. Once I opened my own firm, obviously everything changed. I threw away my watch! But I was no longer just a counselor. I was everything: owner, manager, salesperson, secretary, etc.

Qualifications

Find someone who has a background in either customer service, sales, marketing, counseling, parenting, or any other field where service is a key factor in productivity. The charismatic traits are a good listener, a clear and concise communicator, intuitive, humorous, steady, intelligent, and honest.

It's not crucial to hire someone who has been an employment counselor in the past. In fact, I deliberately chose not to ever hire someone with experience in the personnel field. I wanted to train people to work within the structure I'd designed and use the systems I'd created. When you meet the right counselor, you'll know it intuitively. You'll feel that it's the right match.

Salary

Some personnel agencies prefer to pay their employment counselors on a commission basis. They'll offer a minimal base salary, plus commissions. This means that the employment counselor's income is calculated on the placement of positions, and the counselor is paid the commissions only after the fees are received.

I preferred to pay my counselors with a set salary plus a participation in the profits of the business on a quarterly basis. This method of payment gave the counselors much more leeway in the interview process. It felt much less like a sales-motivated environment and more like a counseling-based business. Their salaries ranged from $1,200 to 1,800 per month, and they earned 5 percent of the profits of the business.

Keeping employee morale high and encouraging team spirit are primary factors in a successful business. It's important to show your employees that you're interested in them and you welcome their ideas on how things might improve. Respect their differences of opinion and accept the fact that they might not see things exactly the same way you do. Treat them as individuals, and encourage promotion from within. Offer criticism privately and only in the form of constructive suggestions. Never embarrass your employees.

SALARY AND PERFORMANCE REVIEWS

Compensation for work well done and a "pat" on the back are the two primary factors that keep your employees motivated. Certainly strong company systems and procedures, policies, and benefits are also contributing factors, but not nearly as much as the pay and the strokes.

Salary

It's important to encourage your staff to work productively all the time, and one of the ways to implement this is through salary-increase incentives. This is one of the best tools available to you to keep your employees motivated and energetic. You give these raises, if justified, three times within the first year of employment. The raises do not have to be exorbitant, but they should certainly be enough to make a difference in take-home pay once taxes are withheld.

All good managers know that each time they take the time to pat someone on the back, they see a marked difference in the employee's attitude during work hours. An increase in productivity can be accomplished in one of two ways: compliments or raises.

It's not fair to expect an employee to have to come to you and ask for a raise. It's the responsibility of the owner to assess the work performance and compensate for that productivity accordingly. If you spell out your firm's pay structure policies from the very first date of hire, there should never be a problem with any misunderstandings or misinterpretations. Don't ever let your people feel that you're a cheapskate, as the word travels around in the industry quicker than you can imagine. When you hire people, be sure to let them know how the salary structure works. This way, they have something to look forward to, and budget for, as they work each day.

Hidden costs of staffing

Employees will cost you, the employer, between 15 and 30 percent above their wages or salaries, depending on what benefits you offer. A full benefits package and required taxes can reach the 30 percent figure quickly.

You must match every dollar of federal Social Security taxes that you deduct from your employees' checks. This is currently more than 7 percent. Also, you must pay state unemployment taxes (which will vary from state to state) and an additional 0.8 percent for federal unemployment taxes. Social Security and unemployment tax rates tend to change from year to year. Some states require the employer to pay a portion of the state disability insurance premiums.

Raises

We've listed the salary increases on the first-year raise schedule for your review:

    1st: This is the beginning salary, and it's calculated by assessing the strengths and experiences of the new employee.

    2nd: The increase at the 90-day review or probationary period. The employee will no longer be asking questions about the position's responsibilities. Because of this, the employee should be producing at a rate of 100 percent. This means no down or wasted time.

    3rd: If the employee has earned it, a merit raise is given within the next six to nine months. This raise encourages the employee to continue to produce at the same level.

    4th: The annual cost-of-living raise is to be given to all employees straight across the board. This is not considered a raise based on merit, but an increase in pay to keep employees within their own budgets.

Bonuses and incentives

I always paid every one of my staff bonuses at the end of each business quarter. This bonus schedule was calculated based on seniority and positions of authority. The longer the employee was with the firm, and the more responsible the position, the higher the percentage. In other words, the office manager received considerably more than the part-time general office clerk from the local high school.

Needless to say, life was pretty exciting around the office four times a year. Each year, most employees in other companies only receive one additional check that's not budgeted for standard living expenses. This is generally the income tax return, and it comes in the spring of each year. If you implement this bonus strategy into your payroll policies, your employees get to look forward to five additional pay-checks each year!

There are many types of incentives you can provide for your people. Some incentives are in the form of bonuses. Other incentives are advancement of responsibility within the firm. And sometimes employees get the small incentives they need when a task they've accomplished well is given compliments. Everyone needs to have goals to work towards, and if you explain in detail the incentives from the very beginning of your new employees' association with your firm, you'll appreciate the reward for their efforts.

Salespeople live for financial incentives. Some larger companies have competition within their sales department, and the awards given for achievements can be anything from cars to cruises. Since your firm will very likely never be that large, we've listed the breakout of the sales commission structure for North Coast. This will give you an idea of what works in the personnel industry.

For example, the first 25 (workable) job orders created in one week will earn $500.00 (this is $20.00 per order). Between 26 to 35 (workable) job orders in one week = $25.00 per order. All job orders over 35 created in one week will be paid at the rate of $30.00 per order.

An additional percentage was paid on the revenues earned from the placement fee. Not all job orders are filled. Some are closed for a variety of reasons. So I paid 3 percent of the paid placement fee. Since the average placement at North Coast was $1200.00, the salesperson received $40.00 of that earned revenue.

The reason I paid the sales staff a percentage of the revenue earned on placements made was to give them an incentive to bring in specific types of job orders. We were able to fill certain types of openings, and this was the area where the sales staff could generate the best return. It was not practical for them to bring orders in that were difficult to place or hard to work with. Once they figured out the standard workable orders, their sales contacts and calls were targeted more productively.

Performance reviews

One of your responsibilities is to provide performance reviews for all employees on a regular basis. This comes from evaluating the day-to-day interaction between yourself and your employee. The review should be conducted on or about the employee's anniversary date. You might want to review newer employees more often.

The primary reason for a performance review is to recognize obvious strengths and identify weaknesses. This reinforces good habits and works toward solutions to improve weaker areas. It also makes employees aware of how their job performance compares to your predesigned business goals and job description. Sometimes suggestions for additional training or classes can be discussed in this evaluation session.

These are the points covered in the performance review:
- Attendance, initiative, and effort.
- Knowledge of the work.
- Attitude and willingness.
- The quality and quantity of the work.
- The conditions under which the employee works.

An example of a performance evaluation form is in chapter 2.

VACATION, HOLIDAY, AND SICK-LEAVE POLICIES

How often will you let your people take time off? Will they get paid leaves, special holidays, and illness compensation? We've devoted a great deal of time and attention to this important facet of staffing.

Vacations

For a new employee, the standard vacation schedule is one week of paid vacation within the first year. Although some companies expect employees to work a full year without a vacation, I never thought this was really fair. Let employees schedule some time off after their first six months. It's acceptable to let them take their time any way they choose. Some will want to create a series of three-day weekends, and others will decide to get away and take it all at the same time.

Employees should be allowed to carry over vacation days each year and not be penalized for not taking the time off within the allotted year. There should be an understanding between you and employees that taking time off should never put you or the business in an awkward position. This is only common sense and courtesy.

After the first year, two weeks of paid vacation is standard. Then, only after five years does the vacation time extend to three weeks. It will remain at three weeks unless you decide to build other incentives into the vacation package. That is your prerogative, of course.

Holidays

There are standard holidays for all companies: New Year's Day, Easter, the afternoon of Good Friday, Memorial Day, Fourth of July, Labor Day, Thanksgiving, and Christmas. I generally closed my business when the banks were closed. This was a good indicator of normal work holidays.

One extra holiday was given to staff members of North Coast. They got paid to take their birthday off. If it landed on a Saturday or Sunday, I gave them the Friday before the weekend. They were all very appreciative of this and thanked me many times over.

Sick leave

Each employee should be given ½ day per month for sick leave. It can be accrued compensatory time or used as a cash payment, but only during the following calendar year.

BENEFITS PACKAGE AND PERKS

It's standard in today's business world to provide certain benefits and perks for your people. It's common in most offices to have a package for a variety of potential problems and situations.

Health plan benefit

A comprehensive health plan package is a wonderful benefit to offer your employees. Unfortunately, because it's extremely expensive, most often it's just not practical, especially if you're just a little company (fewer than five employees).

There are ways to adjust the benefit package to fit your payment plans. Some employers will choose to split the cost of the medical plan for the employees only, and not pay for (but provide) a policy that can cover employees' dependents.

Your selected insurance representative will give you all of the alternative plans available and their costs. It's not necessary to provide medical, dental, and optical. You might only want to pay for a part of the medical. Choose the plan that works the best for you and your budget.

We used the employees' desire for a good medical benefits package as an incentive goal. We all worked toward the goal of being able to afford the policy. Together, as a team, we made it happen. Without the goal being set, and the revenues generated, none of us were insured.

Life insurance benefit

Again, your insurance agent will provide all the information you need to select a life insurance policy for yourself and your staff.

Perks

Automotive expenses

Mileage The standard rate for mileage is $.25 per mile. This is only paid from the office to the location of the businesses contacted. It should never be calculated from the home to the businesses visited. Unless, of course, employees are traveling and are making their sales contacts directly from the motel. The two employees affected by this benefit are the salesperson and the person running the errands.

Fuel Reimburse all of the gas station receipts. Never expect employees to pay for their own gas while on company business.

Company car You might choose to provide a company vehicle for the salesperson. This is certainly not mandatory or expected.

Bridge and toll fares Bridge and toll fares are to be considered part of the automotive expense. Reimburse all receipts.

Parking Your offices might be located in a part of town that doesn't have free parking available for your employees. If this is the case, it's practical that the company pick up the monthly parking fees for the staff. If you don't, it can really put a dent into an already tight budget. Paying for their parking is another way of establishing good rapport with your employees. It's certainly not required, but it's really appreciated!

Lunches and dinners

It's expected that if your salesperson takes a client to lunch or dinner, the agency picks up the tab. This should never be the responsibility of the sales individual.

Motel

If the salesperson is trying to create business outside your normal target area, the company should pick up the motel or hotel expense. If the client contacts are within driving distance, there should be no motel expense.

OFFICE PROTOCOL

Standard protocol for business is simply using common sense when dealing with clients and interoffice issues. It covers areas such as dress code, telephone etiquette, interoffice communication, and business ethics.

Telephone calls

- Don't let the phone ring more than two times before answering—three rings at the very least.
- It's only practical for the closest and least busy person to answer an incoming phone call if the receptionist is busy.
- If the phones are really busy, don't ever answer the call and put the caller on hold without asking the caller if it's okay.

- Never leave someone on hold for more than a minute without getting back on the line to alert the caller of the continued delay.
- Always give callers a choice as to whether they would like to wait, call back, or receive a return call.
- Don't put a call through when an individual has asked for calls to be held.
- Always identify the caller when putting the call through.
- Don't tie up the lines with personal calls.
- Don't ever make personal long-distance calls without recording them on the long-distance calling sheet and reimbursing the company for your calls.

Clients (applicant)

- Greet incoming clients with professional courtesy and make them as comfortable as possible.
- Always keep them alerted as to the time constraints and changes in scheduling.
- Provide coffee, tea, or other refreshments.
- Be polite, personable, and communicative, but not nosy.
- Be aware of their comfort and offer to reschedule if necessary.
- Be professional at all times.
- Don't gossip.

Internal staff

- Delegate clearly, defining expectations and objectives. Welcome opinions and feedback from your coworkers.
- Try to offer help when you see that someone is having a problem.
- Don't create or be a part of interoffice gossip.
- Be supportive and respectful of each other all the time.

Dress code

- Wear clean and neat business clothes.
- No short skirts, heavy jewelry, or heavy makeup.
- No thongs or slippers.
- Jeans and/or pants are acceptable only when working on days when clients are not coming in (Saturdays).

EMPLOYEE HANDBOOK

See Fig. 10-1 for an example of an employee handbook.

Welcome To (Company)

Dear XXX:

We're delighted to welcome you to (Company). Thank you for joining us! We want you to feel that your association with (Company) will be a mutually beneficial and gratifying one.

You have joined a company that has established an outstanding reputation for quality personnel placement services. Of course, credit for this goes to every one of our existing staff. We hope you, too, will find gratification and take pride in your work here.

(Company) is dedicated to two standards:

1. To provide you with a salary and benefits package comparable to others doing similar work within the personnel industry and within our area.

2. To offer our customers the best-quality service at the most reasonable fees.

This manual will give you answers to most of the questions you may have about (Company)'s benefit programs, as well as the company policies and our procedures.

Compensation and personal satisfaction gained from doing a job well are only some of the reasons most people work. (Company) is committed to doing its part to assure you of a satisfying work environment.

I welcome you to our firm and offer my personal best wishes for your happiness and success at (Company).

Sincerely,

XXX, Owner
(Company)

BENEFITS

The value of your benefits amounts to a considerable sum each year in addition to the wages or salary you earn. These are just some of the benefits (Company) provides for eligible employees each year:

Annual Party or Outing

Dental Insurance

Disability Leave of Absence

Education Assistance

Group Term Life Insurance

Health Care/Hospital Insurance

Paid Holidays

Paid Vacations

Personal Leave of Absence

Profit-Sharing Plan

Short-Term Disability Insurance

Sick Leave

Social Security

Unemployment Compensation Insurance

Worker's Compensation Insurance

PURPOSE OF THIS MANUAL

This employee manual has been set up to educate you about (Company)'s philosophy, history, employment practices, and policies, as well as the conduct expected from you, and the benefits given to you as a valued employee.

Please do not hesitate to ask questions if there is a portion of this manual that needs explaining. We ask that you read this carefully and look at it often for reference.

RECEIPT & ACKNOWLEDGMENT OF (COMPANY) EMPLOYEE MANUAL

(Please have all employees read and sign at the bottom of this statement).

This manual is an important document designed to educate you about (Company's) policies. It is only intended to act as a guide. We are fully aware that all people are different, so individual circumstances may call for unique solutions.

Please read and sign the following statement to indicate your acknowledgment of the (Company) Employee Manual.

1. I have received and read a copy of the (Company) Employee Manual. I understand that the benefits, rules, and policies detailed in it are subject to change at the sole discretion of (Company).

2. I know that during the course of my employment with (Company), confidential information will be made available to me. This will be in the form of internal operations of clients' companies, pricing policies, customer lists, and other related information. I know that this information is essential to the success of (Company). In the event of my termination of employment with (Company), whether voluntary or not, I hereby agree not to use or exploit any of this information with any other company or individual.

3. I have received a copy of the (Company) Employee Manual. I also understand that my signature below indicates that I have read and understand the above statements.

Employee's Printed Name   Position

Employee's Signature   Date

Owner's Signature   Date

(Place the signed original copy of this agreement in the employee's personnel file)

TABLE OF CONTENTS

(Insert the appropriate page numbers)

A Welcome to (Company)

Benefits with (Company)

Purpose of This Manual

Acknowledgment of Employee Manual

An Overview of (Company)

1. Employment

Employment Policies

Standards of Conduct

ABOUT (COMPANY)

(Insert a brief description about the history of your company. Make sure to include:)

- When the company was formed

- Your company's location

- Who the founders are/were

- List services that your company offers

- Describe the purpose of your activities

- Consider including a mission statement

What Company Expects From You

Your first responsibility is to understand your job description and how to accomplish these duties quickly, accurately, and with a pleasant demeanor. Secondly, you are expected to cooperate with your fellow employees and management and maintain a positive team attitude. The results of these actions will be better performance for the company overall, and higher personal satisfaction for yourself.

This manual teaches you how you can positively perform to the best of your ability so that you can meet and exceed our expectations.

We have always believed in direct access to management. So we expect you to speak out and voice your constructive opinions and contribute your suggestions to improve the quality of our firm.

We need your help in making each working day enjoyable and rewarding. Your dignity and that of fellow employees, as well as that of our clients, is important. All of us here at (Company) look forward to working with you.

1. EMPLOYMENT

YOUR PERSONNEL FILE

It is important to keep your personnel file up-to-date. This simple action affects you with regard to pay, deductions, benefits, and other matters. If you have changed any one of the following, please be sure to correct the information in your file immediately:

1. Legal name

2. Home address

3. Home telephone number

4. Person to call in case of emergency

5. Number of dependents

6. Marital status

7. Change of beneficiary

8. Driving record or status of drivers license, if you operate any (Company) vehicles

9. Exemptions on your W-4 tax form

Employment Policies

APTITUDE & ABILITY TESTS

We may be giving you job-related tests to help determine your aptitude or ability to perform a specific job within our firm. Some tests may be given to individuals for position changes and promotions, as well as to new applicants. All of the test results will be confidential.

BUSINESS HOURS

Our regular operating hours are 8:00 a.m. to 5:00 p.m. Monday through Friday.

Your specific hours of employment and the scheduling of your lunch period will be determined by the owner of the company. Most employees of (Company) are assigned to work a 40-hour work week. You will be required to take one hour of unpaid lunch daily.

CONFIDENTIAL INFORMATION

Our clients entrust (Company) with important information relating to their businesses. The nature of this relationship requires essential confidentiality. By protecting the confidential information received, we earn the respect and further trust of our many clients.

You are obligated to maintain this confidentiality, even after you leave our employ.

CREDIT INVESTIGATION

(Company) reserves the right to conduct a credit check for financial stability at any time after you are hired. Your employment with (Company) may be conditional upon our review of the information of this credit check.

CUSTOMER RELATIONS

You are (Company)'s public representative, regardless of your position. The more professionalism you exhibit, the more our clients will respect and appreciate you, (Company) and our services.

Please follow these simple steps for good customer relations:

1. Always deal with clients in a courteous and respectful manner and act competently at all times.

2. Take great pride in your work and enjoy doing your very best.

3. Communicate respectfully and courteously with other employees at all times.

4. Follow up on all incoming job orders and any questions quickly. Always provide business-like replies to inquiries and requests, and perform all of your tasks in an orderly fashion.

DRIVERS LICENSE & DRIVING RECORD

(This only applies to employees who are required to drive as part of their job)

Employees must present and maintain a valid driver's license and a driving record acceptable to our insurers whose specific job duties require operation of a motor vehicle. Occasionally you will be asked to submit a copy of your driving record to (Company). If there are any changes in your driving record, you must report them to the owner right away. Failure to do so may result in possible dismissal.

INTRODUCTORY PERIOD

The introductory period is considered your first 90 days of employment at (Company). During this period of time, you will not accrue any of the benefits described in this employee manual unless otherwise required by law.

This introductory period will be a time for getting to know your manager, your fellow employees, and the functions involved with your position. It also is the time to become familiar with (Company)'s services. We will always work closely with you to help you understand the needs and intricacies of your job.

The introductory period is considered a testing ground for both you, as an employee, and (Company), as an employer. During this introductory period, you can evaluate (Company), and (Company) will evaluate your suitability for employment as well. You may resign without any detriment to your record at any time during this first 90 days. If, during this period, your attitude, performance, work habits or attendance do not meet our standards, we may release you from your employment with (Company). If you take approved time off by more than five working days during the introductory period, we will extend the introductory period by that length of time.

JOB DESCRIPTIONS

We keep a detailed job description for each position in (Company). When your responsibilities and duties are changed, your job description will be updated.

NONCOMPETE AGREEMENT

Certain new employees, such as outside/field salespeople and others, may be required to sign a noncompete agreement prepared by our attorney as a condition of employment.

SALESPERSON AGREEMENT

You will be asked to sign an agreement that cites certain terms and conditions regarding your position as a salesperson, when you are hired in or promoted to the position of salesperson. The purpose of this agreement is to clearly establish the terms for territory assignments, commission payments, etc.

WE ENCOURAGE YOUR VALUABLE INPUT

We believe the person functioning daily in the job is in the best position to think of ways of doing it more efficiently and more effectively. We will welcome your suggestions and ideas if you think of a better way of doing your job or the job of a fellow employee. Discuss these improvements with your manager.

These areas of improvement could be in service, communications, equipment, ways to reduce costs, losses, and/or wastes, or other improvements you may see a need for. We encourage you to always give us the benefit of your thoughts and experience. Remember, your individual suggestions could affect your profit-sharing check! These contributions may also affect your wage, salary, or promotion reviews.

Standards of Conduct

UNACCEPTABLE ACTIVITIES

Negligence or any careless action which endangers any other person.

Willful violation of any company rule.

Unauthorized possession of dangerous or illegal firearms, weapons, or explosives on company property or while on duty.

Being intoxicated or under the influence of controlled substance drugs while at work.

Use or possession for sale of controlled substance drugs in any quantity while on company premises except medication prescribed by a physician which does not affect work performance.

Insubordination or refusing to obey instruction by your manager regarding your work; refusing to help out on a special assignment when asked.

Engaging in acts of violence or criminal conduct, or making threats of violence toward anyone on company premises or when representing (Company).

Theft of company property or the property of your fellow employees.

Threatening, intimidating or coercing fellow employees on or off the premises—for any purpose, at any time.

Giving confidential (Company) information to any competitors or other organizations.

Dishonesty, or willful falsification on your job application for employment or other work records, lying about personal or sick leave, changing company records or other company documents in any way.

Excessive use of company telephone for personal calls. Excessive absence or lateness, or failure to report an absence or late arrival.

Immoral conduct or indecency on company property.

DISCIPLINARY ACTIONS

Unacceptable behavior which does not lead to immediate dismissal may be dealt with in the following manner:

A. Verbal Warning

First Written Warning

Second Written Warning

Third Written Warning

Dismissal

(OR)

B. Verbal Warning

First Written Warning

Dismissal

All written warnings will include any supporting evidence and the reasons for the manager's dissatisfaction. At the time the warning is issued, you will have an opportunity to defend your actions and rebut the opinion of your manager. Disciplinary actions may include fines, suspensions, or other measures deemed appropriate by the manager.

DISMISSAL

(For more information, contact the National Conference of Commissioners on Uniform State Laws at 676 N St. Claire Street, Suite 1700, Chicago, IL 60611, (312) 921-0195).

Employment and compensation with (Company) is at will in that you can be terminated with or without cause, and with or without notice, at any time, at the option of either (Company) or yourself, except as otherwise provided by law.

You will be notified of the problem if your performance is unsatisfactory due to lack of ability, failure to abide by (Company) rules, or failure to fulfill the requirements of your job. You may be dismissed if satisfactory changes do not occur. Some incidents may result in immediate dismissal.

2. COMPENSATION & PERFORMANCE

Wage & Salary Policies

We are happy to report that our wage and salary policy is designed to attract and retain the best-qualified people available. (Company) has developed policies to insure wages and salaries comparable to those of other employees with similar jobs at (Company) or in the personnel industry.

DEDUCTIONS FROM PAYCHECK (MANDATORY)

(Company) is required by law to make certain deductions from each paycheck that is issued to you. Included in these are your federal, state, and local income taxes and your contribution to Social Security, as required by law. All of these deductions are itemized on your check stubs. The size of the deductions depends entirely on your earnings and on the information you give us on your W-4 form regarding the number of dependents/ exemptions you choose to claim. When there are any changes in name, address, telephone number, marital status, or number of exemptions, we ask that you report this information to the owner immediately. This is done to ensure proper credit for tax purposes. At the end of the year, your W-2 form that you receive indicates specifically how much of your earnings were deducted for these categories.

OVERTIME PAY

(Overtime pay for work in excess of 8 hours per day or 40 hours per week is only required in certain states. Check with your attorney on state and local laws regarding overtime, and modify this policy accordingly.)

Occasionally it may be necessary for you to work overtime hours in order to complete a specific job in a timely manner. The overtime hours fall into two categories:

1. Scheduled overtime announced in advance.

(OR)

2. Incidental overtime in response to extenuating circumstances.

PAY CYCLES

(As the owner of your firm, you may select a pay cycle from these categories):

1. Calendar Pay Period/Semimonthly

24 pay periods per year. Payday is normally on the 1st and 15th of every month for services performed for the period ending five (5) days

previous—the 25th of the prior calendar month and the 10th of the

month respectively.

2. Fiscal Pay Period/Biweekly

26 pay periods per year. Payday is normally on every other Friday

afternoon for services performed for the two-week period ending the

previous Saturday at 12:00 midnight.

3. Fiscal Pay Period/Weekly

52 pay periods per year. Payday is normally on Friday afternoon for

services performed for the one-week period ending the previous

Saturday at 12:00 midnight.

Changes will be made and announced in advance whenever (Company)

holidays or closing interfere with normal payday.

Performance & Salary Reviews

PERFORMANCE REVIEWS

(Set standards for performance to avoid discrimination charges and

assure fairness at all times).

Your manager is continuously evaluating your job performance. The day-to-day relationship between you and your manager should give you an idea of how your manager sees your job performance.

(Company) conducts a formal review once a year for each employee, to avoid haphazard or incomplete evaluations. These performance reviews will be accomplished on the employee's anniversary date. Brand-new employees will be reviewed more frequently.

During formal performance reviews, your manager will consider the following things, among others:

- Knowledge of your work

- Attendance, initiative, and effort

- Attitude and willingness

- The quality and quantity of your work

- The conditions under which you work

The primary reason for performance reviews is to help you identify your strengths and weaknesses. This will help to reinforce your good habits and give you an opportunity to work on ways to improve in your weaker areas. This review also makes you aware of how your personal job performance relates to the description of your job and the goal of (Company). This is the perfect time to discuss your professional interests and future goals with the firm. Since we are primarily interested in helping you to progress and grow in order to achieve personal as well as work-related goals, perhaps we can recommend further training or additional opportunities for you.

(Company) periodically reviews employee job descriptions to make sure that we are completely aware of any change in the duties and responsibilities of each position. We want to ensure that these changes are recognized and adequately compensated.

SALARY REVIEWS

(The salary review often follows a performance appraisal and is intended to determine if a raise is appropriate. This policy is very important since we know that many employees would rather quit than ask for a raise.)

(Company) wage and salary increases are based on merit and cost-of-living. Having your compensation evaluated does not necessarily mean that you will be given a salary increase.

(Company) has compensation reviews annually at the time of each employee's anniversary date. Any wage or salary increases will appear in the pay period ending after the dates they are granted. Wage and salary increases may be retroactive in the case of late reviews.

Work Schedule

ABSENCE OR LATENESS

(Company) is aware that illnesses, emergencies, or important personal business that cannot be scheduled outside your work hours may come up. We have provided sick days and personal days for this purpose.

If you are unable to report to work, or plan to arrive late, please contact the office immediately and let someone know. Give us as much time as possible to arrange for someone else to cover your position until you arrive. If you know in advance that you will need to be absent, we ask that you request this time off directly from your manager.

ATTENDANCE

You are required to be at work at the beginning of your assigned daily work schedule, and you are expected to stay at work until the end of your assigned work hours, except for approved breaks and lunch.

Be aware that excessive time off could lead to disciplinary action.

BREAKS

You are entitled to two fifteen-minute rest breaks each day. Normally these rest breaks are scheduled during mid-morning and mid-afternoon times. Always be sure to return on time at the end of any of these breaks.

EXCESSIVE ABSENTEEISM OR LATENESS

Five absences within a 90-day period, or a consistent pattern of absence will be considered excessive. The specific reasons for the absences may be questioned. Leaving early or tardiness is as detrimental to (Company) as an absence. Three of these incidents during a 90-day period will be considered a tardiness pattern. They will carry the same weight and penalty as an absence. The degree of lateness may be considered as another factor.

3. BENEFITS

The Benefits Package

You will be eligible to enjoy other benefits, in addition to receiving an equitable salary, which will enhance your job satisfaction. We are certain that you will agree that the benefits program described in this employee manual represents a very large investment by (Company), and we trust that you will avoid abusing any of the program's benefits.

A good benefits package ensures the loyalty of long-time employees and also helps to attract talented newcomers who can help us grow.

ELIGIBILITY OF BENEFITS

You will enjoy all of the benefits described in this manual if you are a full-time employee, as soon as you meet the eligibility requirements for each benefit.

No benefits are available to you during your introductory period, unless otherwise provided by law.

Paid Leaves of Absence

Time off for any reason will count first against your allotted sick days or personal days. These will be deducted, as appropriate, in hourly, quarter-day, half-day or full-day increments. Once you have used up all of your earned personal or sick days, the time will be counted against your earned vacation time. Any time off after that, unless specifically excepted, will be without pay.

HOLIDAYS

Only full-time employees of (Company) are eligible for holiday pay.

You are not eligible to receive holiday pay during your introductory period. Nor are you eligible to receive holiday pay if you are a part-time employee or a temporary employee.

Recognized Holidays

The following holidays are recognized by (Company) as paid holidays:

Christmas Eve (½ day)

Christmas Day

Independence Day

Labor Day

Memorial Day

New Year's Day

Thanksgiving Day

The Friday following Thanksgiving Day

Veterans Day

Employee Birthday

Good Friday (12:00 - 5:00)

Other possible holidays include:

Day Before New Year's Day

Washington's Birthday

Floating Holiday

Lincoln's Birthday

Columbus Day

Martin Luther King's Birthday

Marriage Anniversary Day

Day Baby is Born

Jewish Holidays

Holiday Policies

You may take time off to observe your religious holidays. You must notify us at least ten business days in advance of this holiday. If available, a full day of unused (sick/personal) leave or a vacation day may be used for this purpose. Otherwise, the time off is without pay.

You are not eligible to receive holiday pay when you are on leave of absence.

VACATIONS

(In some states employees become eligible for, and start accruing vacation, after six months of employment. Check with your attorney on your state and local laws regarding paid vacations, and modify this policy accordingly.)

Full-time employees are the only employees who are eligible for paid vacations. Eligibility begins after the introductory period of 90 days. Part-time and temporary employees are not eligible for paid vacations unless otherwise agreed upon by the owner.

This vacation time is designed for you to relax, enjoy your personal time, and pursue any special interests. This paid vacation is one of the many ways we like to show our appreciation for a job well done.

Vacation Policies

We will make every effort to grant you your scheduled vacation time. Since it cannot interfere with your job, we ask that you give us at least 30 days' notice so a replacement can be scheduled during the time you plan to be away.

If you are on an approved leave of absence for less than 30 days, your vacation eligibility will not be affected. If the leave of absence extends beyond 30 days, vacation time will not continue to accrue.

You will receive an additional day off if a company-paid holiday falls during your scheduled vacation period.

Accumulation Rights

Vacation time may not be carried over and/or accumulated in ensuing calendar years. Exceptions to this policy may be made in unusual circumstances, each case to be considered separately by the owner.

Payment in Lieu of Vacation

No additional wages or salary will be paid to you in lieu of a vacation unless advance approval in writing is granted by the owner. We want you to be able to relax and enjoy your free time. We know that it is one of the best ways to recharge your batteries and come back to work with a renewed energy and positive frame of mind.

OTHER PAID LEAVES

Sick Leave

You will be required to complete your 90-day introductory period before any paid sick leave is granted. We allow the sick time to be used in as little as two increments, so that if you have a doctor's appointment, you need not be docked for the entire day.

The sick leave policy will not apply if you are off work because of an illness or injury that is covered by worker's compensation.

These sick days cannot accumulate year after year. At the end of the calendar year, the unused sick days will be totaled and calculated at your regular base rate. A check for the unused sick days will be issued in that amount.

INSURANCE COVERAGE

(Let the employees know which portion of premium costs that the company pays for and how long they have to wait before being eligible for coverage. Provide booklets that describe the insurance package to your staff.)

Group Insurance

(Some insurance policies and laws may require that all employees are covered. Check with your attorney and adjust accordingly.)

We are very interested in the health and well-being of both you and your family. Because of that, a comprehensive health and life insurance program is made available to you. A national insurance carrier underwrites the group insurance we provide for our employees. You are eligible for this coverage after your 90-day introductory period is completed.

The following benefits are provided:

Group Term Life Insurance

Major Medical and Surgical Coverage

Dental Care Coverage

Vision Care Coverage

Medical Health Care Coverage

If you choose insurance coverage, our insurance carrier will provide a detailed booklet describing the benefits package. When you join the program, you will be given a copy of this.

(A participation of cost breakdown is at the beginning of this chapter, under Create Benefits, Perks, etc.)

Disability Insurance

(Each company is required under federal law to provide leave of absence time for disability due to pregnancy to be equal to that allowed for disabilities that affect anyone. You may want to have your insurance carrier review this section.)

If you are a regular full-time employee, you are protected through a short-term disability insurance policy. This is designed to protect you from financial hardship if you are totally disabled because of illness or accident that is not job related.

The definition of total disability is the inability to perform any position (Company) has available. (Remember, worker's compensation benefits protect you if you are involved in a job-related accident or sickness.)

Health & Dental Insurance

(Your insurance carrier should provide you with a brief summary of the health and dental coverage. Include it in this section.)

(Company) has selected the plan we feel provides the best coverage for our employees. Refer to the literature provided by the insurance carrier for details of this coverage.

Life Insurance

(Your insurance carrier should provide you with a brief summary of the life insurance coverage. Include it in this section.)

Regular full-time employees are covered by this policy. It is payable in the event of your death from any cause, at any time or place, while you are employed with (Company). Refer to the literature provided by our insurance carrier for details of this policy.

Termination of Insurance

Your policy will terminate when you fail to make an agreed contribution to the premium when due, when you cease to be eligible for coverage, when you cease to be employed as a regular full-time employee or when the insurance policy terminates.

Government-Required Coverage

(Have your attorney review this section and adjust according to your state requirements.)

The California Worker's Compensation Law is a no-fault insurance plan which is directed by the state and is 100 percent paid for by (Company). This law was designed to provide you with benefits for any injury which you may suffer in connection with your employment. If you are injured while at work, you are eligible to apply for worker's compensation, under the provisions of the law.

Every employee, whether full-time or part-time, is protected by worker's compensation. (Company) and the worker's compensation insurance carrier work together to insure that your medical expenses are taken care of. They also pay you money to live on until you are able to come back to work, if you are unable to work because of job injury.

Coverage begins from the first day of employment and continues until employment with (Company) ceases.

The benefits are:

Medical care to take care of the injury, including not only doctor bills, but also medicines, hospital costs, fees for lab work, X-rays, crutches, etc. There is no deductible and all costs incurred by these injuries are paid directly to the worker's compensation carrier.

Rehabilitation services necessary to return to work. This is simply an extension of your medical treatment. If you are unable to return to work because of the injury, you may qualify for vocational rehabilitation services and job retraining. All costs are paid directly by (Company) through our worker's compensation carrier.

Cash payments for lost wages. The most common kind of payments, for temporary disability will be made for as long as the doctor says you're unable to work. If there is a permanent handicap, additional cash payments may be made after you are able to work. If the injury results in death, payments will be paid to your surviving dependents.

Unemployment Compensation

(Check with your attorney on your state and local laws and modify accordingly.)

If you become unemployed, you may be eligible for unemployment compensation, for a limited period, under certain conditions. We are required to pay a percentage of our payroll to the Unemployment Compensation Fund according to (Company)'s employment history. This compensation provides temporary income for workers who have lost their jobs. To be eligible, you must have earned a certain amount and be willing and able to work. These benefits can be applied for through your local state unemployment office as soon as possible.

Social Security

Our government designed a system of contributory insurance known as Social Security. You are required, as a wage earner, by law, to contribute a set amount of your weekly wages to the trust fund. Benefits are paid from this fund. (Company) is required to deduct this amount from each of the paychecks you receive. We are paying one-half of the cost of your Social Security benefits because (Company) matches your contribution dollar for dollar.

Profit Sharing

PROFIT-SHARING PLAN

(Company) grants a profit-sharing award on an annual basis determined by the profitability of the firm. The amount of any award represents a fixed percentage. All regular full-time employees are eligible for the profit-sharing plan once they have completed six months of employment.

The complete details of the profit-sharing plan will be given to you when you become eligible.

Other Benefits

EDUCATION / TRAINING

(Company) will pay for seminars or training sessions that are designed to enhance your productivity. We know that this will be a personal investment of your time, but the rewards to yourself and (Company) are justified.

We may arrange to have both formal and informal training programs for you. If you become aware of a seminar or workshop that will be educational, contact us immediately, and we will make every attempt to register you in the class. You will receive a normal paycheck while attending these workshops. The expenses for off-premises training will be paid for by (Company).

You are encouraged to ask questions and learn more about (Company) and the services we offer.

4. OTHER POLICIES

ANNUAL PARTY

(Company) schedules at least one yearly party. This annual celebration usually is the Christmas party, and all of our clients and business associates are invited to join us in the celebration of the holidays.

BONUSES

We try to distribute annual merit bonuses when our profits allow. These bonuses are rated on these factors:

Attitude

Cooperation

Attendance

Initiative

Efficiency

Performance

Knowledge

Length of service

Salary

STAFF MEETINGS

Every morning from 8:30 a.m. to 9:00 a.m., we hold a staff meeting to discuss the previous day's business, business of the day, and any other topical points of interest. Suggestions and ideas are encouraged in these meetings, and any news regarding our competitors in the personnel industry is welcomed.

DRESS CODE & PERSONAL APPEARANCE

You will be expected to dress yourself in accordance with the accepted social and business standards in our industry. This is especially critical if your position involves dealing with clients and visitors in person.

It is your responsibility to present a neat and tasteful appearance at all times. This makes a favorable impression with our clients and promotes professionalism in the workplace.

Your self-confidence and poise are greatly affected by the clothes you choose to wear. Evaluate the dress code of your fellow workers, and match this code accordingly.

EXPENSE REIMBURSEMENT

You must submit an expense report to be reimbursed for all authorized expenses. These expense vouchers should also be accompanied by receipts and approved by the owner before reimbursement occurs.

When you are required to use your own vehicle on company related business, you will be reimbursed $.XX per mile.

GRIEVANCE & SUGGESTIONS

We welcome your suggestions, regardless of whether or not you feel a problem or idea is large or small. In order to promote satisfaction in the workplace, (Company) feels that it's essential to operate a successful and efficient company. This only happens through your valued input, your creative ideas, and helpful suggestions.

MANAGERS

The person selected to act as your manager is the one who is closest to you and your work. Since you will have day-to-day contact with this person, it will give you an opportunity to receive counsel and guidance regarding your tasks. This manager will teach you new things, show you how your work fits into the scheme of the business, and help you through any difficult times.

This manager was very likely functioning at some time in the past in your job position. Because of this, the manager is more than qualified to help you in many, many areas.

Your manager has the authority to recommend pay increases, maintain order, assign work tasks, and hire and dismiss.

PERSONAL PHONE CALLS

Please be considerate and keep your personal phone calls to a minimum. Our phone bills are extremely high as it is. We have designed a long-distance report form for you to record any and all long-distance calls made from your station. This report form will be submitted each month to the bookkeeper. They will then be able to charge the appropriate caller for the expense. We appreciate your honesty in this area.

SMOKING

Please don't smoke in areas where it may be offensive to your coworkers or when you are directly servicing a client. Always be courteous and concerned about the needs of the nonsmokers. Smoking is prohibited in the office. Designated areas are made available for the smokers of (Company).

USE OF COMPANY VEHICLE

These are the rules for using a (Company) vehicle for business:

1. You must be a licensed driver.

2. You must maintain and submit weekly mileage reports.

3. You are responsible for paying any tickets.

4. You are responsible for standard vehicle maintenance.

5. You must not allow unauthorized people to ride in said vehicle.

6. You must keep the vehicle clean at all times.

TRAINING MANUAL

Once your company expands to the level of several employees, and/or several offices, you won't be able to train all employees. Because of this, it will be necessary to create an individual training manual for each staff member. Included in the manual are the following:

Job description

A complete and thorough accounting of all the duties to be performed by this person. The personnel agency job descriptions are in the beginning of this chapter.

Hours

Define the work schedule for all of the hours and days that the employee is expected to perform.

Supervision

This is the chain-of-command section. Explain who the employee will be reporting to for guidance and problem solving, and why.

Qualifications

There should be a complete list of the required experiences, per position, for each newly hired staff member. The job descriptions and qualification are covered at the beginning of this chapter.

Expectations

Create a specific and carefully recorded time line for the new employee. This spells out the expectations and additional work duties to be performed within a certain allotted period of time. In other words, how much time will be spent on office protocol, how much time on company policy, and how much time to learn the systems and procedures? When will employees be expected to be up and running and completely on their own?

HIRING AND FIRING

Each state has its own legal requirements for bringing someone on board and for letting them go. The discrimination laws in every state are specific, and these guidelines have to be met or harsh penalties will be paid. The following are the steps to follow when hiring and firing employees:

Hiring a new employee

1. Assess the need to add a new person to your company. This might be recognized when either you or someone on your staff is working overtime

to fulfill the demands. Don't be fooled and think you need to hire someone permanent when it might simply be a seasonal employee who is needed. Hiring might also occur when you reach the stage of expansion, create a new division, or open a branch office.

2. Design a complete and thorough job description and the qualifications you feel are necessary for the position to be adequately performed.
3. Set up the specific work schedule required for this individual (hours, days).
4. Advertise for the position. This might take longer than you expect, so give yourself at least a month to recruit, and don't hire until you've found someone with all the skills you need. Other ways of finding employees are:
   - Preregistered applicants
   - Newspaper help-wanted ad
   - Word of mouth/networking
   - Association contacts
   - Schools
   - Walk-ins
5. Screen the response to your advertisement. It's not necessary to meet all the people who respond to your ad. You can discuss the position on the phone, review the résumés, and pick only the people who you feel are just right.
6. Interview the top three choices. Set up at least an hour in the beginning to meet with these applicants. Follow all the state legal guidelines for nondiscriminatory interviewing. Don't schedule the interviews back-to-back. You need time to think about each person overnight and give yourself that first-thing-in-the morning reaction.
7. Check the applicants' work references. Afterwards, be sure to contact the people they have worked for in the past. Owner-to-owner references are very satisfying. Remember, the names applicants give you to make reference calls to are people who are primed and ready to receive your call. You might want to call applicants' previous employers, whether their names are on the applicants' reference list or not.
8. Call the individual back in for a second interview. This time, introduce him or her to your next in command (office manager).
9. Offer the position. State the salary, benefit package, perks, and any other data that's pertinent. When you do make the offer, be prepared to negotiate until you get what you want.
10. Introduce the applicant to the rest of your existing staff members.
11. Walk the applicant through the offices and show the applicant his or her work station. Don't overwhelm the new employee with details on the very first day. Let the new employee come in refreshed and ready to learn before you begin training.
12. Describe the company policies, and give the applicant your company's employee handbook.
13. Have the new employee fill out a W2 form for accounting purposes.
14. Set up a file for this employee, with his or her job application, résumé, W2, letters of recommendation, test results, and any other data that's pertinent to this individual.
15. Begin the training program.

Firing an existing employee

Please contact your local regulations office and get a copy of the laws pertaining to firing a member of your staff. Each state has its own set of policies regarding this sensitive area.

An employee is far more likely to file a wrongful discharge suit with a previous employer than file an illegal interview and selection situation. This is because an applicant doesn't have an existing relationship with the new firm, but he or she might have an emotionally charged relationship with the firm that's letting them go. Be very, very careful.

Don't confuse the term lay off with fire. The two terms mean two completely different things. When you lay someone off, it means the employee's payroll is not being justified. You might have reached a slow period, or something you thought would work didn't. Either way, there's simply not enough money in the cash reserves to pay this person.

When you fire an employee, it could be for several reasons.
- Low productivity.
- Theft.
- Misconduct.
- Extensive unreported or unexplained absence.

Before you fire someone, it's mandatory that you give him or her three written warnings. Each warning must be on paper, dated, and signed by both parties. The rest of the specifics about firing have to come from your own regulatory board.

11
Marketing and public relations

Some people spend a tremendous amount of time and effort creating the most exciting service or product in the world. But they don't know how to develop a workable system to present their company description and products or services to the general public. These businesses will inevitably fail.

PACKAGING AND MARKETING

Packaging and marketing are the key to all successful enterprises, regardless of their size. Always remember those two words. They really pack a wallop as far as we're concerned. We've seen so many potentially viable and productive companies fail because they didn't understand the crucial need for packaging and marketing. It's really such a simple concept, and yet too many business owners fail to realize the importance of this crucial facet of the company. It's not logical to work diligently toward growth and success for your company and not put every tool you've learned about sales and marketing to use. Refer back to this chapter often for ideas as your company expands. We've listed a few guidelines to follow that we feel will help you create a strong, response-getting advertising campaign.

Sell the sizzle, not the steak!

This is a very old advertising truism. It simply means sell the actions of your service, not the service itself. There's nothing wrong with selling the services and features of your company, but if you don't spell out how the client will benefit from these services, your carefully placed advertisement won't draw the maximum response of your potential clients. Always be straightforward and use plain, simple English. If you keep your ad copy at a level that's understandable by an 11- or 12-year-old child, you won't lose much of your audience.

Repetition, repetition, repetition!

Repetition works because the more times people hear or read about your service, the more believable the message becomes. Also, if you remember that timing is everything, you'll agree that clients might not need your service the first, tenth, or twentieth time they see or hear the ad. But eventually they'll have the need, as all people do. When they have an employment problem, they want a service that's professional, consistent, reliable, and available! Try to keep the sales pitch the same, but consider adding a slightly new slant to the features and benefits every other time you run the ad.

Some of the tools we're going to share with you might be best implemented in the future development stages of your agency. This is because these business practices are most successful once you've developed a solid reputation in the personnel industry. There's a tremendous amount of information for you to review and put into practice. Some call it getting more bang for the buck.

MARKETING PLAN

Gather information about what works for other companies before you prepare your personalized marketing plan for your business. Without this important preliminary study, you could spend many wasteful years trying different methods of advertising before you finally find one that works for you. It's not necessary to reinvent the wheel. As you research the successful companies, glean the most effective ideas for your own service, and tailor them to fit the needs of your unique creation. Learn to emulate the strengths of others who are successful with their advertising.

Time lines and goals are the basis of the marketing plan. Develop a short-term and long-range plan. These are some of the questions you should be asking yourself:
- How much time do I expect these projects to take?
- How much of a return on my investment do I expect to make?
- What goal am I working towards?
- Once I've achieved that goal, what's next?

It's essential that you put all of this information into an easy-to-read reference manual for yourself and your staff. This manual should be reviewed constantly and added to often. Be flexible and adaptable with your marketing plan. Some of the things you attempt will not show the return you anticipate. That's simply the price of doing business. Just be willing to learn from all your mistakes.

Your salespeople should almost memorize this binder and treat it like the valuable tool it is. As they work from your predeveloped system, it will be rewarding to watch them begin to produce effective job orders for yourself and your counselors. This manual will also define your territory, so the salesperson doesn't wander!

Some companies hire professional marketing firms to promote their businesses. This is acceptable, as long as you carefully select the firm that will do the best job for you. Go into their offices prepared with as much information as you can.

We've included a series of questions to ask a potential advertising agency:
- What information is needed from you to get started?
- Does the advertising agency fee include cost of ads: newspapers, television, radio, etc?
- What is the time frame?
- Short-term cost versus long-term relationship. (Project versus ongoing relationship.)
- What does the advertising agency provide in its services package? Cost breakdown?
- Do you have a referral list of previous clients?
- How do we start?

- Do you give us an indication of the return we can expect on our investment?
- How many meetings are required?
- Where do we meet? Your office or mine?
- Do you have a brochure?
- Can you tell us what we can expect for $1,000, $3,000, $5,000, etc.?

Give the agency the list of your business goals, the tools you have to work with, and your budget. The agency will then take this information and prepare a marketing proposal to present at your next meeting. Agency fees are high, but the expertise is invaluable. It can be worth seeing what the agency can do for you.

It's okay to set goals that are high. We're fortunate to live in a country that lets you reach for what you want. Try anything that you want. When you believe in yourself and have a professional attitude and a sound marketing plan, you can and will achieve tremendous success!

EXCLUSIVE ACCOUNTS

Securing an exclusive account takes a lot of patience, consistency, and unwavering business ethics. One of your primary goals will be to work diligently toward developing a high percentage of these exclusive accounts. These are client companies that choose to work specifically with your agency and no other. Creating this one-on-one relationship, with as many accounts as possible, is one of your ongoing marketing strategies.

The right time to approach the company for exclusivity is when you have just completed a successful recruitment. Don't try to win the company's approval until this happens. This is the perfect opportunity to make an arrangement to solidify all future business deals.

Convince the owner or manager that your service can and will offer the most effective placements available. Offer a guarantee. If the placement you make doesn't work out, for any reason, the next placement is provided at no charge! You might have to give up a little in the beginning to get a strong return in the end. But, as we've said many times before, keep your eye on your goals, and don't lose track of the reason for nurturing these valuable accounts.

Some companies will easily switch over to your services with little more than one good placement. Others will take much longer to make the move. A few will need special attention. It will require going the extra step. Go out of your way to prove to them that you're serious about wanting their business on an exclusive contract.

We've included a series of tools that have worked in the past:
- Always be pleasant, thorough, and specific when taking the job order.
- Schedule an appointment with the decision maker to review the job order and evaluate the company.
- Be first with the qualified interviewees when sharing an order with another agency.
- Always be prompt when returning calls.
- Be sure to follow up all business dealings with the appropriate letters on your stationery.
- Always treat company representatives with respect and sensitivity.
- Thank them for their business.
- Invite them to lunch or dinner to discuss your business relationship.

- Invite them to join your business association and take them to their first meeting and introduce them as your guest.
- Send flowers, balloons, or a card to the owner or manager on his or her birthday.

As you can see, it takes special attention to develop these exclusive accounts. You have to work much harder and spend more money and time when other agencies are involved in a shared recruitment process. Once you obtain this valuable relationship, nurture the account and always maintain the same quality business practices that drew them to you in the first place.

NETWORKING

The term networking was made popular in the '80s and has carried over into the business world of the '90s. It simply means spreading the word about your services to as many people as possible.

There are many resources available to you. Most entrepreneurs have strong social connections. These are your family, friends, and business associates that you see at meetings, parties, lunches, coffee, dinners, or talk to on the telephone. Keeping a steady flow of communication with these people also gives you an opportunity to keep abreast of business news. Keep in touch periodically, but don't overdo it.

Networking isn't costly and only takes time from your busy schedule. You will be attending monthly association meetings, visiting friends, or volunteering your time for a committee position. Marketing your services in this manner keeps your image constantly out there. People begin to see and recognize your face. After a period of time, they make the connection between who you are and what you do. It's a good idea to have your staff involved in networking for your business also. Explain to them how effective this advertising strategy is, and teach them how to represent your firm.

Be patient and consistent with this form of sales, as it's difficult to see the return quickly. It's a slow but methodical and effective way to get the positive word out to the public about your wonderful personnel service.

BUSINESS ASSOCIATIONS

Contact your local chamber of commerce and request a current list of business associations for your target area. The chamber of commerce normally doesn't charge for this service, and it will give you a quick review of the association name, contact person, and phone number. When you decide to attend your first meeting, call the contact person first and make the appropriate arrangements.

Since you'll be spending time with this group for quite a while, it's best to attend several different groups and pick the two that feel the most comfortable. Just make sure that the clubs you choose will make productive use of your time. Plan to schedule three to five lunch or dinner meetings, per month, for your association contacts.

Join committees within the associations that interest you and become actively involved in the group. This helps you establish a working relationship with other business people. It's also enjoyable spending time with people who share the same responsibilities as you do. These people are also business owners, and sharing the trials and tribulations of business with your peers is comforting.

Plan to sit next to a new person at each meeting you attend. Get to know them well enough to ask for their card at the end of the meeting, and give them two of yours. If possible, try to schedule some time that's convenient to both of your schedules to meet with this person away from the association meeting place. This is so you can learn more about the person's company and let him or her know all about yours. You might want to suggest a lunch meeting or an appointment at either office.

Once you're involved with the group, try to encourage new membership with the business contacts you make. A personnel agency is one type of company that's in constant contact with all different types of businesses. You have great influence and the perfect opportunity to expand a membership roster.

Your employees should also become members of a different association. They will do the same things you're doing: networking, joining committees, learning, sharing, and being a part of the business community. Attend the first meeting with them and get the ball rolling. Always pick up the expense of annual membership dues and meals.

Our association contacts were some of the most valuable and resourceful revenue generators for our business. Members referred clients to us and we, in turn, constantly sent business their way whenever possible. This is one of the most profitable forms of marketing available to you and your staff. Use it carefully, and watch the revenue increase.

BUSINESS CONTACTS

Almost everyone you come into contact with, have a conversation with, or do business with has to be considered a business contact. Applicant clients are business contacts. So are employer clients. Social contacts made through association meetings and all the people on the association roster lists are potential contacts.

Last, but not least, are your friends and family. These are business contacts, too. Anyone who is interested in hearing about what you do, how you do it, and what you need in order to do more is a good business contact.

PUBLIC SPEAKING ENGAGEMENTS

How do you feel about speaking in front of groups? If the answer is "no problem," then look into giving some luncheon and dinner presentations. This is another form of marketing that's also extremely productive. When you're standing in front of a roomful of people, you're reaching a large number of potential clients in a concentrated period of time. If you make a strong impression with your speech, they will remember you and your company.

Try to select a topic that relates to the group that has invited you. Whenever I talked to a group of women, I discussed the challenges of single parenting and ownership of a business. Many of these businesswomen could relate to the frustrations and see themselves as part of a group, not quite so alone.

When talking to civic groups, I covered topics that were community-based and affected large groups of people. Career change topics are always an interesting area to cover. These topics also encourage some people to eventually come into your business for more information.

You can get things started by contacting your local chamber of commerce again. Get the local public-speaking group roster and put your name on the list. But don't just wait to be called. Volunteer your time when you attend your local meetings, and ask business friends how you would go about speaking to their groups. Get creative with this marketing avenue. It's not only fun, but also extremely profitable. High profile! That's the key.

COLLEGE AND VOCATIONAL SEMINARS

I developed a course on job searching called How to Successfully Control Your Job Search. This was a short course that was originally taught at the local junior college in my community, and I eventually taught it at several colleges and trade institutions. It became so popular that inquiries for registration came to the college long before the catalogue was mailed to the community.

You can set this up by contacting your local junior college and asking for information on developing a short course. After you receive the information, prepare the course outline, course description, cost and time schedule, and send it back to the college for review. My seminar was a six-hour class and was only taught on one Saturday from 9:00 a.m. to 4:00 p.m. I offered the class in the late spring, on three separate Saturdays. The charge was $45.00 per student.

Every time this class was offered, it was filled to maximum seating capacity (about 45 students). Not only did North Coast generate revenues from the students attending the class, but we also saw several students register with the agency for future placement assistance.

Once the initial curriculum was developed and the handouts for the students were prepared, the rest of the work was minimal. This class only took up one day of my time and usually generated about $1,000 for the Saturday. But the revenue generated by the agency for the placement of the students was phenomenal. This can be a great money-maker for your business, too.

ENDORSEMENT REFERRAL SYSTEM

The endorsement referral system is a marketing strategy I developed when in the seventh year of operating my business. I worked under the premise that most new sales contacts would be much more inclined to talk with me, or my salesperson, if they had received an endorsement referral letter from someone they trusted, prior to my call.

Once I refined this system of sales, it became the most exciting program I'd ever had the pleasure to work. It was easy to implement and completely eliminated the frustration of cold calls. It also increased my company's revenues 150 percent in one year! This is how it works:

Make a list of the clients that you, as a business owner, do business with on a consistent basis. This will include firms such as your printer, accountant, attorney, insurance representative, supplier, computer consultant, management consultant, and anyone else you feel especially connected to. These are the types of contacts I call your core accounts. They are the people who have become business friends of yours and that you have a strong working relationship with.

First, contact the companies with a business letter that announces your plans to increase your market base and expand your firm. Since you have been using these business services for several years, it's very likely you have also placed employees within the companies. When you prepare the letter, include the following information:

- Tell them how glad you are to have them as business associates and friends, and how thankful you are for their professional service over the years.
- Let them know you're planning a marketing campaign to increase your client base.
- Ask them for permission to use their business names in any future advertising campaigns you develop.
- Ask them to continue to refer clients to your firm as they have in the past.
- Let them know you'd like to schedule lunch meetings, at their convenience, to discuss the details of your marketing plan in person.
- Close the letter by stating that you will be calling them in a few days to schedule the lunch, and thank them again for their business.

This letter should be brief. Make sure you date it, and then follow up in the time period they expect. When you reach them and set up the lunch dates, tell them you have a really exciting plan to increase your business, and you can't wait to share it.

At lunch, detail the marketing plan with each business. This marketing plan enables you to endorse your clients' businesses while they do the same for you. This exchange not only increases your company's revenue, but also helps them increase theirs, too. After several years in business, both of you should have a strong client base and trusted business associates.

This is what you'll be doing. You'll be exchanging personalized endorsement letters and 20 solid and trusted business associate names and addresses with your core account list. Create a list of the 20 most-trusted associates to your business and ask the other companies to do the same. Then, write letters that endorse each others' businesses and open the door for a follow-up sales contact.

Let's use your printer for an example. Write a letter, on your company letterhead, that describes how satisfied you are with the printer's services. Then, ask the printer to also write a letter on its company letterhead that describes its satisfaction with your firm. Exchange the letters, along with the 20 business names and addresses and also 20 blank letterhead sheets. Then, transfer the printer's letter of endorsement onto its stationery and mail merge to create 20 original letters to the 20 brand-new potential clients.

So, from the printer's office, 20 endorsement letters are mailed to its clients that encourage them to be open and receptive when you make your call. The letter will say that someone from your firm will be contacting them, and they should be expecting the call.

Do exactly the same thing for your printer. Send the printer's endorsement letter to 20 of your associates describing your satisfaction with the service. Tell them a salesperson will be contacting them from the printer's office and to be prepared for the call.

See how simple this is? You'll be doing exactly the same thing with each of the people on your core list. You should plan to carefully implement this marketing strategy when you have adequate time to schedule all the meetings and make all the follow-up calls. Don't begin this valuable program without being prepared for an increase in business!

COMPANY IMAGE

Your professionalism is displayed in many ways. It's apparent in the staff you hire, the advertising copy you create, the business signs that direct clients to your door, the logo that represents your firm, the style of stationery you select, and even the office decor. All of these factors affect your company image.

It's extremely important to develop and maintain a strong company image. This means that your firm will always have a reputation for uncompromising honesty, ethics, and fairness in all your dealings. It also means earning the respect of your peers.

When you have this reputation established, it will automatically ensure the trust that's so necessary with your clients. Personnel agencies have an opportunity to look at the insides of businesses. You'll see how they operate, what mistakes have been made, and how smooth or rough the management systems are. Don't ever divulge this sensitive and confidential information about your clients to any source for any reason. You must always maintain confidentiality with each associate and stand by your code of ethics.

Unfortunately, bad advertising spreads ten times faster than good advertising. It's a lot like gossip. It spreads like wildfire. Set up company policies that make all the people who come into contact with your firm impressed with your business style, warmth, and friendliness. Everything you do and everything you say is part of building your company image.

MEDIA ADVERTISING

When you develop your advertising budget, don't forget to consider the peak seasons in your business. It's a wise plan to expend the highest revenues during these periods. It isn't practical to spend the same amount of money in one source all year long, unless, of course, it's giving you an extremely high return on your investment.

There are several sources of advertising. Make appointments with representatives of each resource and listen carefully to their sales presentations. If there's more than one television station, look at each one. If the radio choices are broad, take the time to learn the policies and programs of each. They each have value in their own way and can be extremely effective in drawing business to your agency. Listed in the following are the selection choices:

Newspaper

The help-wanted section of the paper draws a tremendous client base. We found this to be the most profitable source. It's because most of the general public is conditioned to seek employment alternatives through this avenue. Individuals who are currently unemployed use this as one of their search sources. People who are working and dissatisfied with their current job will also scan the want ads for something interesting. Clients who are looking to relocate into your area will use this natural resource to scout out the area before the move.

Each week, as job orders arrived in our office, we created weekly scatter ads to draw the appropriate clients for screening and selection. These ads are described in detail and shown by example in chapter 9. We also ran a monthly laundry list, as shown in the same chapter. While using newspaper advertising, there was a much higher return on the investment of advertising dollars than with any other resource available.

Television

Television is an extremely expensive form of advertising, but it can be very effective if used properly. Work with the production manager and sales department to develop an ad campaign that will reach as many qualified applicants as possible.

You might decide to develop an advertising campaign that attracts the employer to your services, as well. Describe the long-term relationships you have developed with other businesses and present your businesses ethics policies.

We made a business trade once with our local television station. We recruited an employee as requested, and the station, in turn, put together an advertisement for North Coast. This transaction cost both parties the in-house fees for services only. The ad ran only a short period of time, but the general public response was good.

Radio

The trick with radio is to create an ad campaign that puts the blurb in the exact same time slot again and again. Remember who you're trying to reach. The working-class public is generally up and moving and listening to the radio between 7:00 a.m. and 8:00 a.m. Try to secure that time slot. Although it's another expensive alternative, it can be successful with the right ad copy and a professional station that reaches your selected audience.

Trade journals

There are many trade journals available to job seekers today. Each journal has a concentrated area of focus and draws a specific industry-based professional. You can create a display ad that attracts the attention of job seekers in general, or design a specific ad that will target a certain client. This source is not as expensive as television or radio advertising, but it also doesn't reach the wide range of population or run as often as other media sources.

FREE ADVERTISING AND PUBLICITY

There are many, many ways to get the public to hear about your company without dipping into your advertising budget. Be creative and, without too much effort, you'll be coming up with ideas yourself. These are some of the things that have worked for us:

Business briefs

The business briefs are in the business section of the Sunday newspaper. These are the short announcements of local business news. Your local newspaper might have a different name for them. Some of the announcements are about staffing changes and/or additions, expansion of services or product lines, relocation to a new address in the area, industry awards presented, association officer announcements, or contracts awarded. You might think of another reason to get coverage in this free section. Be creative. Contact your newspaper source and have them mail you information about these notices.

Public service announcements

Newspapers have public service announcements that provide the business and service groups with a place to announce their volunteer efforts. They also let you announce any classes that are offered in your field. We advertised the job search courses for free in this section all the time.

One of the places we chose to offer the classes (since our offices were eventually too small) was at the local office of education boardroom. When we prepared the public service announcement, the board of education was mentioned along with our services. The tie-in was good for us both.

Business association involvement

This form of advertising only costs you a little bit of your time and, in return, the public becomes familiar with your business, your policies, and your personality. The more you get involved, the more you'll see the advantage. Just don't go overboard and get so wrapped up with your volunteering that you lose track of making money!

Hosting a chamber of commerce "mixer"

Once a month, one of the chamber of commerce member companies hosts an after-work wine-and-cheese social gathering. It's designed to let the members socialize and share business information. This lasts from about 4:30 p.m. to 6:30 p.m. The entire membership list is invited to attend, and there's a free announcement in the chamber newsletter telling everyone where the next mixer is and who is giving it.

The only cost to you is the food and drink. You might choose to prepare it yourself or order a cake and serve it with coffee. Some companies hire caterers to serve at these functions. Either way, many new businesses will become acquainted with your firm, and new clients can be developed from this source.

Volunteering

We've talked a bit about giving up your time to work on committees in your selected associations. Just remember the reason for the sacrifice, and don't get lost in the saving-mankind syndrome.

Later, when your company is extremely profitable and you have lots and lots of free time, then you can get wrapped up in more volunteer activities without losing sight of your goals. But, in the beginning, be careful. Volunteering can be a two-edged sword, and you might lose more money in the long run than you gain in the beginning.

Guest speaking

This form of free advertising was discussed in detail earlier in this chapter.

BARTERING STRATEGIES

Bartering is a form of business transaction that has been practiced for thousands of years and is still routine today. It's simply exchanging services or products with your business associates instead of paying cash.

Trading services is fine as long as you let the IRS know what you're doing. The IRS isn't too happy when it discovers that this business practice has occurred without its knowledge. Be sure to alert your trade associates of the need to report the exchanges also, or you might put them in jeopardy if they don't report the barter. Fortunately, almost all companies need the services that you offer, so there's an abundance of business that you can work with. Each time you consider spending money for something your business needs, think barter.

When making the arrangements for the barter, evaluate the cost of services performed and hours worked and make a fair exchange. If your firm will be charging $600.00 for the company's portion of a placement fee, then trade for $600.00 worth of the company's business services or products. Remember to record all transactions and report these exchanges to the IRS.

There are many advantages and a few disadvantages to doing business in a bartering manner. Let's look at the advantages first. Saving money is the strongest advantage. We've traded services with many of our associates. They were all firms that offered a service or product that we would have had to pay for anyway. We saved a considerable amount of cash revenues using this time-honored business exchange. Another advantage was the positive reinforcement we received from these business associates for our willingness to share respected services. Sometimes a stronger business relationship was developed because of this unique relationship. The last advantage is that you might be able to secure something through a barter that you would normally have to do without if the barter wasn't available. This gives you more choices than were available to you before.

The only disadvantage that we discovered was the frustration experienced when a certain trade didn't work out. Sometimes there was dissatisfaction with services rendered or products exchanged. Then things got a little sticky. Since there are no cash invoices, the disagreements can sometimes be a bit more frustrating than you're used to.

CUSTOMER SERVICE SYSTEMS

Customer service means exactly what it says. Take care of your customers and provide the most honorable and ethical services you can. Train all your employees on fair trade practices. Update them continually and watch for problem areas. They simply need instruction to get over some of the small hurdles. Teach them how to satisfy an unhappy client, and make sure they treat each case separately.

Whenever possible, don't hesitate to refer clients to your competition. They will appreciate your honesty and trust. It leaves them with a good feeling about your helpful services, and they will, in turn, spread the good word to anyone needing agency assistance. Don't forget to remind each referral to let the agency know you sent them! Your competitors will also be grateful for the opportunity to help whenever possible. They'll welcome the business if they know applicant referrals have come directly from your offices.

It's easy to see that a short-term loss is acceptable in this type of business, especially if there's going to be a long-term gain. Be willing to put this valuable practice to work in your agency and make it an automatic rule of thumb.

INDUSTRY MAILING LISTS

Some of these mailing lists can be obtained from your local chamber of commerce. Our chamber had two lists available. One was for the major manufacturers in the county, and the other was for the major employers. The chamber charged a small fee for these lists, but they were invaluable when developing marketing campaigns for the business.

The information given on these lists are the company name, address, mailing address, phone number, fax number, and a contact name. The contact name might be the owner of the firm, general manager, president, or even the sales manager. There's also a description of the type of service offered or product provided and the length of time in business. Sometimes you even can find a statement of the most recent annual gross revenue receipts and number of employees.

Almost all industries have business associations that draw representatives from the individual firms from that field. We listed the different associations in the beginning of this chapter, and there's a membership list for each association.

This is an ideal source to use for building your mailing lists for advertising. You can create a personalized target mailing to introduce your services to the business community. A sample copy of the sales letter is in chapter 8.

OPEN HOUSE

This form of advertising is primarily designed to promote good will with your associates and encourage long-term business relationships. It also gives you a great opportunity to show off your invaluable and committed staff, professional office decor, and excellent services. There are three kinds of open house situations that you can offer for public-relations purposes:

Announcement of business opening

When you select the target date for the opening of your company, plan to publicize it well. Invite all your friends, family, and business associates to share the beginning of your new firm. If you're leasing offices in a business complex, extend the invitation to the tenants of the building as well. This gives you an opportunity to meet these neighbors and share business news.

You might want to send an announcement of new business to all of these people too and make it a grand opening. Now is the perfect time to throw a party and celebrate all your hard work in getting prepared. It's a great way to get your new business off to a great start!

Chamber of commerce mixer

As discussed earlier in this chapter, this is another valuable marketing tool for public relations. You'll probably have only one chance to hold this open house, so pick the time that you feel would be best to introduce your services.

Christmas open house

A Christmas open house can obviously be done on an annual basis and can become a standard yearly party that your clients look forward to. Put a great deal of effort into this special occasion, and they'll want to come back to celebrate the holidays with you and your staff year after year.

12
Competition

Nothing motivates a company more than competition. It forces you to constantly stay "on your toes." I've always found competition to be a primary factor in developing and maintaining the quality of my agency. Constantly watch what's out there, see what's working and what isn't, learn from it, and avoid competitors' mistakes. Strive to improve your existing systems to stay ahead of the pack. As a constant reminder, I had the following placard on my office wall:

A TRIBUTE TO MY COMPETITORS

My competitors do more for me than my friends. My friends are too polite to point out my weaknesses, but my competitors are attentive, hard working, and would take my business away from me if they could. They keep me alert and inspire me to find ways to improve my products and services. If I had no competitor, I would be less efficient and inattentive. I can use the discipline they force upon me. I salute my competitors. They have been good for me. God bless them all! (Author unknown)

RESEARCH

While in the developing stages of your business, plan to study all your friendly (or unfriendly) associates. The following are some of the things you can learn by sending a friend into competing companies as a potential job seeker:
- What do they charge?
- Who pays the fee?
- What is the fee repayment structure?
- When are the business hours and days?
- Is an appointment necessary?

- What type of placement do they offer (permanent and/or temporary)?
- What categories of placement do they cover?
- Who pays the fee (applicant, employer, or split/reimbursement)?
- How large is the staff?
- How long have they been in operation?
- How successful are they in promoting repeat business?

You can also learn the employers' perspective by asking a friend who owns a business to contact the competition by phone and request the standard information for placing a job order. Some of the knowledge obtained by this valuable exercise would be:

- How professional is the support staff? Are you left on hold for very long?
- How thorough is the counselor when gathering the appropriate information for the job order?
- Will they send information about their services?
- Do they have a list of client referrals?
- Are you treated with respect and understanding, or hurried through the process with little feeling?
- How positive do they sound in finding the right person?
- Is the counselor familiar with your industry terminology?
- Is there noise in the background—busy phones?
- Do you feel good when you hang up the phone?

These are just a few of the items you can learn when investigating the competition. With a little thought, more useful tips can be gained. It's fun to make the list of points to cover and see just how much you can learn. It's very important to be careful in the selection of your investigators. Do not go yourself or send anyone that you plan to use as an employee in the future. Another important point is to be ethical with your competitors. An agency with a poor reputation does not prosper in this industry or in its community.

SHARING AND SPLITTING THE FEES WITH THE COMPETITION

If you learn during your preliminary research that some of the competition is honest and fair, meet with a few owners or managers to discuss the potential of sharing a few job orders and splitting occasional fees. Sharing is proposing to use another agency's applicant pool, without compensation. This practice, when handled professionally, can create a long-lasting, mutually rewarding, and unusual relationship in the industry. Be sure to stress that the competitors are never going to lose any existing business, but they will be able to satisfy their clients with even the most difficult of orders.

About once a month an order came into my office for an immediate temporary placement, and I couldn't reach any of my qualified applicants on the phone. So instead of calling my client to report a failure, I telephoned my friendly competitor with an SOS. It was never necessary to release the name of the client, only the job description. The competing counselor would release several names of qualified applicants and, more often than not, the order was filled. In return for the favor, I was more than willing to help whenever my friend had the same problem.

Another competitive arrangement is the fee-split job order. This situation occurs when you lack qualified applicants for a permanent position. If we couldn't find a match after reviewing my existing applicant files and advertising for the position, all we had to do was call one of the other agencies and offer a split-fee arrangement. If another agency provided someone who was hired, we would split the fee based on our company's payment schedule, and all parties would be satisfied. There must be an agreement that the agency that received the order retained the client.

Set up individual files on your competition, and constantly add any bits of information you learn. Try to include a copy of their applications, fee schedules, and contracts. Watch for any changes in advertising, association involvement, staffing, and management.

Always be alert to any feedback when interviewing applicants. Often, they will register with all the agencies to increase the chances of finding work. When asked, they are more than willing to share any news, good or bad, about their experiences with the competition.

Sometimes an employer chooses to list the job order with more than one agency to speed up the placement. Be alert to responses from the employer about the quality of service provided by the competitor, the suitability of the applicant sent to interview, and general business practices. Before long you'll develop a very reliable picture of your competition. Be sure to update it, and remember to let your staff review it periodically.

Competition doesn't have to be difficult. You can work with them or against them. The choice is yours. In the long run, if you're willing to give a little, share a little, and trust a lot, you'll see far more profit in the end, and you'll feel good doing it!

13
Taxes

The tax information provided in this section of the book is prepared based on the current laws of our government. Since Congress has been passing tax legislation at the rate of one major act every two years, we strongly suggest that you check for any major tax changes that might affect your new business.

As a business owner and employer, you'll be required by law to pay certain taxes yourself, and you'll also be responsible for collecting the various state and federal taxes due for your employees. These tax payments need to be submitted on a timely basis to the appropriate governmental agencies.

FEDERAL TAX IDENTIFICATION NUMBER

One of the first things you must do, as a new employer, is obtain an employer tax number from the federal government. You can do this by using the IRS form SS-4. If your individual state requires an income tax also, you'll need to obtain a tax number from the state as well. You can contact the federal and state agencies by calling the phone numbers that are listed in the white pages of your telephone book under United States and the name of your state.

Your new employer tax identification number will be mailed to your new offices immediately, along with charts that determine the payroll tax deductions, W-4 forms, quarterly and annual forms, tax-deposit forms, and an instruction manual on filling out forms. The government doesn't charge a fee for this service.

When you hire one or more individuals into your agency, you will be required to withhold the Social Security and income tax from each of your employees' paychecks. Then these withheld portions of their paychecks are to be remitted to the proper tax-collecting agencies.

SOCIAL SECURITY (FICA) TAX

The acronym FICA stands for Federal Insurance Contributions Act. This act requires that all employers pay the exact same amount of Social Security tax as the employee. You will find the charts and instructions for these deductions when you receive your IRS payroll forms. You'll see on the charts provided that the U.S. Congress has accelerated the requirements for depositing FICA and withholding taxes. Substantial penalties are applied for failure to comply with these remittances.

You must file, with the IRS district director, four different reports in connection with the payroll taxes that you withhold from your employees' salaries.
- Quarterly return of taxes withheld on wages (Form 941).
- Annual statement of taxes withheld on wages (Form W-2).
- Reconciliation of quarterly returns of taxes withheld with annual statement of taxes withheld (Form W-3).
- Annual Federal Unemployment Tax return (Form 940).

INCOME TAX WITHHELD

The amount of income tax you must withhold from each employee's wages depends on several factors: the number of exemptions claimed on the W-4 form, the marital status, the length of the payroll period, and the level of income. The IRS percentage tables will be included in your packet of information for weekly, biweekly, monthly, semimonthly, and other payroll periods.

STATE PAYROLL TAX

Payroll taxes are required by almost all states. These taxes must be collected and submitted to appropriate governing agencies. The unemployment tax is paid entirely by the employer in most states. This tax is calculated as a percentage of your total payroll and paid at the end of each year. The percentage will vary according to each state and individual employer.

As an employer in some states, however, you might have the added responsibility of deducting taxes from your employee's paycheck and remitting it to the state. There is also disability insurance tax in a few states that must be deducted from the employee's pay. This tax might be split between employer and employee.

The federal government has set the standard that most states have used for the tax collection systems. Employer numbers are issued, and instruction booklets and similar forms are distributed.

PERSONAL INCOME TAX

If you choose to operate your new business as a sole proprietor or partner, you will not be paid a salary like an employee. Since you don't fall into the same category as your employee, no income tax is withheld from the money you draw from your business for living expenses.

Instead, you have to estimate your personal tax liability each year and pay it in quarterly installments on form 1040ES to the IRS. You can request the *Tax Guide for Small Business* when requesting the forms and instructions for filing these estimated tax returns.

The amount of your personal tax liability is based on the profits earned in your company for each year. You're required to file an income tax return as an individual. We've included a list of the standard tax requirements for your new business (see Table 13-1).

Table 13-1 Tax requirements

Type of tax	How often
(Federal)	
Income tax	Yearly
Estimated Income Tax Deposits	Quarterly
Self-employment Tax	Yearly
Income-Tax Withholding	Quarterly
Income-Tax Withholding Deposits	Quarterly*
FICA (Social Security) Tax	Quarterly
FICA Tax Deposits	Quarterly*
FUTA (Unemployment) Tax	Quarterly
FUTA Tax Deposits	Quarterly*
(State)	
Income Tax (State of Residence)	Yearly
Income Tax (State of Business)	Yearly
Estimated Income Tax (State of Residence)	Quarterly
Estimated Income Tax (State of Business)	Quarterly
Withholding Tax	Quarterly*
Withholding Tax Deposits	Quarterly*
(County)	
Personal Property Business Tax	Yearly
(City)	
Earnings Tax	Annually
Earnings Tax Withholding	Quarterly
Business Earnings & Profits Tax	Annually
(*) or more frequently	

EXPENSE DEDUCTIONS AND DEPRECIATION ALLOWANCE

Individual tax items, such as expense deductions, are in constant flux, and the last change severely limited the amount of these deductions. The depreciation allowance was also recently accelerated in certain categories.

PAYROLL

Prompt reporting and accuracy are essential, and payroll software such as INSTINC-TIVE™ PAYROLL will help immensely.

For payroll, you need a good accountant and a good accounting software program with accompanying tax programs. The accounting software will properly record your daily entries, and the tax program will add the data and place these totals in the appropriate form or schedule. These tax programs also usually give some basic advice. The main purpose of employing the talents of an accountant is to ensure accuracy and to see that you receive every legitimate deduction you're entitled to.

TAX AUDIT

If you keep good records, any audit should go smoothly. You'll be informed what items are to be examined during an audit. Get together with your accountant, and bring along the physical records and your trusty accounting program, including the data files. If your accountant did your taxes, he or she will go with you.

Audits can be randomly chosen, or they can be caused by a red flag sent up by your return. Your accountant should know what causes a return to cry out for an audit. Don't try to get your accountant to give you false deductions or make a fraudulent return. The majority won't. There are some who will, but you will bear the brunt of a bad audit. Ethical business practices extend to tax returns. Claim everything you're entitled to, but don't ruin your reputation to get that last dollar.

A
Industry associations

Employment Management Association
Five W. Hargett Street, #100
Raleigh, NC 27601
(919) 828-6614

National Association of Personnel Consultants
1432 Duke Street
Alexandria, VA 22314
(703) 684-0180

National Association of Temporary Services
119 South Saint Asaph Street
Alexandria, VA 22314-3119
(703) 549-6287

National Employment Counselors Association
5999 Stevenson Avenue
Alexandria, VA 22304
(703) 823-9800

National Personnel Consultants
P.O. Box 1379
535 Court Street
Reading, PA 19603
(215) 678-8230

B
National industry publications

Personnel Managers Letter
Bureau of Business Practice
24 Rope Ferry Road
Waterford, CT 06386
(Monthly, 8-page newsletter)

Employment Marketplace
P.O. Box 31112
St. Louis, MO 63131
(314) 569-3095
(Quarterly publication, approximately 40 pages. Products and services for the recruiting, search and employment professional)

California Job Journal
1800 Tribute Road
Sacramento, CA 95815-4314
(916) 925-0800
(800) 655-JOBS
(Fax) (916) 925-0101

Employment Newsletter
Employment Management Associates
20 William Street
Wellesley, MA 02181
(617) 235-8878

Employment Review
A Recourse Communication Publication
1655 Palm Beach Lakes Blvd., Suite 600
West Palm Beach, FL 33401
(407) 686-6800
(Fax) (407) 686-8043

Journal of Employment Counseling
National Employment Counselors Association
5999 Stevenson Avenue
Alexandria, VA 22304
(703) 823-9800

National Business Employment Weekly
The *Wall Street Journal*
420 Lexington Avenue
New York, NY 10120
(800) 323-NBEW

Occupational Outlook Quarterly
Superintendent of Documents
U.S. Government Printing Office
Washington, DC 20402
(202) 275-3345

Personnel Consultant
National Association of Personnel Consultants
1432 Duke Street
Alexandria, VA 22314
(707) 684-0180

Index

About the authors

Kristi Mishel is a successful business owner, entrepreneur, career counselor, author, and lecturer. She has taught employment strategies classes at California universities, colleges, and vocational schools.

Her 20 years of experience in the personnel industry has provided a thorough knowledge of business structuring, staffing, systems analysis, administration, and expansion. In 1982 she created her own personnel agency and expanded to three locations within 2½ years. Using her business and career-change counseling skills, she has assisted in the development and start-up of 29 businesses, including two personnel agencies. She is a current member of American Business Women's Association, Business Connections, and Women's Entrepreneurs, Humboldt County, California. She is the author of *Hidden Market Strategy*, a comprehensive job search guide for the professional in transition.

John Thomas is a business owner, computer consultant, commodities trader, author, and fine woodworking craftsman for North Coast Services & Products, a combination business-consulting service and woodworking company. He is the coauthor/editor of *Hidden Market Strategy*. He has also been a California Highway Patrol officer (15 years, retired) and he is a Vietnam veteran.

His business experience has involved computer consulting, wholesale buying, refinishing, reproducing and selling antiques, and producing and selling fine woodworking products, ranging from furniture to traditional crafts. He is proficient in computer applications for spreadsheets, databases, accounting (including tax programs) and other related products. He has 16 years of experience in technical analysis in stock and commodities trading, and he is a member of American Association of Individual Investors.

* The authors can be contacted at
North Coast Services
39512 Highway 36
Bridgeville, CA 95526

FACING CANCER
WITHOUT
GOD